The Path Within

*Break Through Harmful
Programming and Doctrine
to Experience Happiness and
Harmony in Your Reality*

By Anthony Santen

BALBOA
PRESS
A DIVISION OF HAY HOUSE

Copyright © 2015 Anthony Santen.
Path Within® is a registered trademark of Anthony Santen.
Path Within® Program and Path Within® Practitioner are trademarks of Anthony Santen.
Cover Photograph of Ewelina Haratym Copyright © 2014 Anthony Santen.
Author photograph Copyright © 2014 Ewelina Haratym.

All rights reserved. No part of this book may be used or reproduced by any means, graphic, electronic, or mechanical, including photocopying, recording, taping or by any information storage retrieval system without the written permission of the publisher except in the case of brief quotations embodied in critical articles and reviews.

All scripts are Copyright © 2014 Anthony Santen. All rights reserved. Do not publish without permission. These scripts may be used as-is in a professional practice and are for educational purposes only. The author does not assume responsibility for the use of these scripts.

Balboa Press books may be ordered through booksellers or by contacting:
Balboa Press
A Division of Hay House
1663 Liberty Drive
Bloomington, IN 47403
www.balboapress.com
1 (877) 407-4847

Because of the dynamic nature of the Internet, any web addresses or links contained in this book may have changed since publication and may no longer be valid. The views expressed in this work are solely those of the author and do not necessarily reflect the views of the publisher, and the publisher hereby disclaims any responsibility for them.

Although the author and publisher have made every effort to ensure that the information in this book was correct at press time, the author and publisher do not assume and hereby disclaim any liability to any party for any loss, damage, or disruption caused by errors or omissions, whether such errors or omissions result from negligence, accident, or any other cause.

The author of this book does not dispense medical advice or prescribe the use of any technique as a form of treatment for physical, emotional, or medical problems without the advice of a physician, either directly or indirectly. The intent of the author is only to offer information of a general nature to help you in your quest for emotional and spiritual well-being. In the event you use any of the information in this book for yourself, which is your constitutional right, the author and the publisher assume no responsibility for your actions.

Print information available on the last page.

ISBN: 978-1-5043-2520-2 (sc)
ISBN: 978-1-5043-2522-6 (hc)
ISBN: 978-1-5043-2521-9 (e)

Library of Congress Control Number: 2014922107

Balboa Press rev. date: 3/19/2015

Dedication

No work is truly from a singular source. Influences and collaborations work in symbiosis to create a book such as this. I'm truly grateful for all the amazing influences in my life.

My courageous clients, who asked seemingly endless questions, created the forum that allowed me to work through the theories and helped create a depth of clarity that would have been impossible otherwise. I want to thank A. MSc. Eng. who insisted on working through each detail in scientific terms, enthusiastically and relentlessly laying parallels and uncovering axioms to create clarity. I want to thank Dr. D.S. who allowed me to refine my tables, exercises, *mental-models* and background research to include medical information, which created clarity about where the Path Within and medicine are in alignment or separated. And Dr. R.P. with whom I spent days working through methods of delivering the various *mental-models* and exercises to patients, who gave invaluable support while remaining within the scope of an emergency physician. The girl I will name Tracey who gave me her worry stone after she no longer needed it. And many, many more...

My parents, most notably my mother, without whom I would have never questioned my own existence and without whom I would have never applied myself to such an arduous and ostentatious task as solving some of the mysteries of the Universe and our interactions with its magic.

My grandfather, for showing me the kindred souls who opened my heart to the world.

My beautiful and wise daughter, who embodies the Path Within with such natural grace and innate wisdom.

My friends Marci and Rochelle, who encouraged me to start capturing my work, which had been written in various notebooks and computer files, but never recorded methodically enough to be read and used by anyone other than myself.

My soul teacher and inspiration Ewelina, who sought me out and helped me to discover the most meaningful separation between soul and ego to a depth I had not previously experienced within my own awareness.

Realizing that now much of this information is, indeed more structured and comprehensive and hopefully useful for others gives me great joy. I hold the hope that you will find your own way and that others, in search for a foundation to build upon, find better ways to help loved ones get their lives back on track and find the courage to step away from the issues in their lives that don't serve them and embrace and nurture their passions and souls.

Being able to reach out to many more people using this medium has always been a dream of mine and through the encouragement and support I received from my clients and my friends, who felt my passion for this work, I've been able to accomplish just that!

LIVE! It's your life!

Enjoy

Contents

SECTION 1: INTRODUCTION 1
  Chapter 1 – What is The Path Within Program About? 3
    Life to the Fullest 4
    The Quest for Happiness 5
    Being Authentic 6
    Authentic Relationships 7
    Being the Change 8
    What Is The Path Within 8
    Why Use Hypnosis 11
  Chapter 2 – Are You Ready for The Path Within? 12
  Chapter 3 – Book Structure 15
    Alone or With a Guide? 16
    Results 16
    Exercises 17
    Discovery 18
  Chapter 4 – Purpose / Mission 20
    Balance vs. Harmony 21
    Medicating Healthcare 23
  Chapter 5 – Shaping the Journey of Life 25
    Our Super Power 25
    Intuition 28
    Cat Moves 29
    The Suspicious Rat 30
    The Omnipotent Baby 31
SECTION 2: PATH WITHIN FOUNDATIONS 33
  Chapter 6 – What Came First? 35
    If a Tree 36

Chapter 7 – The Hippocampus - The Stage of Life 38
- The Stage of Life 39
- Blanks and the Closed Box 39
- Safe or Danger? 40
- Construction 42
- The Presumption of Threat 44

Chapter 8 – You and "The Problem" 46
- Biting off More than We Can Chew 46
- Identifying with Problems to Conquer Them 47
- Believing We Have Problems 48
- The Power of Playing the Victim 48

Chapter 9 – Competing with God 49

Chapter 10 – What Isn't to What Is 51
- Time as an Illusion 51
- Time, Money, Language 52
- Growth as a Function of Resistance 52

Chapter 11 – Fear Is Healthy 54
- Why We Fear 54

Chapter 12 – Why Do We Fear? 56
- What You Don't Want 56
- Providence 57
- The Puppy Nightmares 58

Chapter 13 – Axiom of Fear 60
- One Future at a Time 60
- Intuition and Fear Combine 61
- Unhealthy Fear 61

Chapter 14 – Guilt, Shame and Blame 63
- Shame 63
- Guilt and Blame – The Quick Way Out 64
- Guilt and Blame – Holding On 65
- Regret 66

Chapter 15 – Simple Truth 68
- Accept, Not Like 69
- Perfectly Flawed 69
- For Better or For Worse 70

Chapter 16 – How We Store Memories 71
- 100% Brain 71
- Efficient Storage (and How We Count) 72

    Three Second Clip 73
    Reconstructing the Car Accident 73
    Generalizations... 73

Chapter 17 – Mind/Brain Healing Response Cycles 75
    Common Cold 75
    New Paradigm on Mental Illness 76
    Who Feels You? 78
    You Make Me Feel 80

Chapter 18 – Anger- A Feeling? 81
    Danger and Anger 82
    Limiting Beliefs – Limiting Possibilities 83
    Self-talk 83
    First Time in the History of the Universe 84

Chapter 19 – Anger Escalation in Relationship 85
    Anger 85
    Threat 85
    Ultimatum 86
    Resolution 86

Chapter 20 – Anxiety 87
    Root Causes 87
    You Are Not Alone 88
    Discovering the Root Causes 88
    Understanding Anxiety in a New Way 89
    Freedom from Fear and Anxiety 89
    Exercise: Connecting with Peace - The Three Things Exercise 90
    Complete Moments 92
    Reality of a Moment 92
    Thought Awareness 93
    Exercise: The Four Questions and the One Answer 94

Chapter 21 – Depression, Grieving and Sadness 96
    Foundation of Reality 97
    What Is Grieving 98
    The Grieving Process: An Overview 99
    Elisabeth Kübler-Ross Model 100

Chapter 22 – The Amazing Brain 102
    Understanding Severance 102
    Processing Severance 102
    Re-learning 103

Chapter 23 – Sleep and Depression ... 105
- Sleep Cycles ... 105
- Processing Sleep ... 106
- Hippocampus ... 107
- Revealing Dreams ... 108
- Overwhelm ... 109
- Mind Overload ... 110
- Creating Separation ... 110
- Clearing the Cache ... 111

Chapter 24 – Strategies for Effective Depression ... 113
- Reduce Input ... 113
- Sleeping Pills and Drugs ... 114
- Set a Reasonable Time ... 114
- Find a Guide ... 115
- Feed Your Mind ... 116
- Curb Escapes ... 116
- Don't Hope for Miracles - Participate in Creating Your Own ... 117
- Find Your Own Normal ... 117
- Fall Back on Rhythms and Tradition ... 117

SECTION 3: PATH WITHIN SESSIONS ... 119
- First Threshold: Understand ... 120
- Second Threshold: Embody ... 120
- Third Threshold: Relate ... 121

FIRST THRESHOLD – UNDERSTAND ... 123

Chapter 25 – Accepting Responsibility ... 125
- Most Complex Life ... 126
- Who is Responsible? Externalizing vs. Internalizing ... 127

Chapter 26 – Happiness ... 129
- Unhappiness by Design ... 130
- Action Is Profitable ... 131
- Our Economy Depends on Your Unhappiness ... 131
- Unhappiness Is Big Business ... 131
- The Origin of Happiness ... 133
- Defining Unhappiness ... 133
- The Basic Rules of Happiness ... 134
- The Meaning of Happiness ... 136
- The Word Happiness ... 136
- The Happiness Experience ... 137

Contentment 137
Bliss 142
Being Happy 143
Chapter 27 – Laws of Self-Preservation............................ 146
1st Law of Self-Preservation 147
How We Make Motivated Decisions 152
Strategy: What, Why, What Else, How............................. 157
2nd Law of Self-Preservation 163
3rd Law of Self-Preservation.. 167
In Summary 169
Chapter 28 – Assumptive Life 170
Shaping Personal Truths 171
Distilling Reality 171
Neural Pathways... 173
Reality or Belief?... 173
Participation or Control 174
Expecting an Answer 175
Deserving Reward 176
Chapter 29 – Negative Thinking... 179
Positive Outlook 180
Chapter 30 – Effective Self-talk... 183
Affirmations... 183
Examples Of Effective Affirmations.................................. 184
Creating Your Own Affirmations 184
SECOND THRESHOLD – EMBODY 189
Chapter 31 – Energy and Focus... 191
100% No More. No Less. 191
Working in Overdrive 192
Planning.. 193
Leverage.. 194
First Step 194
Where Your Focus goes your Life Goes 195
Reframing 196
Manifesting 101... 196
The Power of Focus.. 197
Hindsight 198
Energy Shorting.. 199

Chapter 32 – The Hierarchy of Motivation 201
    Why We Avoid Accountability 201
    Language Motivates 202
    Highlight the Word TRY 203
    Replacing Try 204
    Should 205
    Need and Want 206
    Want - Fuel of Life 208
    Short vs Long-Term Gain 208

Chapter 33 – Creating Change 210
    Asking Better Questions 210
    Remove Prerequisites 212
    Strategy: Making Anything Better 213
    Strategy: Forgetting How of the Future & Why of the Past 215

Chapter 34 – Connecting to Self - The Three Skills 217
    Re-connect with *Core Self* (S-BridgeMeditation) 217
    Connecting to Your Highest Purpose (Spirit Guide Meditation) 218
    Connecting with Our Personal Power 219
    Advanced Personal Power 222

Chapter 35 – Action First 224
    Re-choice is Progress 225

THIRD THRESHOLD – RELATE 227

Chapter 36 – The Power and Reward of Vulnerability 229

Chapter 37 – Lean into the Direction of Resistance 230
    Highway of Life 231
    The Illusion of Control 231

Chapter 38 – The Power of Resistance 234
    Our First Answer Is No 234
    Complicated or Complex 235
    Resistance is a Function of Growth 235
    Flow 236
    Outsmarting Resistance 236

Chapter 39 – Becoming Sovereign 238

Chapter 40 – Strategy: Influencing Others 240

Chapter 41 – Human Needs Psychology 243
    The Six Human Needs 243
    Column C 246

Chapter 42 – Forgiveness: An Act of Power 247
Chapter 43 – Bestowing Trust 250
Chapter 44 – Circle of Potential 252
Chapter 45 – Being Yourself 255
    Exercise: Recalling the Present 256
Chapter 46 – Identities and Belief Systems 258
    Three strategies 259
CONCLUSION 265
INDEX 267

Section 1: Introduction

My Wish - Forgive me my clumsiness. Forgive me my lack of finesse. For if I took time to learn the ways of the author, the beautiful prose, the amazing wit, the deep and gritty point and the book world, this book would be delayed and its message and teachings lost for another decade.

This book is by no means rough, yet it was never meant to be a slick, poetic stimulant of language, either. I've spent years in my little office talking with amazing people, living with my observations and philosophies, determined to take these messages to the world; determined to inspire you to participate more deeply and authentically in your own inner journey, your Path Within.

I've spent more than twenty years submerged in subjects such as God and Life; creating methods to overcome Depression, Guilt and Anxiety; and learning about Relationships, Parenting and Human Needs and Interactions. Experiments and research added to my findings. In my office, I coached my clients through The Path Within Program. I learned from them, adjusted the program, refined and simplified the tools, the metaphors and the messages. And now it's time to publish the work; to share this transformative work with you and to create a new awareness and authentic experience.

At first, realizing that my writing experience was limited, I thought I would need to hire someone to hammer out the details, to make the book more suitable for a wider audience. Not so. I've spent years creating this work; writing down the philosophies and methods I use in my daily sessions with clients to help them overcome their current situations. I've decided not to rewrite it for a wider audience. That might have caused the book to lose some of its message, hidden in the unrefined parts of this work. My hope is that you'll find this book inspirational and meaningful and that you'll be able to use the philosophies and *mental-models* to understand, interact, view and create your world – your way!

Anthony Santen

Chapter 1 – What is The Path Within Program About?

This book is not an instruction manual on best practices or methods by which to live your life. This book leads you through a self-discovery process to help you discover and develop your authentic self within the context of your own unique life.

This book promises to demystify and challenge some of the popular notions of our time. To restore your faith in the Universe as a diverse and benevolent whole that sustains life within its harmony, to understand the origins of the belief systems that enslaved us and to challenge the modern day philosophers who complicate and confuse us by telling us how we should reinterpret our life, thereby making life and happiness more difficult to achieve - as if following a single protocol and lifestyle could ensure happiness.

For starters, you will have the opportunity to observe the world with fresh eyes on a basic level, similar to how a Taoist would see the world. You will learn that most people really don't care much about you.... yet in a good way! You will also learn that the Universe is not out to sabotage you, nor can you hold it accountable for your wellbeing. The Universe doesn't owe you and it doesn't seek you out to harm you. You will even learn that Murphy's Law is most unlikely to be true and how you choose many of your experiences.

You'll learn how the law of attraction and manifestation really work within a real and logical world.

We will discuss and liberate desire. Not suppress this motivating force that is the single most influential force in evolution and the fuel of life. We will put shame and hell back where they belong, in the obscurity of religion-based fears and control. We will discover why we fear and the true amazing power of our fear mechanism. We will discover that time is not an illusion and that manifestation and the law of attraction, while interesting ideas, are widely misinterpreted.

Section 1: Introduction

We will discuss the origins of anger, fear, depression and anxiety. Not the symptoms, but the root causes and mind-responses that lead us into these states. Simple and practical knowledge will help you understand and reengineer your own responses and reactions.

Being able to observe behaviours, your own and others' and understand them through the eyes of an authentic sovereign being, will lead to a sense of well-being, peace and happiness. Ultimately, we are not looking to overcome all fear, but to see it for what it is: part of our predictive warning system, one that attempts to protect us and is most often, thankfully, wrong.

The power of living an authentic life and the freedom that such a life promises will require a change in mindset and an understanding of the reality of the world. Understanding what is real and what is drama.

Life to the Fullest

Do you wonder if you are living life to the fullest? Have you pondered the meaning of life itself, or wondered why we seem trapped in a consumeristic life filled with competition and unhappiness?

Misery and unhappiness are everywhere! Entire industries have sprung from humanity's unhappiness with life. From eco-adventures and vacations, shiny new gadgets and entertainment, to meditation retreats and weight rooms (or if you prefer, yoga classes), to recreational drugs, sex addictions and the all-too ubiquitous anti-depressant drugs. There seems to be no end to the ingenuity of mankind in finding ways to escapes and fill the alleged void and the daily drudgery of life. But do these escapes make us happy?

The big question remains: What is happiness and, once defined, do we actually want to be happy? Is this your goal? How do we achieve any goal without first defining it? Do we find our own happiness? Do we create it? I believe that we want to feel connected to life itself. I believe we want to live in a relatively autonomous way that allows us freedoms and to transcend the fears and worries that threaten our survival. But do we want to be in a state of glee all the time? I challenge that notion.

We want to feel alive, yes. But this means something completely different than feeling "high on life" all the time. Walking through nature, listening to a brilliant piece of music, building something, creating, nurturing, participating... these experiences are what feeling alive is all about. Having a purpose, knowing that we significantly contribute to the world, learning, growing, witnessing and being witnessed; these are our souls' needs. This is when we feel truly alive as we wipe off the sweat and dust at the end of a hard day's work, looking upon the experience of life: the contributions we made, be it lives we saved, the houses we built, the storms we weathered, or the beauty and art we manifested for others to connect with and admire...

To feel alive, we must feel life, which is fulfillment and growth. The question is how?

How do we find our place in this world? How do we harness our life's energies and participate in life, without falling into the energy-draining competitive traps set out for us, while still creating the security and attaining the rewards we desire?

The Quest for Happiness

Are we searching for meaning in life, or are we searching for happiness? Or both? Are they mutually exclusive?

I believe the reward of living is felt in the connection. The connection that exists among people, with oneself and with the world around us. I also believe that we measure our experience by how we feel and that feeling is the reward of experience.

There is contentment in the knowledge that we contribute to life around us and from within this contentment we are able to find the desirable feelings we seek. Rewards in life are ultimately a matter of feelings. Why, then, is feeling euphoric not an end goal in itself? Euphoria is a feeling many people escape to when they lose their sense of wellness, but why is this not the route to happiness?

There is a feeling associated with our souls' growth, without which we lose the ability to define Self. This feeling is the feeling of significance: the sense that we matter, a knowing that we contribute our abilities to the world, the feeling of having a sense of purpose.

Our connection to life, our ability to contribute and the rewards we strive to experience are rooted in the connection, the communication, the sense of togetherness and belonging and the contribution of our unique strengths to life. This gives us our "raison d'être" – our reason for being, our ultimate Soul purpose.

Section 1: Introduction

Being Authentic

What is being authentic all about? Aren't we always already being ourselves?

Authenticity is a question of self-integrity. How we view ourselves in relationship to others. Authenticity is when we can be ourselves without fear of judgment, from others or from ourselves. Being authentic is being able to create genuine agreements with oneself, other people and the Universe. Being genuine requires an ability to connect with reality: with *What Is* and detaching from the illusion of *What Isn't*. Being ourselves does not mean we must be consistent. Being ourselves means we can be what we want to be in any moment including naughty, playful, inquisitive and even wrong! And all this happens while we are continuously exploring our world, having the freedom to make mistakes, to invent and create and to explore our boundaries be they environmental, self-imposed or imparted by our belief systems.

Being truly authentic requires a level of self-reliance that allows us to be independent of the reliance on charity or pity for our well being; being able to be selective with our relationships and the agreements we create within them. When we were much younger, we were constantly pleasing others, catering to their belief systems and judgments in the hope of not being abandoned by our caregivers. This behaviour of pleasing others to get our needs met is a difficult habit to break, but once we do break the habit we are immensely rewarded.

Giving yourself permission to be authentic allows you to be different from or the same as those around you, whenever you please and in whatever way you desire. Of course, this means being fully aware that others, in their entitled autonomy, may still judge you. Being authentic, therefore, also means that you permit others their judgments, or at least their comparisons to their value systems and beliefs.

This book is about becoming an authentic sovereign being. In many ways you already are authentic and sovereign, in which case this book can highlight areas of your life where you might further develop your ultimate freedom from fear and judgment.

Authentic Relationships

A major component of happiness is our ability to have rewarding, functional relationships. When we talk about relationship, we often refer to intimate partnership. We concentrate so much on this type of relationship– out of need for validation – that we overlook the other relationships that facilitate our wholeness and sense of wellness.

Of course there are the relationships that are not intimate, such as the relationships between friends, family, colleagues, neighbours and others. We often get lost in maintaining relationships with the many individuals that colour our lives. So lost that we completely overlook the two fundamental components that make this type of relationship even possible: the relationship we have with ourselves and the relationship we have as individuals with the world around us.

The relationship we have with ourselves is greatly influenced by our self-talk, the constant observer/narrator in our head who represents the voices of our parents, teachers, caregivers and idols in their absence.

Re-observing and re-evaluating our behaviours affords us the ability to change what we believe about ourselves and to re-evaluate what we believe about how we ought to behave. Understanding that we have limited time here on earth and releasing the incessant judgments and imposed belief systems gives us the freedom to live new identities; ones that are more becoming of our authentic selves.

Changing the relationship we have with ourselves, our bodies, our minds, our behaviours and the ways our behaviours affect our interactions with the world around us, frees our attention. The attention and energy previously captured by our belief systems and others' doctrines and control, can now be freed and returned to its rightful owner: You. Being able to dedicate more of your precious time, energy and attention to your passions, causes and personal growthis the key to being happy, contented, truly free and able to follow your path on the journey of life. The Path Within.

Later in the book I describe how unhappiness creeps into our lives and how others, by hijacking our attention, keep our attention focused on our inadequacies, flaws and failures which causes us to stay focused on our unhappiness. In marketing companies this ability to capture our attention, to highlight inadequacies, flaws and failures followed by offering us their antidotes, is known as "driving the want "by "stirring the hurt."

Re-learning the relationship you have with yourself and how you interact with the world around you gives you your power back.

Being the Change

I often speak to people who voice their dismay at the state of the world, the poverty, the abuse, the pain and suffering that so many must endure. They wish there was something they could do about it, to contribute in some significant way. In some cases their expression of powerlessness over the state of the world is their reason for feeling stuck in their own lives.

My response is almost always the same, I respond with questions. Questions about their parents, their spouses, other relationships, especially their children and almost invariably I find that these people are quite willing to help others, far away, but overlook the needs of the people in their immediate environment.

Don't save the world, save yours.

You have the greatest impact on your local world. Not only are you able to direct your energies more efficiently locally, any energy applied locally always has further reaching effects through propagation. What you do with your immediate relationships causes a significant ripple effect in the direction you intended. The biggest impact you can have on the world is learning and creating peace and harmony in your own life. With that peace and harmony, you can improve the world with every interaction and finally break a long and prolific cycle of which you may have become a part. What your parents did to you, they learned from their parents, who learned the same behaviours from their parents and so on. Children are influenced by their parents, not so much by the parents' words as by their actions and most especially by their reactions. Changing the way you react to the world around you will encourage your children (and peers, colleagues, etc) to learn with you.

Your children will teach their children, their neighbors and their communities. The saying really does work: change the world by changing yourself.

What Is The Path Within

The Path Within Program was originally developed as a follow-up program for people who have "done the work." That is, people who have explored their problems and thoughts and become aware of their triggers and frustrations.

Chapter 1 – What is The Path Within Program About?

This exploration would have led to an understanding of the basics of their reactions to their environment. Once people have this understanding, then they are capable of asking the next big questions.

The Path Within Program was a response to the need to answer a question that remained for many of us even after having "done our work." When we arrive at the point in our lives of understanding how much influence our parents had on us and how much responsibility we now have for our own lives, we start asking the questions "so, what's next? What does it all mean, what is my purpose, how can I participate and contribute?"

Often, we start looking in the metaphysical realms for meaning way before we look to our own roles as autonomous authentic beings within this Universe.

Before reading on, I would like you to consider how you accept, participate and contribute in the *"Here and Now"*. Consider how you find meaning, happiness and reward in your current life and consider whether you look inside before looking externally for answers. Let's first work with the current manifestation of our souls and how our souls grow within this current Universe. I'd like you to consider spiritual growth as more than reaching out and worshiping and begin to learn how to honor our souls' roles as active participants in creation itself.

Many other programs address the spiritual side of life as a separate topic, or ignore the needs of the soul altogether and treat life and the world as some kind of shopping-mall that abundantly provides everything we could possibly desire (if only we believe hard enough).

If you investigate some of these programs, you can find several that look somewhat like this:

"If you know what you want (have a clear and focused goal) and you have a true sense of where you are right now (your starting point), then break down the total gap into smaller, more achievable goals (chunking-down) and keep motivated until you close the gap (chunking-up). Develop a strategy and action plan for success..."

In essence this approach is a "life coaching technique" in another wrapper. These Napoleon Hill – based philosophies make it sound very achievable:

Section 1: Introduction

1. Clearly understanding your goals.
2. Clearly understanding your starting point (where you are now, relative to your goals).
3. Create a step-by-step program to achieve your goals and manifest them.

But there is always a missing piece. And not just one but several:

Missing piece #1: You NEED to figure out your goals for yourself and this is one of the most difficult parts. Most people don't know what they want. They look at their future in terms of what they can have and can live rather than developing an understanding of what they truly want. We've lost our childlike ability to dream; to embrace and believe that what we truly want and desire... is actually possible.

"Follow your dreams" and "manifest your journey" are wonderful messages - if you know the goals you're headed towards.

Missing piece #2: Most people look for answers outside themselves. Not because this makes sense, but because popular marketing and a commerce-based society tells them that their solutions come from the OUTSIDE... (From buying things!)

I have studied many coaching programs, but I was disappointed in the way they approached the topic of goal-setting. To solve this puzzle, they talk about goal-setting as if you live in a "shopping-mall of life" filled with cars, money, bigger houses, trips, anything money can buy and measure....

Worse, they tend to teach techniques that help you maintain your idea of constantly bettering yourself and never finding the inner peace of being "abundantly ENOUGH!" Ultimately this is missing piece #3.

The Path Within Program addresses these points. In individual sessions that are geared towards understanding what drives your *authentic core being* and fortifying your *foundation of reality*, I help you discover your own *personal power* and your place within the Universe. This is why I've been asked to write this program down. To make it available for individuals as well as for practitioners who can use these techniques in their own sessions.

By learning personalized skills and practical self-actualization from within, we can address the questions that keep coming up; demystifying the secrets that give us access to our happiness and living the life we truly desire.

Why Use Hypnosis

In my practice, there are various moments in which I like to use hypnosis. I use hypnosis to provide a focused "channel" to work on specific topics in a concentrated way.

Some people are worried about hypnosis. Various myths are propagated about this tool. Some believe it can be used for mind-controlor coercion. Nothing is further from the truth. Hypnosis simply provides a way to concentrate on specific topics without all the mind-clutter getting in the way.

This program is filled with knowledge and methods but there is still no way I can make you reach within yourself and connect with your innermost personal wisdom and *truth*. I can be but a guide and give you tools to help you find your own answers. The *truth* you already know was created within yourself and can only be accessed by you. The real value of this program to you then is the practical application of this knowledge within your own life. You must be the one to find your own *truth*, answers and metaphors which are but vehicles to journey through the necessary changes in your own life. Hypnosis is a very practical way to go inward and work on your own solutions without needing to worry about convincing the always-present critical factor of the mind, the gatekeeper to the inner mind. This critical factor, also known as the vigilant mind, is convinced that it is "always right," and can therefore create much resistance in psychotherapeutic exercises. Hypnosis solves this problem and allows you to work on your own problems, in your own way, at your own speed - often faster and more successfully than any other method currently available - without needing to rely on conversations with a convincing therapist.

The speed at which hypnosis can help a client realize and facilitate transition from old to new beliefs allows progress to be made quickly, sometimes almost immediately and effortlessly. Using more traditional "talk therapies" requires that the facilitator or therapist convinces the client. Specifically, the client's critical factor, also known as the logical reasoning, the ego, or the vigilant self, needs convincing before it allows change. Within a hypnotic state, the client allows a deeper understanding of the newly seeded idea, which then has a chance to grow, to percolate and become a new awareness within the client - without relying on the critical factor to evaluate the entire novel thought before being convinced and passing it along in a translated, filtered and re-coloured state to the subconscious, where the idea may do its healing work.

Chapter 2 – Are You Ready for The Path Within?

The most frequent obstacle I encounter when a new client comes for an exploratory session is obstinacy. My exploratory sessions are two-way interviews that are designed to allow me to get acquainted with an individual client and to help my new client decide if this is the best next step in his or her life's journey.

This type of work requires a person to have a particular mindset. Not everyone has this mindset, although it can be developed. In order to be able to complete The Path Within Program, you must understand that this type of work requires the individual to create the changes from within. There's simply no way that the realizations and changes can be enforced by an external source. In these modern times we easily pass-on our responsibilities to the "professionals" and assign the responsibility for our wellness to others. People who do this tend to <u>externalize</u> their responsibility and therefore lack the accountability to take their life into their hands and create the change they want.

On the other hand, there are people who are a bit skeptical in nature, but this is not the same as externalizing. After spending time in genuine presence and after only a few sessions, skeptical people soon embrace the work, be it cautiously at first. These people can be very successful at this work. I have many clients who can attest to being reluctant to the initial change of thought, but who found it difficult to ignore the logic and practical applications of these simple truths and did find their paths.

No, the truly impossible ones are the obstinate ones, the ones who claim to be in need of change but refuse to do any real work. They believe that they can simply continue their old behaviours and thought patterns and that the practitioner will override their behaviours and "install" a better program without their participation or effort. Alternatively, they want to continue

Chapter 2 – Are You Ready for The Path Within?

with their problems and use the work as a justification: "See, my problem is much more real and terrible than anyone else's. I still have the problem, <u>even</u> after going to sessions."

Many people who come to this work have been through forms of "traditional therapy" and tried other methods without success and are "sick of being sick." This is a good indication that they are ready to embrace the journey through this approach. The logic and the refreshing, brutally honest support they receive resuscitates their faith and keeps them going. In the end they are invigorated and delighted with the relatively brief period of time we spend together compared to the years of dead-end therapy.

I'm sure you'll find many similarities with approaches you've encountered before. I hope to show you much of what you already know in a new and more practical way.

Are you ready to make a change in your life? Are you ready to be a participant in creating your future, even if this means you must learn what part of your perception of life is reality and what part is illusion? Are you ready to invest time and a little effort into creating lasting change?

I often ask my clients if they truly understand that they are finite, that they live <u>this</u> life once and that they may not have time or opportunity to correct their choices in the future. I get mixed responses, but most people understand that one day you will be looking back on your life. When that day comes for you, will you be grateful for taking the time and effort to turn your life around, or are you still hoping that your lottery ticket will pay you a lifetime of happiness?

There are many other self-help programs available. Each highlights its own unique viewpoint. Some are more spiritual, others are religious and yet others quote much science or extrapolated scientific terms in an attempt to prove that their approaches are sound.

While I embrace the use of any attempt to help others, no matter what metaphor is used, I'm often surprised to learn that many programs are still claiming to offer the secret to life while making it impossible to actually achieve the ecstatic claims promised in their marketing.

Many programs require you to ignore parts of reality to effectively use the program. The Path Within Program is aimed at using clear reality to explain what influences us and how to navigate the Universe to create a realistic place for ourselves and everyone around us. You don't need to believe in religious concepts, you don't need to be advanced in meditation; you don't need to declare allegiance, ignore pain, fear or time or adhere to a certain lifestyle. Just be yourself and learn how your mind interacts with your *core Self*, your Universe, your fears and illusions.

The Path Within approach is realistic and observant. There are plenty of spiritual metaphors in this book but they do not require learning a new religion or becoming more spiritual; these metaphors support a deeper understanding of your inner relationship with your *core Self* and your Universe.

So if you too have come to realize that while life itself is infinite yet your life is finite, then maybe you are ready to take your journey further and grow towards healing and awareness; to understand yourself better and how and why you interact in certain ways with others and especially the relationship you have with yourself.

This book goes beyond awareness and knowledge alone. When you are ready to direct your energy and focus to changing your life, examine how you interact with the Universe and everyone in it and are ready to see yourself as the creator of your life, then The Path Within becomes your resource to create your own personal, rewarding future.

Chapter 3 – Book Structure

This book is divided into three sections. You're reading the first section, which is the introduction to the program. Section two helps you understand the foundations and underlying logic of The Path Within Program and section three takes you through the levels, or thresholds, of the program in the way that I do with my clients.

To get the most from this work I recommend you read this book from cover to cover and to take your time absorbing the material. Typically, sessions with a Path Within practitioner are 90-120 minutes, spaced approximately seven days apart. This would give you time to absorb the material and to seed the changes you want to embody.

Don't be in a hurry. Take your time. Digest the concepts slowly and allow yourself to observe the insights in your awareness in everyday life. It is well-worth the patience to set yourself a reasonable pace to work through the exercises and material in section three.

Of course, The Path Within Program will not do the work for you. Only if you have the intent to find a better way to live your *truth* and purpose, with meaningful relationships, peace within yourself and the curiosity to learn how and why people relate at their core levels – then The Path Within Program is your perfect next step.

For now, let your curiosity be your motivation. As you become more deeply involved in the teachings and ideas of the Path Within, your motivation and participation will increase exponentially.

If you make it to the end of the book you may want to challenge me on these notions, but first I would recommend you follow along, absorb and connect with the concepts and philosophies presented in this book. Individually, each of these concepts and notions may conflict with what you were taught by your well-meaning parents, your teachers, your society and other influences in your life, who were themselves heavily influenced by marketing, social policy and lobbying. But once you embrace multiple overlapping thoughts, you will stand before a new outlook in life, filled with opportunity and possibility for you to embrace.

Alone or With a Guide?

Working with this book and the accompanying audio meditations is all that is required to realize the benefits of this program. Clearly, working with a Path Within practitioner would be a useful resource as Path Within practitioners, having knowledge of the complete program, have the ability to introduce modules in a different order than how they are presented here in the book. This personalization allows for more rapid progress and a level of customization that is a more personal approach to a client's individual life. Working with a Path Within practitioner provides other benefits as well, such as being able to receive a second opinion, the presence of a motivator/coach and the support to linger on a difficult topic or skim over topics that are more easily assimilated by the client. But this does not mean you need a facilitator or guide for every step of this program.

I would recommend that if you have a difficult past that may influence your current behaviours and thoughts, that you consider therapies that specifically address these issues. Often, properly administered Regression Therapy using Reframing techniques or Gestalt-type work allows sufficient processing to disassociate main triggers related to the past.

If you have a relatively healthy relationship with your past and you can recall your memories without having to relive the emotions associated with these events every time you recall them, you can be confident to embark upon The Path Within Program on your own, without a skilled practitioner.

Results

The people who have completed The Path Within Program, either with me or by themselves, report high levels of Self-Confidence, Self-Esteem and Self-Worth, for starters. You will learn a clear and intimate knowledge of your *authentic core being* and the blissful awareness that it survives ALL. You will come to understand that your *authentic core being* is indestructible.

Chapter 3 – Book Structure

You will come away with an absolute knowing that your uniqueness and differences are to be celebrated and nurtured, not normalized or dampened.

The Path Within Program provides tools to help you to re-learn your old *truths* and behaviours and understand their triggers. Not in the classical psychotherapy sense, but more simply - how these old *truths*, or belief systems, no longer need to be obstacles to accessing and developing your potential.

Exercises

If you want to create change in your life, then I would highly recommend you practice the skills of your new self progressively. This book is structured so that each chapter builds on the strengths of the previous chapter. You are a master at your old behaviours, thought patterns, emotional triggers and other habits through years of practice. Consider the Path Within as a new skill. Practice each skill and master it, knowing that each skill builds upon the foundation of the skill before it.

There's a huge difference between knowledge and *knowing*. The deep understanding that you can gain from learning The Path Within Program is useful, but practicing the mind skills and learning new ways to resolve the factors that influence your life will produce invaluable results. Imagine being faced with a difficult situation that overwhelms you. At a moment of decision, a moment of resistance, or a moment of opportunity, what will you do? You will do what your habits and your core nature is trained to do. It is in these moments that you would benefit from the mastery of the Path Within skills, as with those skills embodied in your core nature you will effortlessly follow your authentic *truth* rather than fall back on habits from your past.

Once you have mastered the Path Within and are living your clear and conscious self, you will effortlessly make the decisions that would allow you to continue along your authentic path. It really is up to you now... are you ready to become master of a life that works <u>for</u> you?

Be aware how every day influences may continue to "nag" at you and steer you slowly into the direction of their influence. A master doesn't waiver. A master follows his or her own path; a Path Within, serving your authentic and autonomous self.

Section 1: Introduction

Discovery

I won't teach you that the world is vastly different than you know it to be now. I won't teach you a new religion, nor that your religion is somehow flawed. I won't even teach you a better way of being yourself. What I will show you, throughout this book, is another way to see the world for what it is and then to interact with the world from this place of embodied knowledge.

Throughout my life I have been fascinated by the way people interact with each other, with themselves and with the Universe around us. More interesting to me, however, has been the ways people interact with what they imagine to be true – their perceived realities, emotional drama and adopted belief systems. I've been interested in the reasons we create these augmented realities, believe them to be true - to the point of defending them - and attempt to build our lives and grow our souls on these unstable foundations, using perceptions and hallucinations as anchors. Are we so attached to the safety of the idea of a stable reality that we'll invent one and live in illusion rather than live in the uncertainty and reality of an authentic life?

All I am able to promise you right now are the tools to make new discoveries for yourself. No one but you can make these discoveries; can enter the vault of your mind and start freeing that beautiful soul of yours, the part that has been imprisoned by perceptions and belief systems. Ultimately, the goal is to discover an intimate personal knowledge and awareness of your own personal journey – your Path Within.

We will discuss and discover concepts such as living in the moment, working with forgiveness, trusting the Universe while letting go of our *illusion of control* and living with harmony versus insisting on fairness and balance.

Let me ask you a question: can a lone swimmer move a big boat?

Yes, of course! It will take time and sustained effort, but the boat will slowly move and once the boat is moving, it will require significant effort to slow it down again.

Imagine driving slower than all other traffic around you. You'll be in everyone's way and they will attempt to pass you. Now imagine wanting to drive faster than all other traffic around you. You'll find that now everyone is in your way and the additional effort of driving around every slower vehicle is disproportionate to the gain you make.

Now imagine driving at approximately the same speed as the traffic around you and also looking for opportunities, openings and obstacles along the way. You will find that your ability to anticipate changes in traffic will allow you to react nimbly to quickly and exponentially create advantage, with virtually no additional effort than if you were simply driving at the same speed as everyone else.

Force requires effort and is met with resistance. Agility requires no perceivable effort and obtains better results. Let's work with harmony and agility.

Chapter 4 – Purpose / Mission

With this book I intend to contribute to the restoration of harmony in the world; an inclusive harmony with room for everything and everyone.

In a world of harmony there is also room for negatives, problems and illnesses. In a world of harmony we don't fight wars with soldiers, but with understanding and learning. In a world of harmony we don't fight the symptoms of disease, but we work with the root-causes which act as indicators for choices we made or circumstances to which we are exposed.

In a "just" world, on the other hand, a world of right and wrong, of balances, fairness and justice when we are in distress we retaliate and feel justified to do so. In a world of harmony we remain inquisitive, ask questions and learn. We wonder what sequence of experiences would prompt someone to attack us or we think, "what about me do you fear enough to behave this way," or "what is it you are trying to show me? And how can we restore peace" and how do we avoid creating more cumulative harm?

My purpose for this book is to look at mental wellness (not illness) as a holistic topic. Working <u>with</u> rather than <u>in opposition to</u> our own natural abilities to survive and heal, both mentally and physically.

Harmony of mind (mental wellness) requires a different viewpoint than "fixing the mind" (mental illness).

At times I touch on and even welcome, the indicators and symptoms surrounding depression, anxiety, relationships and the meaning of life itself, but I don't see these cases in terms of illness. Please take care when dealing with medical issues. If a medical illness is suspected, it must be dealt with by a medical professional – such is the law in many countries. Once the symptoms of the illness are of no further concern to a licensed practitioner, the actual path to healing the underlying root causes can truly begin.

Chapter 4 – Purpose / Mission

Balance vs. Harmony

Imagine a scale in front of you, a balance-type scale. An old-fashioned scale made of 2 baskets on either side of a rod. And the rod is balanced in the middle by a hinge; the fulcrum.

This scale can represent anything you like, the balance of life, the balance of power between countries, or an everyday problem. The following principles of Balance versus Harmony are equally applicable.

In the first example (Illustration A) each side of the scale applies minor pressure to the scale and life looks in balance, equal and in harmony. The scale is level.

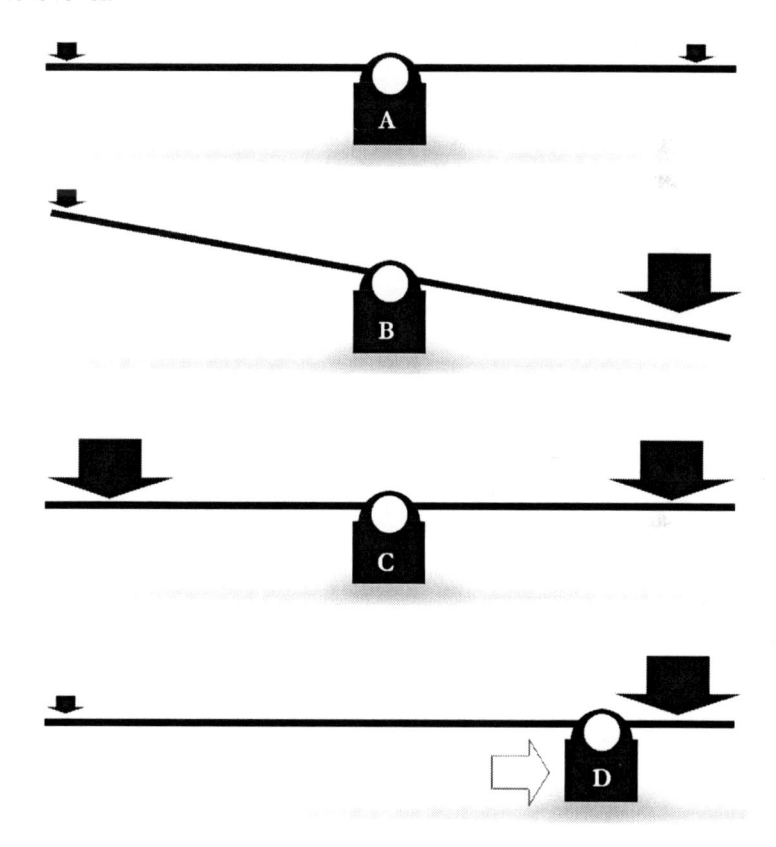

At this point, I would like you to imagine placing an issue on one side of our scale. The scale is no longer balanced and leans towards the side of the additional "weight" (Illustration B). We have a strange and unnatural reaction to this issue being placed on one side of the scale. As thinking

Section 1: Introduction

humans, we tend to place a "solution value" of equal and opposite "weight" on the other side of the scale for balance (Illustration C). Yet nature tends to use its resources more frugally and I would like to advocate learning from nature.

It seems that by placing a solution with equal weight to the opposing side of the scale we have dealt with the issue. When you look at the scale (Illustration C) it does appear to show that balance is restored, because the scale is level again. But the overall load on the fulcrum has now doubled! Not only is the fulcrum taking the weight of the issue but it is now forced to support the weight of the solution as well – in our example the fulcrum is now carrying twice the "weight."

Not only is the issue itself not addressed, it is challenged. In my experience and discoveries, when anything is challenged its resistance becomes stronger. Adding a "solution value" of equal and opposite force doesn't solve the problem! This merely stabilizes the problem without dealing with it and the system as a whole needs to take the entire load. In order to eradicate it, we must overwhelm the "issue" with "solution" and thus, for good measure, we load the "solution side" of the balance with additional "solution" – overloading the fulcrum which must bear the total load of both issue and solution! And if the issue has any built in survival mechanism, it will start to resist the "solution" in response, creating a bigger or more complex "problem."

Nature takes a different approach. Nature is not a system "in balance," but a system "in harmony."

As the "issue" is placed on one side, the harmony of nature attempts to restore harmony by moving the fulcrum towards the issue (Illustration D). The closer the fulcrum gets to the issue (the symptom), the more the system learns the issue (the root cause) and the quicker harmony can be restored. For example, pain killers don't restore harmony they mask the symptoms so that you can continue your routine without interruption; only attending to the issue i.e. rest and healing will actually work from the root cause and restore harmony.

The harmony of nature works in every aspect of the Universe. By constantly shifting its fulcrums, it is constantly adjusting to maintain universal harmony. Of course, we tend to think of harmony as something pleasant and resist the notion that harmony is non judgmental; not good or bad, not pleasant or

Chapter 4 – Purpose / Mission

unpleasant, but the overall sum of all factors within a system, collaborating without one dominating the others. Yin and Yang. Life.

Medicating Healthcare

Imagine a basement with two rooms. The total of the rooms occupy the entire basement. One of the rooms is the game room and the other is used as your office. Now, you want to expand the size of one of the rooms. Naturally the other room becomes smaller. This is how harmony works. You might be the occupant of the expanding room, or the occupant of the shrinking room.

In a world of balance or justice, it would stand to reason that if one of the rooms is expanded, it's only fair that the other room is also enlarged. But this fairness doesn't exist. Not in basements and not in the Universe! Life and the Universe are not "out to get you" by giving you the unfairly shrinking room. The Universe finds harmony first, regardless of "fair or unfair" judgments or justifications. The fair/unfair judgment is only one side of the discussion. In its totality, the Universe enforces harmony. Balance can be upset, harmony cannot. Take from one, add to another... just like physics, but unlike physics, our Universe is ever expanding.

And as I advocate that we stop sending soldiers to war zones, maybe we would also be best served by ending the fight against cancer and other auto-immune disorders and starting to work with them; alongside them. In this book I'm restricting my focus to issues such as grief, depression, anxiety, bi-polar disorder and other mental labels. In my opinion, these conditions benefit more from understanding, harmony and collaboration than from our current approach of "masking the symptoms," "overcoming," and "coping."

Fighting a problem within you means that you're only fighting yourself.

It's in your best interest to find permanent answers for your troubled mind. So why is the healthcare industry more interested in "fighting mental issues" and "coping with symptoms?" Largely it is because mental illness is a huge industry with companies constantly marketing and finding new ways to sell their legalized "happy pills". Without much regard for your actual issues, the mental health industry is looking to sell you drugs that will obfuscate your issues temporarily – and only while you continue to use the drugs they sell. This approach is not meant to be a long-term solution that serves your wellbeing, but is likely a structured attempt at creating a long-term dependence on their products, while serving only your short-term needs for relief.

The corporations make much more money on these drugs when you don't actually get better and they don't address the underlying causes. While you are on drugs you can go back to being a productive citizen, earning money, contributing to the GNP, paying taxes, etc. Others think they stand to gain more from your productivity than from your healing. Suppressing symptoms and ignoring the root causes of illness seems to have been the main focus of modern healthcare. Dealing with the root causes of mental and social wellbeing would put parents back at home, pulling them out of the work-force; would teach people to purchase only what they need, not what corporate enterprise tell them they are entitled to; and would enable us to address the other institutions that stand to gain from your unhappiness, unbalance, disharmony, or whatever else you want to call it.

Harmony and healing are the main focuses of the Path Within work. Breaking through to health, healing the root causes, learning to recognise and promote our own minds' healing responses, catching the symptoms earlier and finding permanent solutions without side effects or addiction are the ways to create true mental wellness.

Does this mean we let nature run its course? Often the answer is "yes," but sometimes it is necessary to assist nature. Rather than looking at these corrections as controlling nature - which cannot really be done anyway - we change the way we participate in the harmony of nature itself. When we make attempts to overcome nature, nature always wins. If, however, we participate with nature, as part of nature and the Universe, then we can influence the ways in which the harmony of nature manifest and work in collaboration with the Universe itself. It's all part of working in collaboration <u>within</u> the harmony of the Universe rather than attempting to enforce fairness, balance and justice, which would put us in challenge and opposition to the Universe.

Life is neither fair nor just. Life is harmonious. As individuals, we might believe we would prefer for life to be just and fair. And I'm sure we would like this fairness to be in our "just" favour. The truth is that a Universe that is not in perfect harmony is not stable enough to sustain itself, so the Universe enforces harmony. Life favours the perpetuation of the Universe itself and harmony within it.

Chapter 5 – Shaping the Journey of Life

Do you know when and how you have influence on your life? Do you know when your perceived reality is based on extrapolated perception? Or that your sense of control is mostly illusion?

It is difficult and fruitless to create a life that is largely based on illusion. We can handle the truth. We are adults. Even if the truth is painful now, we will never escape its discomfort if we don't start from reality.

Our Super Power

Animals evolve over generations, that includes humans. Does it not surprise you then, how humans evolved without obvious super powers? No retractable claws, no wings to fly, no particular speed, no big teeth or enormous strength, etc. While every species on the planet took its evolutionary place among other species and created a symbiosis, humans seem to have gone another route. Or have we?

While most species adapted physically to their environments, humans have developed our ability to develop. That is, we have developed a way to learn from our own development and then to augment our experience of real-time learning with virtual learning. Other species are also capable of learning from their own behaviour and extrapolating their knowledge and abilities into future possibility, but we are able to extrapolate much further into the future than any other species on the planet. What we are capable of – our *super power*– is more than just learning habits and creating learned responses as most other species do.

Humans can observe our own thoughts! Our *super power* comes from this ability. The ability to observe our thoughts is known as metacognition. Our ability to learn from our observations is our *super power*. There is some evidence that there are other species that have some abilities in this direction, but none as highly developed as our own.

Not only are we able to observe our thoughts, we're able to manipulate the thoughts and results they produce, all while learning from each virtual situation as if it had occurred in reality. Like actors on a stage, we can conjure up new thoughts, concepts and ideas and think our way through the possible outcomes of adding the imagined thought to a virtual world, without exposing ourselves to the real consequences of experimenting in the real world.

For example: Imagine for a moment that you remember a conversation you had with your best friend. You recall having different views on a situation regarding a third and mutual friend. Now, imagine that this conversation ended badly. You disagreed on "what really happened" and you leave upset. A few days later your mutual third friend told his or her story and resolved the conflict. In the mean time, you and your best friend were upset at each other.

Now, let's use our *super power* for the same situation, still in hind sight. With metacognition, we observe what happens from the safety of our minds. Restart the scene where you and your friend disagree over the behaviour of your mutual friend. And now, the third friend joins the conversation while you're still disagreeing and resolves the conflict right away. The way you felt about your best friend would have been different for the following few days, right? The exercise we just participated in caused you to use a "what if?" thought pattern during the replay, while observing your own thoughts at the same time.

This is how we, as humans, have evolved our ability to learn rapidly. We are even able to predict the future, or at least attempt to predict it with relatively high accuracy. Our metacognitive abilities have allowed us to create a virtual, unlived future in our minds. A true *super power*!

The Good News
In every study about winners, that is, when success stories are analysed, we're able to observe a clear trend. The majority of successes were born from two major factors: Tenacity and agility. The sheer belief that there is a solution makes the winner hold on (tenacity) and continue to look for another way to make it work (agility). Our ability to experiment with outcomes in our

minds, without needing to put everything into practice, saves us time and energy in our quest for solutions.

The agility of the mind works at its most efficient when we use this power of metacognition. We can experiment with the viability of new ideas without needing to test them in reality. Just a thought can hold a possible answer to a real-life question. In thought, we can even play with ridiculous and unlikely scenarios to find possibilities in the vastness of our imaginations – and observe our own thinking processes while doing this. We can even evaluate ideas and select the better ones, all without executing any of them (yet).

Reality vs. Metacognition
When you look into a mirror that is angled so that you can view another mirror, you end up with a strange repeating visual pattern. Metacognition can work in a much similar way and we have thoughts that observe thoughts that observe thoughts and so on... But it is important to get back to a sense of reality outside of our reflected thoughts. Observing our feelings can be the key to keep us from getting too entangled in our inner-virtual world. We'll discuss how to observe our feelings in the third threshold of the Path Within.

In all studies of trends and especially in business models, we find that the most agile entity survives and ultimately determines the outcomes of trends and models. It is agility itself and our ability to discriminate between workable ideas and possible resistance or harm that creates success- but only once translated back from fantasy to reality.

Our *super power* is like a double edged sword.

The Bad News
Metacognition has a shadow. Our *super power* is a true force and as with all true forces, it can be used to serve us but metacognition can also be a source of discomfort. The double edged sword of metacognition is that we are able to convince ourselves that the discomfort we create in ourselves is for our own good. And this is where this book truly begins.

As we predict the future and look for possible outcomes that could manifest in real time, we adapt our "predictor machines" to have selective memory. When we predict situations that work in our minds, we store them as "learning." If, however, we predict situations that might harm us, we store the prediction with a connection to our fear; a trigger for our fight or flight response mechanism that we may need to invoke at a later time.

Interestingly, when we study the root of the thoughts, the original notion of fearing the future, we actually see a different pattern emerging. We are not really afraid of the future itself, we are simply looking out for the possible dangers that might arise along the path. Unfortunately, we often cannot distinguish the fears from the possibilities, nor find the courage to see the fears for what they really are: warnings for <u>possible</u> danger, not actual danger. This results in inaction and the continuation of the fears that we perceive to be "real threats," and we stop moving forward. The truth about fear may set you free, releasing you from your limiting belief systems and the safeties and controls your mind so carefully constructed to give you an illusion of safety.

Using Our Super Power
Agility and adaptability are less taxing on our systems – both mentally and physically. In my opinion, using *mental-models* to work within your new mental framework and creating belief systems that serve you is a more efficient approach to mental wellness than remodeling or coping with existing belief systems and habit patterns that drain your life's energies, motivations and ultimately your purpose.

Most of the modern therapies that are available today advocate using coping strategies as a way of working with the symptoms and behaviours of mental issues. The Path Within Program works <u>with</u> your metacognition, assisting you to create *mental-models* that will help you find your own connections within yourself and thus helps you embody the new you. This is, in my opinion, the most efficient way to utilize our *super power* and create change, leaving energy for the creation and enjoyment of life itself.

Intuition

Extrapolating possibilities by learning with metacognitionhelps us to intuit the future. This might sound more like a psychic power but this process is a "subconscious learning of patterns" or "extrapolating possibilities through subconscious deduction."

Our abilities to learn, adapt, predict in the way that we do and deduct answers with the assistance of fictitious scenarios allow us to function at the top of the evolutionary "food chain". While our abilities to intuit and self-monitor give us great advantages, they have shadow sides. Allow me to explain.

Our ability to imagine and then learn from scenarios that are not real allows us to test reality without becoming part of it. Staying at a safe distance, or practicing ahead of time. In other words, we are able to learn from situations that are neither here, nor now.

We have a built in fear of the unknown and a lot of stored knowledge. When we combine the two, we quickly find ourselves assuming that our conclusions might pose threats to our personal safety. We all employ this mechanism to attempt to keep us safe in the future.

Our memory awareness has the ability to trigger associated pleasure or pain stimuli alongside memories. Unfortunately, we sometimes focus on what might hurt us in the future rather than focusing on the reality of *Here and Now*. We all too often find ourselves in thought patterns that use all our mental capacity for predicting future possible threats and we torture ourselves.

Our metacognition is one of our most valuable tools, but also one of our biggest challenges, considering we often focus too much on what can harm us. This causes us to suffer from the effects of memories or imprints that have never occurred. We become fearful of experiencing harm from many situations that are unlikely to occur and these thought patterns prevent us from taking actions.

The underlying issue is that we were taught to believe in the likelihood of harm. The way to avoid this action paralysis is to begin to recognize when your brain enters into a harmful metacognitive cycle. You will notice that you are associating physical pain with predictions that are not real. Begin to recognize these thoughts and fears, for what they are: metacognitively produced hallucinations. Then, focus on reality. In the section "Thought Awareness" in Chapter 20, I discuss a useful exercise to identify the difference between a hallucination and reality.

Cat Moves

My cat loved sitting on a tiny rug on the hardwood floor. Every time the cat would pounce, the rug would fly in the opposite direction and the cat would move towards her target at less than half her anticipated speed, having lost most of her energy when the rug flew in the opposite direction. One day I placed a small rubber mat under the rug. The next time she pounced, the power she was able to use was amazing. I remember the height of her jump!

I would like to use this anecdote to illustrate two things: 1. With only the illusion of a solid base, the cat gained very little return on the energy she invested in her endeavor. 2. Without resistance there is no traction, nothing to push against, no resistance to harness from and no power to convert into relative distance from the starting point.

To be able to create real change in your life, you must start from reality; a solid and real *foundation of reality* that will support the changes you are working towards. Change can only be made in relation to this *foundation of reality*. This interaction between what you want to achieve and reality is felt as resistance. Resistance to the force you exert upon the *foundation of reality*. As you are overcoming the resistance you feel traction and momentum. Only then can you feel a sense of progress.

The Suspicious Rat

I was reminded recently of a study with rats in a book by Paul Watzlawick called: "How Real is Real." In this book he describes a behavioural study with rats in a box that had a little door to an outside area. At the end of this outside area, there was a feeding trough. The experiment went as follows:

Open the trap door to the outside area
Wait 10 Seconds
Drop the food in the feeding trough
Repeat

What the observers observed was that the rat believed it had an influence on the food being placed in the feeding trough. When the rat looked side to side to see where the food came from and then the food appeared, the rat would remember this side to side motion as the cause of the food's appearance and repeat the behaviour in the next experiment. The truth was unknown to the rat; the food would come after 10 seconds, regardless of the rat's behaviour. The rat would continue to come out of the trap door, repeat its behaviour and receive a "reward" for its behaviour.

Different rats created different repeating behaviours in their attempts to influence the food rewards.

Interestingly, we too think and behave like these rats at times. We believe that our behaviours have much more influence on the world than they actually do. Much of what happens to us is not caused by us yet we continue to live in our illusions of control and taking too much responsibility for what happens.

The Omnipotent Baby

One of our first impressions of the way our world works is as a baby. We feel tummy aches and complain of discomfort. Then we're fed by our mommies and our tummy aches disappear.

From the baby's naive viewpoint there is only one explanation possible: "We were fed because we felt a tummy ache," therefore "everything that happens to me happens because of me."

While this notion is partially true, especially for babies, we never really learn of disappointment and the injustice of reality until we're much older! And we still throw temper tantrums whenever the world isn't fair according to us....

We make incorrect conclusions as babies that our world revolves around us and that our awareness alone is enough to influence the world. This narcissistic approach and notion remains with us throughout our lifetimes. Isn't it time to understand the truth of reality and understand the world in ways that allow us to grow within it? Isn't it time to stop resisting the world because it does not match our infant-like notions of omnipotence and to interact with it in deep understanding and in true collaboration?

Section 2: Path Within Foundations

The purpose of this section is to introduce and explain many of the principle theories and applications that underpin the practical work of The Path Within Program.

It is recommended that you work through this preliminary section that contains the general philosophy to lay a solid foundation for moving into the deeper work. The Foundations section also introduces some exercises which will be of use to you in your everyday life but are optional to The Path Within Program. After you have worked with all the Tools and Exercises in the Sessions section these chapters will serve as a reference guide in the future.

Chapter 6 – What Came First?

Let's begin this journey inward with an age old riddle: which came first - the chicken or the egg? Hidden in this simple question is a profound metaphor that provides clues to understanding our existence.

Path Within Foundations starts with this conundrum because I believe that exploring this seemingly unanswerable question may provide a doorway to connect with this material through experiential mental participation.

So, to examine the question of the chicken and the egg; if one must precede the other, then what started the cycle? This question highlights a fundamental thought pattern that we may all need to re-examine. That is, the idea that everything in relation to each other is causal: the belief that everything is caused by something else. While every action has a reaction, not everything happens for an obviously present reason. Many things are caused, some things are created and other things can simply be attributed to *magic*, which we'll discuss in depth later in the book.

With the awareness that not everything has a cause in mind, the answer to this riddle is that one was not created before the other. Over time, they co-created each other as they are one and the same. At no time was there suddenly a chicken or egg. They evolved together, as they needed each other to continue the evolution of the species.

This understanding is the first step on our path and we will apply it to understanding ourselves. If the chicken and egg evolved concurrently, what about the brain and the mind? The brain is the physical flesh and blood organ in our heads, which processes our perceptions of the world and interacts with our bodies. The mind is our non-physical reality of thoughts, identity, intellect, imagination, perceptions and all that we understand as our selves. At any given time we harbor many a thought and we accommodate these thoughts and processes with our relatively large brains. But did we always have such large brains? Did we always have so many thoughts and processes to accommodate? Just like the chicken and the egg, over the course of human evolution, our minds and brains also co-created each other. In fact, mind patterns, self-talk and repeated behaviours physically alter our neural networks. And the brain as a self-regulating, self-modifying organ continues to evolve in co-creativity with the mind, to have an influence over the way we think, how we remember and the ways we behave. Our moods, our illusions and the reality around us persistently interact with us, influencing the physical makeup of our neural networks, which in turn assist our minds to perceive, learn, etc.

If a Tree

To more deeply explore our *super power* of self-observation, I would like to invite you into one more question you may have heard before, but that has often been poorly examined:

"If a tree falls in the forest and there's no one there to hear it, does it still make a sound?"

Please observe yourself thinking about the solution to this interesting question without looking at the answer below just yet. Some might argue that a physical object that normally creates a sound when it falls still makes that sound on impact with the ground. Others might argue that our ears create the experience by converting air-pressure and the impact of vibration on our ear drums into what we call "sound," and without our ears there is nothing to make the sound in the first place. Even others have spent hours convincing me that reality is created by the perceiver and if there is no one in the forest, then the forest does not exist. This would mean that without the observer the tree does not exist either and non-existing trees don't make perceivable sounds.

Clearly, opinions differ when you approach this question as something that can only be answered with a "Yes" or "No." But there is simply no yes or no conclusion to this riddle and these various viewpoints obscure a deeper philosophical challenge:

"If there's no one to hear the tree fall, does it matter?"

Maybe it matters that a tree fell. Not only is the tree no longer standing and growing, but its demise could have an impact on the entire ecosystem of the forest, etc. But to concentrate on the actual question – if there is no observer, is there a reason for the sound? The sound in this riddle was created for the observer and removing the observer removes the reason for the question, regardless of the existence of the sound.

There are many lessons in this little riddle, some of which give us insight into deeper *truths*. It especially highlights how we tend to project meaning onto otherwise simple experiences.

Chapter 7 – The Hippocampus - The Stage of Life

When a human's mission is to evolve and grow, then surely we can only grow when we are in reality? Initially this may seem true, but upon further examination it becomes clear that learning through the use of our virtual reality is faster, more efficient and less messy. But growing through an imaginary world only provides us with imaginary results. Our only hope of creating real results comes through learning from and growing through real world situations. Yet our *super power* is metacognition, it gives us the opportunity to learn and grow at an accelerated pace by using our imagination. The answer to our evolution seems to be a collaboration of the two worlds, reality and imagination.

In order to understand how we learn we need to take a fresh look at how we perceive and construct reality. The mechanics of perception are a clue to the complex ways by which we obtain and process information from the outside world. How we obtain and process information from our internal and external environments determines how we experience and understand our reality.

Let's examine these mechanics of perception briefly: we have sensors for light, sound, touch and the other senses and we process the inputs from these sensors into cohesive images in our imaginations. Then we observe and further process these images in our amazing brains and comprehend them in our amazing minds. While this explanation is true in essence, reality is actually much more complex than this simplified version would suggest.

Our eyes, for instance, do not see complete images. They see light intensity and colours and our stereoscopic vision (two eyes in the front of our heads) allows us to perceive depth and distance. While this is a masterpiece of nature, what we see is much more than what our eyes perceive. Only after the visual cortex of the brain processes the information taken in by the eyes do we "see" shapes. Then our brains further process those shapes into images. Look at any thing and you'll be convinced you are looking at the entire object, even though you can only see part of it. In actuality, we only imagine a world filled with complete, three-dimensional objects.

For instance, look at your hand. You can see the front or the back of your hand but never both sides at the same time. Yet you perceive the hand as a whole object. How does this work, if we can only see part of the picture?

The Stage of Life

We use the hippocampus, which is a seahorse-shaped distinct region in the core of the brain, as a repository of processed images, thoughts, concepts and other fragments of reality. We hold a model of the world and ourselves within this world, as representations on a stage in our minds. Upon this *stage of life* the world is three-dimensional. It is perfectly fine to receive mostly two-dimensional, stereoscopic, partial information from the world around us, because the mind simply combines the information it <u>already knows</u> with the information that is <u>being observed</u> to create a <u>complete</u> scene upon this stage. And because the mind is the filter through which we experience reality, our entire <u>world</u> is this stage.

If you look at your hand, you don't perceive a flat partial image; you believe you are looking at all of your hand - including the parts that are hidden from view. You might even unconsciously turn your hand over to reacquaint yourself with the other side, without realizing you were not actually seeing that side until you turned your hand. The image in your mind and the image that you see are distinctly different! You see only part of your hand, yet your mind creates an experience of seeing your entire hand when you look at it.

The mechanics of this are completely transparent to us, but unless you think about it you could easily believe that you are looking at a whole hand - even though that is impossible.

Blanks and the Closed Box

So, how are you filling in the blanks of your knowledge?

Your brain is housed in the skull; a closed box. It relies completely on the information it has gathered about the world through sensory input from a diverse set of tools including the eyes, ears, nose, etc. But this information

Section 2: Path Within Foundations

is only used indirectly. The brain employs an ingenious mechanism of assembling the various partial inputs into a coherent picture using a temporary memory store. The temporary memory store is called the hippocampus and it functions as the *scratch pad* of the mind.

Instead of perceiving reality directly, our brains assemble the characters, images and thoughts by temporarily storing these partial inputs in the hippocampus as if they were placed on a staging area of the brain. This stage functions as a multi-media platform that represents our perception of reality, resembling perhaps a holographic projection of the world around us. We use this space to "create" a representation of the world around us, yet this cached version of what we observed and assembled is but a staged copy of our reality, augmented with "what we already know" about the impressions we have gathered: partial information is therefore enough to create the total complexity of this staged image. We simply fill in the gaps where our observation was lacking.

This hippocampal space actually exists in your brain; we all observe reality via this mechanism.

We may only observe only around 20% of actual reality, but that is enough to create a functional model of reality. The other 80% of this perceived reality is composed of assumptions, educated guesses, related thoughts, constructs and outright hallucinations. We use this information to play out reality in a way that matches what we know and can therefore, more easily comprehend. And then, we use it to start predicting the future! Actually, right away and with only partial information, we start predicting many futures!

Safe or Danger?

Our limbic brain understands that "same is safe" and "different is danger" and aims to preserve our safety. And it seems as if we interpret the information we observe and construct, much of it from sources outside of reality, as biased towards possible harm. This is an ancient protective mechanism that serves to ensure our survival.

Much of the information we process is imagined, deducted, or constructed. If we interpret each initial construct as negative and then deduct our next thoughts based on this negative outcome, we're bound to spiral into only one direction: negative thought. No wonder many of us battle such negative and even threatening thought patterns! No wonder we can have such negative views of the world! This means that we augment our observations of the world with mental projection that perpetuates this fearful perspective, keeping us in a highly alert state that robs us of our energy reserves.

Did you know that we have a huge influence on how threatening we perceive the world around us to be, by how we interpret and augment the reality we observe?

All we must do to alleviate most of our experience of feeling consistently under threat is to:

4. Understand that 80% of the observation is internally constructed and influenced by our thoughts, habits, beliefs and behaviours.
5. Observe the information with clear perception and make a conscious effort to separate the assumptions, hallucinations, lies and augmentations from our true awareness of the present moment.
6. Shift the focus from negative influences to positive influences for the augmentation, or filter through which we view reality (the assumptions, educated guesses and related thoughts we add to our observations of reality), to encourage your perception of the observed experience to be viewed in terms of possibility rather than threat or detriment.

Interestingly, how we react to our experiences is based on the way we habitually filter reality. Our filters begin to influence the outcome of the very reality we're experiencing. As our filtered reactions to experiences are interactive with the experiences themselves, we direct our outcomes and influence the paths of our futures just by interacting to the filtered experience.

We use the hippocampus to assemble our predictions, intuitions and the information we gather through temporarily living in and observing this "virtual reality," and to create a "staged experience." We can co-create a more positive experience of each moment by mindfully shifting our focus, using tools such as guided imagery, meditation, positive affirmations and hypnosis. These tools can be useful in adjusting our perceptions and therefore can indirectly influence the outcomes of our experiences by instilling suggestive direction for the filters we use while completing our "staged experience."

Construction

I would like to take a moment to examine the aspect of our *super power*, the part that makes our intuition and prediction possible, the "engine" of our *super power*: *construction*. This engine is what fabricates, deducts and predicts, using memories, guesses, beliefs and assumption as mortar between the bricks upon which we build our *foundation of reality*. Construction is the way for our brains to connect the dots between what we already hold to be true and complete our images of reality. In the simplest form, construction is imagination or assumption. When we have some knowledge but do not have the full information, we simply make up the rest!

The process of construction is even more complicated than it might at first appear. Once we fabricate a construction, we use the constructed "conclusion" as the foundation for new thought. We create new assumptions, new deductions, new *truths* based on constructed conclusions – and so on. Noticing this process as it happens is not as easy as it might seem. Most of the embedded reality we rely on for comparison and evaluation is based on either construction or dogma. Our perception of life based on beliefs we have either previously constructed ourselves or adopted from others' constructed beliefs, assumptions and teachings.

Our brains' prediction systems are so well evolved that most of our awareness is filtered through these constructions. Our mind produces "what if" scenarios at lightning speed and new possible deductions, opportunities and fears are created from what are otherwise reasonably ordinary circumstances. Our lives have become rich in construction and poor in reality. We live in a dangerously virtual world, made up primarily of imagination, dreams, pre-programmed belief systems, externally imposed values and rigid morality.

We seem so obsessed with understanding everything that we fill in the very reality we observe with illusion and construction. We might better understand this obsession with knowing, labeling and judging if we explore the feeling of discomfort that arises when we have incomplete information. We fear the unknown because it might be dangerous and quickly fabricate the missing information in order to make sense of our world and feel secure in thinking that we now understand the circumstances in which we find ourselves. This illusion of understanding allows us to be better prepared for the possible dangers of the unknown and even help assist in the creation of opportunities that would give us advantage over others.

The information we construct in an attempt to quench our fear of not-knowing is comprised of various fabrications with both benign and harmful possible outcomes. At some level we know we are living in an illusion that may not completely match reality and so we look at our constructions with discernment and suspicion. This makes us err on the side of caution in the construction process and primarily construct the negative outcomes first, often leaving no room for positive ones.

Construction can be a wonderful way of complementing an incomplete reality so that we can have some semblance of comfort, but the answers we fabricate usually prove to be a poor and hurried substitute for the often slower and more genuine answer that result from curiosity. We're not usually in immediate danger and might gain from taking the time to create more beneficial meanings by remaining open to possibilities within our realities. When we maintain a positive attitude when presented with a new observation and stay curious when parts of the puzzle are still missing, it is easier to create these beneficial meanings and even more positive outcomes. Remaining positive, inquisitive and flexible contributes directly to our ability to experience calmness, happiness, resourcefulness and peacefulness.

Example
Here is an example of how our *stage of life* would work in a real-life situation:

We observe two people in intense discussion. Our eyes observe the images of two people and process them into the memories we know as "John" and "Chris." We add auditory information to this image, assuming that the loud sounds we are hearing are related to these people because our binaural hearing tells us that the sounds match the location of the two people. We cannot make out the words, but we take clues from their body positions and gestures.

Our eyes place the images and our ears, the sounds of the people on the *stage of life*, as if we're putting together an animation in our heads. Our mind constructs a perception that these people must be fighting over something and as they are pointing to a car beside which they are standing, we assume that the fight is about a collision.

At this point we need to stop for a moment and think. The only real thing we have observed is two people in heated discussion next to a car. From that small amount of information we have assumed that the car belongs to one of them, that there is a problem with the car and that the people are fighting each other because of that car related problem.

Upon closer examination, we might discover that the two friends were upset because the government has raised the cost of driving and John and Chris were in heated discussion over taxation on foreign cars. They were pointing at a foreign car they happened to be standing near, but which neither of them owned.

This is just a quick example, but it illustrates how easy it is for us to assume an entire negative situation from only a small amount of information.

How many times have you assumed the worst when someone has not replied to your text or email in a timely fashion? Did you jump to some negative conclusion based on your construction mechanism, thinking that maybe the person was upset at something you said, or had an accident, a broken phone, or had been kidnapped by aliens...?

Seriously though, in these examples, you can easily spot the many assumptions we add to our observations. Can you imagine how we would see the world if we trained ourselves to become aware of the difference between what is actually observed and what we construct in our versions of reality? What if we were to assume very little, stick to the facts and ask questions instead of jumping to conclusions? As we augment the reality we observe anyway, what if we were to do so with more positive assumptions and possibilities and focus on desired outcomes rather than negative ones? Would we live a less anxious life? Would we influence our destiny? I believe we would!

The Presumption of Threat

Let's begin by noting that most situations we find ourselves in do not actually pose a serious threat to us. Most people live well into old age, with the current trend moving towards higher life expectancy. Once we understand that we are not constantly in danger, we no longer need to imagine the worst outcome for every situation we find ourselves in.

Ultimately, how you bridge the gaps in your awareness determines how your life will proceed from each moment. The combination of observed reality and your interpretation of it is the foundation for the rest of your life! Even small incidents, tiny happenings and seemingly trivial conversations have enormous influence over your future, based on the interpretation and meaning you give each moment.

You have a great deal more control over the way you experience your life than you may think. You can overcome your brain's bias to look for the negative in every situation, a bias that comes from well-meaning parents and teachers, but you can start to override this bias using the simple power of observation and intention to retrain yourself to look for alternative, more positive answers. You can even begin to see the path towards creating positive outcomes that are still rooted in reality.

Exercise
Here is a simple exercise to experience the *stage of life* for yourself. The next time you speak to someone, close your eyes for a moment. Notice that even though you no longer see that person with your eyes, you are still imagining his or her face and animated features.

When you call someone you know, notice how you can "see" that person speaking to you, without any reference to his or her actual facial expressions.

This is a way to observe how you perceive other people from your *stage*, rather than from reality. We fill in the knowledge gap, adding any details necessary to complete our construction of reality.

Chapter 8 – You and "The Problem"

People identify with problems. Literally! Taking on problems has become a way of life for which we seem to be hardwired. The Universe, however, does not seem to work in this way; there is no obvious direct connection between problems and individuals. Sharing, collaborating and cooperating are the ways of the Universe. However, our individualistically trained minds associate us with "the problem," whenever we encounter one. We may even think in some way that we ARE a problem.

The truth is that "the problem" and "us" are two distinct things. You are not the problem; you do not even have such a thing as a problem! The Problem is the Problem. You are YOU. You get to decide to take on the part of the Problem that you believe you can <u>solve</u> – and discard the rest. Why take on problems that are not yours to solve, or over which you have no control? That would be a waste of your energy. And yet, by involving yourself in problems that are not actually yours to solve, you could be hijacking them, ensuring that they never resolve properly. Letting go of (the part of) the Problem that you cannot solve frees it to be resolved either by itself or through the work of another.

So, why do we so readily identify with problems? Even those problems that are beyond our control or that are better solved by others?

Biting off More than We Can Chew

Truthfully, I wholeheartedly advocate the "bite off more than you can chew" concept. Why not see what we are capable of? Why not challenge ourselves? Why not take on a little more than is comfortable or familiar? People in challenging situations often surprise themselves with what they are able to accomplish.

But, it is important to spit out what we cannot swallow! Once we have challenged ourselves to our personal limits, after we have worked on creating the best solutions we can attain, we need to release the remainder back to the Universe. This may upset our egos' desire to receive credit for the whole solution. Someone else might complete the challenge and be recognized and celebrated for finding the solution.

Often, a juvenile part of our psyches still believes in our own omnipotence. When we were young children the world seemed to revolve around us. This carry-over of juvenile omnipotence believes in two powerful certainties: "I'm the only one who can solve this problem," and "There are no circumstances beyond my control." These beliefs then cause us to become afraid of losing control over the situation, because then someone else might screw up the one possibility of "getting it right." The ego is also afraid of admitting that anything could be outside of our abilities to control. But holding on to a problem often keeps it from being solved! This clinging also keeps us from devoting energy to challenges that serve our purposes. Always remember: "Bite off more than you can chew, but spit out what you cannot swallow."

Identifying with Problems to Conquer Them

The possibility that there might be unsolved problems "out there" challenges our desire to live in a perfect world. Only once we have confronted and conquered each and every one of these problems, do we believe we might find peace. But even then we would still have to live with the fear of being surprised by an unexpected problem. And so we work ourselves into frenzy, trying to be prepared. For what?

Part of the reason we take on problems is to experience a false sense of growth and purpose, or even to distract ourselves from more meaningful personal growth work. Familiar examples of this kind of addiction are the always-busy mother or the workaholic dad.

The truth, of course, is that there will always be new challenges as long as we live. These challenges do not mean that we live in a dangerous world, only that we will be confronted with many opportunities to grow. We do not need to make up challenges or try to fix everything we observe as a problem. Instead of connecting with every potential problem we encounter, we might be better off conserving our energy until we need to deal with the actual problems that are laid out before us on our journey. It's quite exhausting to seek more problems than we need to handle.

Believing We Have Problems

Everyone has problems, right?

Actually, we don't own problems, nor do they own us. We agree to take them on, because we believe there is a reward to be had if we solve them. An underlying or secondary gain is that when we have a problem, we can use this as a kind of currency in our interactions with other people. The person with the most troubles dominates a conversation or relationship. Having problems also exonerates us from performing additional, perhaps less exciting tasks. But taking on problems that are not ours interferes with our ability to solve meaningful challenges that are relevant and can contribute to our lives.

There's a saying that we're only given as many problems as we can handle. There may be a notable truth to this statement. Clearly, we have a say in how many problems we partake in and so we can choose to only take on as many problems as we can handle. In most cases, once we get overloaded or overwhelmed, we stop participating in (solving) problems.

The Power of Playing the Victim

Playing the victim is a way to create artificial power in a relationship. At first glance it might seem that a predator position is more powerful and that the victim is at the mercy of the predator. But in truth, someone who chooses to play the victim can manipulate everyone else and ultimately controls the outcome of the situation. In the absence of a predator, a person taking the victim position has the most negotiation power and can command attention and assistance.

In addition, a victim can selectively avoid taking responsibility for problems yet continues to feel entitled to the energy, pity and help of others. From a victim's viewpoint, victimhood serves well in the short term, yet in the long term it can cause loneliness as friends slowly withdraw their support.

It is easy to rationalize victimhood. Having insurmountable problems prevent us from taking any further actions, however small, to overcome the challenges in our lives. Once we have our victimhood firmly established, our environment and even society itself, will support this victimization. It's like we have tapped into an unlimited source of free energy, all we need to do is behave like a victim and advertise our problems.

Chapter 9 – Competing with God

I'm sure you have heard of "Original Sin," an idea some people focus on for much of their lives. I would like to invite you to redirect your focus and instead begin to contemplate "Original Miracle," which is Life itself.

God or Spirit or Universe or Higher Wisdom is sometimes expressed in the words "I AM." This phrase both defines the all encompassing Being and contains the essence of that being within it. The Creator and Creation lives in and through us all. We, as Creators, experience Creation and participate in it through the Original Miracle of Life.

Happiness is: understanding and accepting *What Is* and the feeling we get from being part of the Universe. Bliss is the reward we feel during active participation in creation.

Not accepting *What Is*, feeling entitled to more than we have at the moment, or wanting to manipulate the Universe to give us the "more" we believe we deserve, are all signs that we are not in collaboration with Creation. We are competing with Creation and competing with its Creator. The truth is that we don't get to adjust reality after it has already come to pass. We don't get to control the Universe to make it alter itself to stack the deck in our personal favour. We have relatively little influence on the Universe; we are simply a part of it. We are but a drop in the ocean, while at the same time being that ocean. We can move towards change, we can even lean towards a desired outcome, as long as we are willing to accept this outcome as it comes and to flow with life, adjusting our efforts and directions as the tides shift. And we are neither entitled to, nor capable of, altering the past or present. We may only assert our energy upon the present harmony of the Universe towards our desired outcomes, without holding a feeling of entitlement to those outcomes.

Section 2: Path Within Foundations

Let's not beg, grovel, or negotiate with the Universe as it is in the present. Just accept that we start with *What Is* and be willing to participate in co-creating the future in collaboration with the Universe. This is a theme throughout The Path Within Program, which we will explore more deeply in the chapters on happiness.

Chapter 10 – What Isn't to What Is

Everything in life starts from the realm of *What Isn't* (yet) and transitions to the realm of *What Is*. Most things remain in the realm of *What Isn't*. Time is the essential indicator that reveals this transition. Just like a blank tape in a tape recorder, time moves past the recording head to be permanently inscribed with the "now," saving the recording forever in the past.

At first, time is in the future and does not yet exist. In this state, time holds but potential, a blank slate upon which people wish to apply their influence, each according to his or her own desires.

Then the ribbon of time passes through the "now" recording creation into a record of *What Is*, a permanent addition to the "Foundation of the Universe." Events are recorded and thus they become permanent, leaving space for the next moment of time to pass over the recording head of reality.

Time as an Illusion

It is often said that time itself is an illusion. Presumably this saying is so popular because we are able to experience time in a special way, where the sense of time disappears and we experience "timelessness," moments of perceived time compression, or time expansion. Unfortunately, this doctrine can be greatly distressing for people attempting to heal from past experiences and create a future that aligns with their true potential.

Being present in the *Here and Now* may be a powerful way to connect to the moment of creation, but stating that the future and the past are only illusions is, in itself, an example of delusional thinking. Worse, the popular media has propagated this message, which confuses people who have realised that they cannot function without their memories and skills from the past and desires for the future. These people may worry that happiness is unattainable for them because their minds are unable to ignore time.

Time, Money, Language

While we are able to experience the transition from *What Isn't* (yet) to *What Is* and recognize that being present in this "now" moment gives us the most powerful interaction with and fullest experience of Creation, to say that time is an illusion is misleading and confusing and causes unnecessary suffering.

Time is a concept we "buy into": we agree upon having time as a part of our collective reality. But there are many concepts that we choose to live within, such as money, marriage, countries, rules, laws, language and even thought itself. As long as we agree to the measurements, the signs, the symbols, the metaphors and the meanings, we participate in these concepts as part of our reality. Time is made real by the same agreements, which are rooted in a law of physics. The very same law that allows any progress or growth: resistance.

Growth as a Function of Resistance

Time resists potential. Without this resistance, we would not be able to measure progress or growth. Movement in time is at the moment of traction; creation occurs at the very interaction between time and potential. Observing creation in progress is becoming aware of the moment where time passes through the "now" and a creation becomes permanent: the transition from *What Isn't* into *What Is*. It is at this moment where traction causes movement or change and change is the indicator that evolution and creation are in progress.

Time has two distinct states and an infinitely brief transition between the two: An amorphous state that we call the future and a solid state that we call the past. It is in constant and never ending, one-way transition between these two states.

Time has some special characteristics which make for interesting harmony and discovery.

The future belongs to the realm of *What Isn't* and is transitional. That is to say it is subject to expiration yet expiration itself is finite, sooner or later the future transitions from potential to reality and becomes the past and is thereafter no longer the future. The time it takes for future to become past is a fixed time, yet unmeasured.

The past belongs in the realm of *What Is* and is therefore permanent. Permanence has no expiration, can no longer be changed and is therefore infinite; it can never be altered and remains forever.

The transition between these two states is magical and paradoxically both infinitely short and infinitely endless. Time's transition is one of life's miracles that we are able to experience reliably, yet we can only influence HOW we experience it, in the illusion that we have control. Most other dual state phenomenon we are not able to experience and can only observe very rarely. Scientists around the world spend millions of dollars to create particle colliders in the quest to discover the moments of creation and still find observing the actual change of state an elusive target.

Chapter 11 – Fear Is Healthy

Many people have a tendency to spend too much time focusing on the negative. Are we really in constant danger? Should we be focusing on the threats in our lives? Surely the answer is "No!" Statistically there is overwhelming evidence that we are not actually in constant danger. Then why do many people perceive so many threats and live a relatively fearful existence?

Why We Fear

The mechanics of fear are ancient in origin. Emotions act as couplers of memory, anchoring impressions as memories in our brain. In the absence of emotional pain from actual experiences, fear appears as a special feeling to couple memories with dangerous experiences we have only imagined in our future. The ability to understand dangers that have not yet occurred is an evolutionary tool for making future plans. In the balance of things, being ignorant of dangers does not serve our quest for survival. Evolution soon eliminates all but the luckiest. Inviting and embracing danger is also not sensible, unless danger itself is the goal of your endeavor.

In our current modern world threats are less about our personal survival and more about the potential loss of our luxuries and significance within our communities. Why then do we experience so much fear? Dangers are less life-threatening than before yet are so persistent and are not easily mitigated by simply finding physical safety. When a danger is life-threatening we can deal with it directly, either by changing the situation or removing ourselves from it. But modern threats are often virtual and pervasive. Nowadays we're unlikely to be visited by a lion in our cave, but our bank balances might dip or our jobs might become insecure.

Chapter 11 – Fear Is Healthy

Our minds do not function in isolation. When it comes to fear, we employ our mind-body connection to induce bodily responses. In a time of feeling constantly threatened about our quality of life many of us live in near absence of peacefulness and harmony.

The way our ancient brains process potential threat has remained virtually the same throughout generations. On the journey of life, we imagine threats and fear them. The fundamental reasons we fear haven't really changed much in all that time yet due to social and commercial influences we are constantly reminded of our need for safety and the possibility of danger.

I want to clear up a pervasive notion that fear is to be avoided or ignored. Our ability to experience fear has a lifesaving function when appropriately channeled. But we focus so much on the possibility of being harmed that we may turn our fears into reality merely by concentrating our thoughts on the fears, rather than on creating solutions. When we focus on our perceived threats our behaviours can move us towards these fears yet if we ignore them we could be harmed by them. The solution is to observe our fears without letting them take over our whole awareness and energy that is needed to proceed.

Some people focus on their fears so much that they stop living their lives.

Chapter 12 – Why Do We Fear?

Fear is always in the future. Understanding this provides a vital clue to the puzzle of our fear.

The reason we fear is to have a virtual memory or placeholder of where we can expect possible dangers along the path of life. Fear's purpose is to ensure that we take these potential dangers seriously: that we use our courage to move towards our desires, while remaining vigilant for potential threats. You see, if we are aware of potential threats we are safer than if we were to ignore the possibility of danger. We are unable to predict all our threats in advance, of course, but being prepared for known or likely threats gives us more chances of survival than if we were to pretend we're safe and open ourselves to being blindsided by the simplest things.

To reiterate the message of this chapter: Fear is a healthy response to certain situations and performs a potentially life-saving function. The goal is not to become fearless, which would be foolish even if it were possible. The goal is to learn, understand and prepare for potential threats and, without ignoring our fears, courageously forge ahead towards our goals.

What You Don't Want

People who relentlessly focus only on their threats find themselves so preoccupied with the potential for danger that they lose sight of their goals. Instead of working towards and manifesting what they actually want, these people tend to manifest their threats. Where we place our focus determines what direction we go and, ultimately, where we end up. Threats are not to be ignored but when you focus solely on the negative things that might happen – and not on your goals – you are steering toward the threats, not towards the goals. And if you are not focusing on your goals your subconscious mind will believe that the threats are the goals.

Chapter 12 – Why Do We Fear?

When clients come to my office I often ask them the question: "What do you want?"

And the response is usually the same answer: "Just to be happy." When I ask the follow-up question: "And, what does happy look like to you?" My clients' eyes lift to the heavens and they say: "I don't know, uhm... I don't want to feel like this anymore, I guess more money, happy family, better relationships... You know, happiness."

Their responses give me a lot of information:

7. They don't actually know what this promise of happiness entails.
8. Their main focuses are how they feel now and all they can think about is that they don't want those feelings anymore.
9. They are thinking only in relative terms (more, better) that have no specific measure (how much more, better than what?)
10. And they have an externally imposed idea of what they think happiness is supposed to be, because they follow their thoughts with "You know, Happiness." As if to say: "You watch the same commercials and advertisements, don't you know what I mean when I say 'happiness?'"

To me, the most important parts of these answers are the "I don't knows"... Our minds are only capable of working towards goals upon which we are focused. You cannot create something you cannot first imagine and then desire- crucial factors in our ability to work towards what we want.

The interesting responses "more money, happy family, better relationships, etc" are the product of effective advertising. We are shown "the good life" by commercial enterprises, which use the understanding of how our minds work to their advantage. We are told what we need and what is available to us in a way that inspires feelings of lack and consumerist thoughts; leading to the typical vague responses rooted in a "more is better" or "the grass is always greener" mentality.

Providence

When you focus on what you do not want, your mind's outlook and available energy is spent on creating more of what you do not want. Your mind gets filled up with only thoughts about what you do not want and is incapable of focusing on what you do want at the same time. Over time, this negative focus causes the fears you focus on to manifest into your reality.

Manifesting what you DO want requires that you take dedicated time away from distractions to actively create an image in your mind of the life you desire for yourself and actually apply effort to work towards it. Once you replace your fearful thoughts with thoughts of what you DO want (and action), you will stop manifesting your fears (while effectively avoiding potential threats).

Don't ignore fears and don't tempt fears. Be aware of them as potential situations to avoid, but focus on your desires. It's that simple. When you look west, you go west. When you look right, you go right. When you look at the danger, you go towards it. When you look towards possibility, you go towards possibility.

The Puppy Nightmares

A great real-life example of focusing on what you don't want is a typical child's nightmare. At some point, children learn that their unwelcome dream is called a "nightmare," and that there are monsters and primeval animals living under the bed.

A typical parent might get into the habit of demonstratively checking the closet and under the bed to assure the child there is nothing to fear, but in reality this behaviour is more likely to re-enforce the idea that those places are truly home to monsters.

The true antidote to nightmares is the highlight of this chapter. The parent who tells the child to stop thinking about the nightmare unintentionally reinforces the thought and the child's subconscious continues to focus on nightmares. Whether the child focuses on the nightmare or focuses on not having a nightmare, the child's focus is still on nightmares.

Even if the parent were to say: "Don't focus on the nightmare, focus on something wonderful instead," the "instead" implies "in comparison to the nightmare." This keeps the nightmare well within the *horizon of awareness* of the child's mind. In resisting the urge to think about a nightmare, the nightmare is actually given more focus!

Reverse psychology provides an amazingly simple answer. Tell the child: "Before you go to bed, say to yourself: 'I will NOT dream about puppies' ten times. Don't think about them, don't dream about them.... not the fluffy, clumsy, licking puppies with the little wet tongues, sniffing you all over, rolling around the bed, playing and getting so tired they all come snuggle with you and keep you warm when they fall asleep, exhausted from a whole day of playing... don't dream about puppies!"

Clearly by "NOT thinking about puppies" on purpose, a child will put thought-effort into it and in their attempt to "NOT think about puppies" their minds will focus intently on puppies.

Don't invalidate the fear of nightmares, either. Depending on the child's stage of development, invalidating a fear by telling him or her that nightmares aren't real, or by telling the child not to worry about things like that, may have an adverse effect on your future relationship with the child. Acknowledging the fear initially, then mostly ignoring the monsters while encouraging the child to focus on the attempts to eliminate puppies from his or her mind will often have surprisingly effective and positive results.

If the child complains about dreaming too much about puppies, just switch to bunnies, balloons, water slides, clouds, etc....

Chapter 13 – Axiom of Fear

There is an absolute truth about fear that is all too often ignored or misunderstood. Knowing this truth will make you infinitely stronger and help you overcome your biggest fears without needing more courage than you already have:

What we fear is not likely to come true.

This truth is known by all leaders and is inherent to all success. I wish more people taught it to their children and opened their friends' eyes to the truth about fear.

Here is an example of this truth:

Imagine for a moment that we encounter a situation on the path of life. Our mind quickly calculates five predictions – all with negative outcomes. In a real scenario, our mind would calculate many more outcomes, but to facilitate understanding of the Axiom of Fear, let's restrict our example to only five possible outcomes.

In real life we would fear the worst case scenario, which is that "all five negative outcomes come true at once." All too often, this is the first mistake my students make when I present them with this exercise. Clearly only one future is possible at a time. Therefore only one of the five negative outcomes can come true at once. A new combination outcome might make for a sixth possibility, hence our brains would calculate many more potential outcomes, but in reality only one future can actually happen.

One Future at a Time

So after that tangent, let's focus on reality for a moment and look at the truth about fear. We fear many futures, yet when we follow through we can see

Chapter 13 – Axiom of Fear

that only one possible scenario could actually happen! It doesn't matter how many futures we conjure up in our minds, only one actual future is possible.

Understanding this truth is useful, but we haven't discovered fear's Achilles heel; the Axiom of Fear. To understand the Axiom of Fear, let's look at the whole picture, add reality to the mix and work the statistics. If we fear any number of possible negative outcomes, the likelihood of any one of them coming true as predicted is extremely unlikely. A more positive outcome is much more likely than the outcomes we actually fear.

When we look at the statistics surrounding negative future predictions the following truths stand out:

- In most cases "something else" happens, something other than the feared outcomes is what actually happens.
- Only in the WORST case scenario does ONE of the feared outcomes happen, but in most cases something else happens.
- In the BEST case scenario, something else happens, also. Therefore the penultimate worst outcome is no likelier than the best outcome.

Intuition and Fear Combine

Since we live in a Universe of infinite potential and we know that fearing the future gives us a clear disadvantage, why then do we hold onto fears that are unlikely to manifest (unless we make them real by focusing on them)?

The main factor in the Axiom of Fear is that the things we fear are unlikely to come true. Our ability to predict possible harm scenarios gives us the ability to avoid the harm. Intuition isn't the only factor in our ability to survive. Fear is part of our *super power.*

Our ability to combine fear with intuition is our ability to survive! Fear is part of life. Understand it for what it is. Use it as a tool for our survival. Don't ignore it. Don't sugar coat it. See fear in all its reality and then use it to navigate life, to steer clear of danger and inspire your courage and motivation.

Unhealthy Fear

While fear can be a natural and healthy function, I believe it is possible to experience unhealthy fear. When the obstacle or danger is replaced by the

Section 2: Path Within Foundations

fear of the obstacle or danger, then fear itself becomes paralyzing. Thankfully, based on the understanding that the Universe is in harmony, it is possible to perceive when fear levels are beyond what we need for a healthy life.

I compare my fear with my courage. When my fear overrides my courage, then I know the fear is no longer healthy and has taken on a significance of its own. In order for fear to assist us, we must understand it as fictitious and based in the future. We cannot let it drown our courage and debilitate our actions in the present. Fear must remain useful by helping us make informed and courageous decisions that allow us to participate in Creation. Fear that debilitates us is unnecessary and merely an excuse to disengage from our accountability and responsibility for our actions.

Chapter 14 – Guilt, Shame and Blame

First I want to identify shame and guilt as distinctly different.

Shame is when we hear a voice inside our mind that tells us "you should have known better" – a concept that, upon further examination, is completely incorrect by virtue of being impossible.

Guilt is when we claim responsibility, deciding or agreeing that we are at fault: it is a form of self blame.

Shame

Shame requires very little energy. There's no need for further research, our brains can simply make up that there was a "better way" to resolve the situation than the action we chose. Based on the sense of making a poor decision, we feel ashamed that we did not handle the situation better. Clearly there is a flaw in this way of thinking, but it saves us from having to deeply analyze a situation, our responses to it, or our place in the world.

Had you known better and been capable you would have taken another route. But the truth is, you DIDN'T actually know better. It's true: "You don't know what you don't know!" Let go of shame. Forgive yourself for not knowing. Understand that your reality at the time was too limited to comprehend the full implications and eventual outcome of your choices. Hindsight is 20/20, they say. Foresight is very limited. Spend some time feeling your way through this truth: Shame is an interesting concept, but in practical terms it is an illusion.

So why do we still feel shame?

We experience shame, even if we know it to be an unhealthy illusion, because we have not yet examined it. We have simply accepted shame as truth, because caregivers, leaders and advertisers have shamed us. The pain we experience surrounding shame is actually the pain of stress. Upon further examination, it becomes apparent that we <u>intend</u> well in every situation, but end up becoming responsible for an <u>outcome</u> we did not <u>intend</u>. The dichotomy happens when we wish a situation had unfolded in a different way than it did and we realize after the fact that a different choice on our part may have created that preferred outcome. The stress of not being able to change the outcome despite your intent causes pain, guilt and regret but shame is not applicable, you didn't know better.

Ask a child: "Why did you do this (bad thing)?" and their most honest answer will be: "I didn't mean for that to happen!"

The simplest truth is that while we are implicated in the cause of an outcome, we cannot be judged for unintended outcome. Instead, we must be evaluated based on our intent. Let's stop imposing the stresses of shame on our children. Maybe it's time to say: "You intended well, now let's clean up the mess," or "So now you know the outcome of that experiment, next time we'll try to do it another way," and save them from the life-long suffering of shame.

Let's examine guilt, blame and regret instead.

Guilt and Blame – The Quick Way Out

The brain is an energy management system. We are constantly surrounded by novelty and everything around us is competing for our attention. When we experience an unintended outcome we would be most served, in the long run, by learning from the situation and choosing to never repeat the sequence that led to this unintended outcome.

But examining every situation is not very efficient. Especially in cases where the outcome had been unlikely or was a singular isolated event then it may be much more efficient to take the blame and move on. Taking the blame is an excellent way to avoid expending energy on re-thinking a situation that warrants no further attention, even if this could keep us from learning from the situation as it is likely that we will never be faced with that issue again.

Our brain tells us: "just take the blame and move on." We do this in many situations without even realizing it. We make a traffic mistake and move on. We blurt something unintended and no one reacts or seems to notice and we move on. We sing the words of a song incorrectly and we move on. We give back the wrong change, we move on.

Chapter 14 – Guilt, Shame and Blame

Often it is simply more energy efficient to take the blame than it is to learn. When you choose the option of blame you don't expend further energy; no need to step-up, no need to rethink a situation, etc. You simply assume fault and move on. Just be aware that in these situations you might still experience the recourse of your actions at a later time and you might still have to deal with the situation. Clearly, having to deal with a situation later is not the intent of this blame-and-move-on behaviour but it at lets puts off the work for the time being with the chance of never.

Guilt and Blame– Holding On

While it is true that some issues are not worth examining and we learned in our early years that "taking the blame" is the quickest way to move on from a parental correction, there is a part of blame that is very toxic. When we are younger and live in the illusion that everything happens for us and because of us, we come to believe that holding on to an issue, claiming it, gives us ownership over the solution.

By holding on to the part of the problem we cannot solve, we believe we can accomplish two things: one, solve the problem later, when we have more skills, knowledge or resources and two, claim the admiration and approval for having been instrumental in its solution.

Often we're not interested in the effort involved with solving a problem unless we can claim the rewards and praise of solving it. We also don't like letting go of problems for fear that someone else might solve the remaining part of them without referencing our instrumental role in their solution. And so we hold onto problems over which we have very little or no control and label them "our responsibility."

This is especially true for those of us who are still under the *illusion of control* blaming ourselves so that we can become the "cause" of a problem or situation. Claiming to be part of the "cause" or "at fault," and therefore in ownership, makes us believe that we might be able to change something or get control of the situation. This way of thinking may seem logical in a mind that otherwise has difficulty grasping the idea that some situations are beyond our cause or control, nor "because of us."

If you look at these situations from an external viewpoint, you can clearly see that the person taking the blame and feeling shame is not actually at fault, nor could the situation have truly been handled better given the circumstances. With the knowledge and emotional build up to the situation, there was, really, only one way it could have played out. In hindsight, of course, it may have been better if... but that's in hindsight.

In the first threshold of the Path Within, we will talk about our limbic programming, the *Laws of Self-Preservation* and their effects on decision and shame.

Regret

For shame we have a solution: Forgive your naïveté and let it go, since you never <u>actually</u> knew better. Hindsight is no substitution for current knowledge.

Blame, however, is trickier. We must let go of the part of the problem that we are unable to solve because the problem is outside of our reach, jurisdiction, or skill range. But the other part of blame is accepting responsibility and learning from the situation. When we understand what went wrong, we create the opportunity to make better decisions in the future.

Focusing on **why** something went wrong is futile. The answer is always the same: "With the information I had at the time, I intended a positive outcome and did the best I could."

Focus instead on **what** went wrong, explore the real shortcomings of the situation and prepare for a potentially better outcome to a similar scenario in the future. This process uses the *regret circuit* of the brain. This is a useful tool for self-growth, but be aware of its energy cost. The *regret circuit* is a learning circuit and learning requires energy. The brain may be reluctant to allocate energy to learning, especially if something of higher priority is demanding attention. The time and energy invested into processing events as regret: examining the situation, acknowledging the damage and devising alternate routes for the future, is a worthwhile expenditure for the long-term benefit of personal growth, especially for problems that are recurring.

Quiet moments of reverie and retrospection are perfect times to run "what if" scenarios and learn from the outcomes we create, so we can move on in our lives with more practical knowledge. Don't allow yourself to be distracted by unimportant things during these times of retrospection, especially by seemingly urgent details. The world around you wants your energy and attention and will do almost anything to stop you from taking care of yourself by diverting your energy to something external. Stay focused on self-care and take time for your own mental health and self-awareness.

Chapter 15 – Simple Truth

The simplest way to interact with the Universe is to say "it is what it is" and leave it at that. Leaving the universe to be. Passivity and apathy are by no means routes to happiness. But there is a deep truth to this simple saying and it warrants further examination.

In this simple phrase lies the key to acceptance, which is crucial for happiness. We must, at some rudimentary level, understand what "it" is. Even if all we know is **that** "it" is. We can name it "magic" or "miracle" but those names are still attempts to define "it" rather than simply accepting "it." At some level we come to understand that *What Is* cannot be defined because *What Is* defines reality itself. Connecting in the most honest and direct way to reality itself is one of the key ingredients to finding happiness. We'll explore Happiness in more detail in Chapter 26.

I'd like to suggest that we give more thought to the proclamation "it is what it is" in times when, for instance, we have a tendency to reluctantly tolerate situations that are not optimal for us. While this seems like a perfectly logical and benign tactic, when we tolerate something we place ourselves in a superior position to whatever we are tolerating. We place ourselves "above" the situation.

Tolerating, enduring and putting-up-with reality are all ways to describe our position of superiority and judgment. The true "it is what it is" statement inspires us to focus on acceptance, without judgment or tolerance. Only in equality can we become part of reality and truly participate in it, with the possibility of truly living in joy and bliss, free of illusions.

Being the "judge" of a situation or behaviour presupposes an illusion of separateness and puts us in competition with that situation. Being in separation and competition with the Universe precludes acceptance and therefore precludes happiness.

Chapter 15 – Simple Truth

Accept, Not Like

Acceptance is often associated with the idea of liking something.

Liking and acceptance can be related, but one is not a prerequisite to the other! In order to accept reality, we don't actually have to like it. This may be a strange concept for many people. They judge the world and everything in it based on their liking. If they don't like something, they don't accept it.

The Universe is in complete harmony unto itself. The Universe even accommodates people who don't live in acceptance of it, because of their likes and dislikes. It maintains complete harmony regardless of our opinions. Not accepting reality brings us into direct competition with the Universe itself. A sure and direct route to unhappiness is to accept the Universe only partially and attempt to ignore or change the parts you do not like.

Accepting the Universe is to be aware of it without judgment. To judge is to assume the delusion of superiority, resulting inevitably in disappointment as the Universe fails to defer to our liking.

Accepting the Universe and its seeming indifference to our good or harm does not mean remaining passive to it... Accepting the Universe for what it is brings us into the most intimate relationship with it and thus allows us to work in active harmonic collaboration with it. Working <u>with</u> the universe, being <u>part of</u> the Universe as an active co-creator, is the way to actively partake in creation itself; a direct route to happiness in its most blissful state.

Perfectly Flawed

Flaws are a perfectly imperfect part of life. The whole idea of flaws is flawed. Flaws are part of nature. Flaws are how nature experiments with change. The Universe is perfectly flawed. It is within these perfect flaws that newness and change are able to occur.

Perfection is when everything stops being dynamic, when boundaries are no longer tested and all growth ceases. Perfect is the end, there is nothing left to do, everything has its place and change has become unnecessary and impossible.

When the process is to perpetually work with flaws, combine flaws into yet other flaws, learn and overcome those flaws and grow through this process, then change and growth with those flaws and imperfections create a movement and fluidity that allow for new opportunity and possibility.

When we're perfect we're done... Perfection is the end. The dynamic of life is in perfect harmony as it creates constant change and new opportunities. In the perfection of dynamic harmony we can find peace and happiness.

For Better or For Worse

"Better" only exists in relation to "worse" and bears no relation to the totality of universal harmony. The Universe is never better or worse, good or bad, the Universe simply is. Observing and accepting the Universe is the most obvious beginning of our journey to happiness.

Successful businesses are successful because they constantly seek to improve themselves. Their leaders learn what can be improved by concentrating on what is flawed or failing as their success is quickly duplicated by other businesses and any advantages previously had are quickly equalised by the competition. This does not mean the owners of successful businesses are looking for ways to feel bad. Not at all, they recognize that success and failure are both outcomes of progress. Neither is better than the other. And the most progress is made when both success and failure are recognized, embraced, celebrated and then used as a starting point for the next phase in the life-cycle of the product or business. A successful life has many similarities with the life-cycle of successful businesses. If you want to be successful, you must embrace your failures with the same enthusiasm as your successes. Leaning towards the difficult prevents you from becoming stagnant in your success. Learning is a journey in traction. Traction is the point of highest resistance, where potential interacts with reality and change results in growth.

A person who lives life to the fullest has the same reaction to success as to failure: he or she does something new or different after the experience of success or failure. Success and failure are both starting points for the next challenge, the next leg in our journey. It really is the journey, the experience that we seek in life, not the goal.

We don't seek life, we seek to experience life.

Chapter 16 – How We Store Memories

I want to highlight and dispel two popular myths:

1. We use 100% of our brain's capacity, not just a small percentage.
2. We do not remember everything that we have ever experienced.

So, before the "myth police" take me to a dimly lit room and feed me popular and well-intentioned myth let me share my truth as this information is vital for understanding our brains' need to go into the healing cycles that are popularly known as "depression."

100% Brain

A popular myth that misinterprets a scientific fact states that "we only use 10-20% of our brains' capacity." Doctors, scientists and the like use this myth to explain all sorts of things. Often this statement is followed by "if we could only find a way to tap into the rest!"

The fact of the matter is that we have an adaptable neural network housed in our skull that is so tight on resources and uses so much energy that it can barely keep up with its own demand for computing power. Our brains adapt to our mind-patterns and our minds demand computing and storage from this highly sophisticated system that relies on relatively few inputs (and many, many assumptions) for our survival, awareness and functioning.

We may only be consciously using 10-20% of our brain capacity, but the rest of our brain is providing us with subconscious computing power, such as interpretation of signals, memories, habits, storage of new information, regulation and data maintenance, among other things.

We use 100% of our brains' capacity. Most of it happens in the background. The brain is in a brilliant state of harmonious flux and the quest to possibly use more of our brain consciously would rob it from using the subconscious computing power. In fact, the subconscious is so much more efficient at its amazing and mysterious work than the conscious mind, that when the brain needs additional capacity to process we tend to fall asleep and disconnect from the interruptions and novelty we're consistently presented with during consciousness.

Efficient Storage (and How We Count)

Do you recollect your childhood? Do you remember playing in the street or playground? If so, how many times did you play outside? It must have been many, many times!

Now concentrate. Can you remember exactly how many times you played outside and the details of each playtime? Can you remember only a few incidents or can you remember each and every time? Could you recollect, with reasonable accuracy, the number of times you played outside during your entire childhood? Maybe you can deduct an approximation?

Let's change subjects. Can you remember how many people you have kissed? How many potatoes you have eaten? How many cups of coffee you have drunk? Count how many watches you have owned, how many computers, how many intimate partners, how many jobs, how many homes, etc.

When you ask these questions in conversation with another person you get answers such as: One, a few, many, a lot, once or twice, three, etc. Analyzing verbal responses gives us clues as to how our memory stores imprints. We tend to store imprints as:

Singular events – our response: once
Countable events – our response: two, five, etc.
Non-countable, notable events – our response: some, a few, etc.
A pool of similar events – our response: a lot, many, etc

We don't remember each and every impression we have ever had. We tend to group impressions together and quickly lose count as the occurrences accumulate. Only singular, remarkable, or separately recorded events are noted as significant. The brain, in its efficiency, records only the key ingredients to events.

Three Second Clip

The way we tend to remember is to hold on to a three second clip, which we play to represent all the memories of that type of event. For instance, remembering playing outside is stored as a three second representation and the association of "often" or "rarely" or some other quantifier is attached to that memory clip. The three second memory is cross-linked to singular incidents and labels to give us a reasonably coordinated recollection of a part of our lives. The rest of memory is mostly constructed. We connect the dots, we make assumptions, we extrapolate and generalize, but we only truly recall a portion of the actual event in memory.

Reconstructing the Car Accident

Most people who are interviewed as witnesses to a car accident will swear under oath that they saw the accident happen.

Interestingly, most people <u>heard</u> a crash, then turned their attention to the direction of the sound and saw the <u>result</u> of the collision and then made assumptions as to the sequence of events. They did not, in fact, see the collision itself. They did not see the cars before the collision or the moment of impact. All they saw was the outcome of the collision, moments after they heard it, yet they will swear under oath that they witnessed an accident.

What happened was that the witnesses placed the sounds of the crash on the temporary stage in their minds (the hippocampus), added the visual scene to the sounds in order to make sense of it - and then simply constructed the rest! They made up seeing the moment of impact!

We do this all the time. We have only part of the information and instead of leaving most questions unanswered we start constructing a "complete" picture of what must have happened. The "complete" picture is sometimes a matter of extrapolating the information to connect the dots. The "most likely" additions are assumptions based solely on our own experiences and prejudices. This mechanism is often referred to as our "filters."

Generalizations

We combine this tendency to construct memories with the way we process thought based on "worst case scenario." When we experience a negative outcome to one of our experiments, we may develop a habit of making sweeping generalizations regarding other, similar situations based on even a singular occurrence.

A good example is when we solicit a customer for a sale. If the customer says "no" it is likely because they have no need for our product or they believe they can find a better value elsewhere. But hearing "no" to our questions feeds the fear of future rejection and may cause us to stop offering our products to a following customer. We generalize the singular response and extrapolate that no one wants our product. The truth, of course, is that we have not yet found a matching customer to the product, or we have not made the true value of the offering match the perceived value to this customer.

My sister was bitten by a dog once. She has been afraid of all dogs ever since. This is just one of numerous examples of generalizations. Typically the older we get, the more we avoid risk and become "set in our ways." Not because the world is so dangerous, but because our ever-increasing collections of generalizations make it impossible for us to allow for new outcomes.

The truth about generalizations is obvious. They limit our range of possibilities and keep us from being present with *What Is*. At first, a skill or experiment has many outcomes, including possible harm. Once a skill or experiment has been practiced a few times, you become more skilled at creating the desired outcome and respect and anticipate the possible pitfalls and dangers. Just because we have a fear of the unknown, or think we already know everything about everything, does not mean we should stop experimenting with life. Learning and personal growth are only possible when we do something we have never done before and look at our world with fresh eyes.

Chapter 17 – Mind/Brain Healing Response Cycles

In this chapter, I would like to highlight some of the ways the mind processes and facilitates its own healing. The mind co-exists with and co-creates the brain, collaborating to make the brain most efficient. This process is called neuroplasticity; it enables the mind to become smarter, more efficient and more skillful.

It is so obvious to me that our minds and brains, like our bodies, are constantly reacting to external and internal influences. Similar to the body's immune system that efficiently neutralizes the numerous attempts to influence the homeostatic states within our bodies, I believe the mind is capable and indeed does employ a mechanism to repair or neutralize influences on its wellness. Our mind uses various methods to defend itself from damage and heal itself when needed. I call this *psychological homeostasis*. Unfortunately, current societal beliefs are such that we believe the idea that when our mind is responding to an upset in equilibrium, we are merely suffering from a temporary chemical imbalance, which can be fixed by using drugs that hide the symptoms and disable the healing response. This way of thinking is based on belief systems that were imposed on us by people seeking profit, who were using <u>short-term profit-based</u> motivations, rather than <u>long-term healing</u> strategies.

Common Cold

Commercial industry habitually presents us with short-term options that suppress the symptoms of a problem, with little responsibility to inform us of the likelihood that these options may not serve us in the long-term, or even may have the potential to harm us in the long run. Take, for instance, healing from a common cold. The common cold is caused by an opportunistic virus that uses our bodies as a temporary host to propagate itself.

Section 2: Path Within Foundations

When we contract a cold our bodies respond with viral healing responses. Typically, we produce more mucous, which makes it more difficult for other infections to penetrate our systems while we concentrate on fighting the current infection; we elevate our temperature, which produces more white blood cells and makes it more difficult for the virus to replicate; and we feel aches and pains, which are sure signs that our bodies are producing and digesting more white blood cells as they are healing.

There is no cure for the common cold. We can, to some extent, boost our immune systems and prevent initial infections, but once contracted our bodies must overcome the virus using the various healing response mechanisms available to us.

Now, imagine taking cold medicine.... The short-term benefit of taking cold medicine is that we will no longer feel the symptoms of our healing responses. The clear long-term problem is that cold medicines disable our bodies' ability to fight the virus. Cold medicine reduces mucus formation, which makes us vulnerable to additional infections during our state of weakened immunity. Cold medicine brings our temperature down to a level where we and the virus, are more comfortable. Instead of being killed by the high heat of a fever, in this temperature zone the virus is free to reproduce and mutate. The analgesic effect of cold medicine helps us to feel more comfortable as we fight the virus, but this is marketed as giving us the ability to go about our "business as usual" and not slow down to deal with the cold at all and likely infect other people.

Using cold medicines in this way can result in being sick longer, becoming vulnerable to more infections and as our bodies are unable to create immunity at the same rate as the virus mutates, possibly susceptible to the <u>same</u> virus in the future while infecting others.

Not only did we willingly disable our healing responses for a little temporary relief from our symptoms, we also set ourselves up to be more sick, more often, which means we will purchase more cold medicine, continuing the cycle.

New Paradigm on Mental Illness

The moment I became aware of the vicious cycle caused by drugs that target and suppress the healing responses of the body, I felt motivated to find new answers to questions I had previously not been able to examine. I began using a new approach to mental health, starting with the understanding that the mind is a self-healing system. This helped me to see mental illness as a collection of symptoms from a mind/brain in healing state. Approaching mental issues with the understanding that the symptoms we observe are not the illness itself, but rather symptoms of a mind in the process of repair, led me to ask new questions regarding our medical response to mental illness. I began to see that current medical treatment for mental symptoms may have a negative influence on the very process that is healing our minds naturally. How is it possible for a mind to heal itself when we take drugs that target and suppress these healing responses?

The irony of the situation became immediately apparent. How could our medical, symptom-fighting approach be better than millions of years of successful evolutionary selection? How can a few minds outsmart their own evolutionary creators? Clearly we have changed priorities from long-term *healing* to short-term *functioning* and changed our values along the way. We have little understanding or regard for the far reaching consequences when our very humanity is altered by promoting drug use over healing.

I invite you to observe evolution and natural selection with the utmost respect. It stands to reason that our minds are subject to evolution and that is how we survive. The ability to adapt and heal our *super power* is a key to our ability to participate in evolution; our survival. There is a deep wisdom to evolution that should not be ignored. We all have the innate ability to become angry, fearful and depressed. Evolution must have a reason for us to experience anger, fear, anxiety and depression. Maybe we should not suppress the symptoms but rather examine and deal with the causes behind these healing responses. Instead of suppressing nature's response we can learn from its innate wisdom and ability to evolve and survive – through healing.

If we let commercial industry sell us the short-term benefits of living with suppressed symptoms, we all become robots, without the ability to learn from our situations, overcome our challenges and evolve beyond our issues. As role models to our children, we would then propagate our own inability to cope with life and make it more likely that our children will look externally for relief and become drug users like their parents before them. Unable to transcend their own challenges, they would also become subject to the "feel-good" addictions and life-long dependence of legalized pharmaceuticals.

Let's examine some of these mental health symptoms and approach them not as disease but as healing response. Using our new paradigm and associated knowledge, let's break the cycle. Let's teach our children and anyone who wants to learn this new approach, why and how we create these healing responses and how to encourage healing and maintain healthy minds.

One such symptom of healing that is too often treated as an illness is our emotional responsiveness. Strong unpleasant feelings often cause an alarm response or the desire to immediately suppress and ignore the feelings; to just "get over it." But emotional responses, even very strong ones like sadness or anger, are not symptoms we can simply repress or ignore without lingering long term consequences. Nor does it mean that something within us is broken. Strong emotions are a tool the brain uses to help us work through and integrate our experiences.

In addition to thinking that experiencing unpleasant emotional reactions means that something within us is broken, we also tend to feel that our emotions are created by the world around us. We believe that the world around us makes us feel a certain way. But how we feel is actually caused by our interpretation of the world and is a symptom of our internal struggle to understand our world. While our emotions may be triggered by outside events, ultimately they are an evolutionary healing response designed to help us adapt to our constantly shifting perception of reality and help us relate better to the Universe around us.

Who Feels You?

Emotions are personal reactions to observations. It is important to note that each individual interprets his or her world in a unique and personal way, based on that person's existing understanding of the world. Most people learn to interpret the world by modelling their parents and caregivers during their early years and subsequently build on these experiences later in life.

When we interpret our observations we do this through a set of "agreements" and assumptions based upon these agreements. For instance, when I mention the word "cell" what is your first associated impression? Is it a biological unit of an organism? A mobile phone? Or a small room in a prison? It's different for different people. This demonstration shows that we all have different meanings and simply assume that others give the same meaning to words as we do. This means we have "agreed" to the same meaning or bought-in to the same concept.

Our emotional triggers work the same way. When we become aware of an emotional trigger, we react to this trigger based on our assumptions about it. For example: When I say "bitch" do you feel yourself reacting to an insult, or are you looking for a female dog? What if you understood a completely different meaning to this word, or spoke another language?

Emotions are felt internally by each individual and cannot technically be transferred from one person to another. Emotions are not like viruses; you can't "catch" sadness from another person by breathing the same air or receiving a blood transfusion. Emotions are learned through agreement, through modelling. This is, of course, one of our best survival mechanisms. Dian Fossey observed in her gorilla studies that the members of the group looked to the matriarch for clues about their own personal safety. For instance, if a loud noise was heard, all eyes went to the matriarch of the group. If the matriarch calmly went about her business, the entire group remained calm. If, however, the matriarch reacted, the whole group would react in a similar way.

Reacting in collaboration and agreement with others is undoubtedly an ancient safety mechanism. So now, when we observe someone emoting (laughing, crying, etc.) we may quickly empathise in agreement with the person's reaction. Similarly, when a person is upset or in love with us, we react from an internal agreement to those behaviours. In order to understand the feelings this person is experiencing, we imagine "being in a similar situation" and emote according to our own interpretation and training, in an attempt understand and adequately interact with the feelings within the other person.

You can see that a change in interpretation immediately changes our associated feelings. We are mostly unaware that our interpretation of our observations is a crucial factor in our ability to choose appropriate emotional responses. It is typically untrue that another person can "make" us feel emotions. Before we feel that person's emotion, we first <u>agree</u> to experience an emotional response based on the behaviours within the circumstances. We then imagine that we are (or could be) the other person and make various assumptions regarding his or her emotional state and reaction to these circumstances. Essentially, we model the other person. Then and only then, do we react to the agreed, intended and previously learned emotion attached to the interaction.

You Make Me Feel

When we interact with the world around us, we trigger our own, internal feelings. When someone says: "You make me feel good" as flattering as this may feel for you, they are technically incorrect. Whatever that person might consciously think about her feelings, the fact remains that she feels good because your presence and behaviour reminds her of a time when she felt cared for or safe.

It turns out we don't need other people as a source for our own feelings. We can easily take care of ourselves and create feelings of safety and other desirable emotions within ourselves. Knowing now that our feelings are internally generated, we can understand that no one <u>makes</u> us feel anything, except ourselves.

Using this model of internal feelings, we can begin to explore some of the essentials around anger, anxiety, depression, sadness and other emotional issues that might challenge us.

Chapter 18 – Anger- A Feeling?

Anger is a reaction to our inability to solve the problem before us. Anger is the recognition of our own impotence in a situation.

In studying anger, I have become reluctant to categorise it as a feeling. Instead, I've learned to view it as a reaction. This is mainly because anger comes and goes so quickly. Feelings tend to linger. When anger is presented with opportunity, it changes to passion or determination and converts the associated angry energy into a fuel for our determination, which we feel as motivation or drive. Other emotions do not behave in quite the same way.

How is anger manifested? What is the sequence of events that leads to an anger reaction?

Imagine the road of life as it leads from where you are now to a goal in the future. You can imagine this goal at any distance in the future: Maybe your entire life's mission, a medium-term goal such as getting a new job, or a short-term goal as simple as opening a jar of mayonnaise. To reach any goal you will need time, energy, focus, skills, resources and perhaps a little providence.

The ability to reach your goals is not completely up to you. There may be more time or energy required to work towards your goal than you have available, or you may be lacking in the necessary skill or focus. Or, as luck has it, the Universe may seem to be resisting your plan when a resource becomes unavailable or some challenging event appears in your way. While we still believe we can achieve the goal, we can be quite inventive. We find innovative ways to solve the presented problems along the way. We become more present and aware, which might allow us a better, more detailed view of the situation we are striving to overcome.

It is in this moment of "temporary alertness" we deploy adrenaline, which heightens our ability to focus on the situation. And as the adrenaline courses through our veins and we realize that the solutions we're coming up with are falling short of solving the problem. Eventually the adrenaline reaches levels that trigger the amygdala, an almond shape node in the brain at the end of our hippocampus that is closely tied to our fight or flight behaviour and causes us to see fewer and fewer options. This phenomenon that we are all able to experience is part of the brain response that Daniel Goleman coined as the *amygdala hijack* in his book Emotional Intelligence.

Danger and Anger

The evolutionary reason for the *amygdala hijack* is to create a funnel of concentrated energy that enables us to focus all our attention on a singular option. We actually treat this singular option as if it was the only threat to achieving our desired outcome and we deploy the same response mechanisms in our body as we would if we were under threat. This reaction gives us maximum survivability and boosts our ability to reach the outcomes we want.

But in its inability to find answers, the now vulnerable mind senses real danger and stops looking for additional possibilities or solutions. This type of focused efficiency is necessary in a life or death situation and in such a case a singular focus of concentration and energy might save your life. In the reality of an everyday occurrence, however, this intense focus on a singular solution unnecessarily triggers the danger mechanism of the brain. This stresses the body, frustrates the mind and keeps us from seeing more obvious solutions that would be available if we "kept our cool." I help my clients to remember this mechanism by removing the letter "D" from the word Danger, which then spells Anger.

The anger reaction in the brain is triggered when the brain senses its own inability to solve a problem. This causes the brain to feel in "Danger" of losing control of the situation and in a last attempt at forcing an outcome, it focuses all energy and attention on a single option. This single option is the object, situation, or person towards which we direct our energy.

Next time you have the opportunity to observe anger in creation, notice that the person in anger is angry at the object, situation, or person they are unable to control. The reason, however, for becoming angry is the realization of their own inability to overcome the situation. Anger is an outward display of the recognition of our impotence, our inability to effect change.

Chapter 18 – Anger- A Feeling?

Limiting Beliefs – Limiting Possibilities

The inability to overcome a situation is not always due to circumstances beyond our control. Most people limit their opportunities simply by the way they self-identify and by setting boundaries around their identities.

For instance a "good girl" may be stuck in a situation that she wants to overcome. She runs out of possibilities for creating a solution within her belief system and becomes frustrated. There may be opportunities that would solve the situation, but pursuing these opportunities would violate her identity as a "good girl." She feels just as impotent as if these opportunities were completely unavailable to her. Her belief systems have effectively created a boundary around her abilities to solve the problem before her.

Simply shifting her identity away from the idea of being a "good girl" may give her the necessary freedom to look beyond her usual belief systems and find the solution that would keep her from becoming angry: she would no longer feel impotent. Open-mindedness and flexibility are crucial for experiencing acceptance and preventing anger triggers.

Self-talk

We re-imprint our own values and beliefs with the stories we tell ourselves daily. The voices inside our heads constantly reiterate our identities, but those voices are often wrong. Knowing that all skills are learned skills and that with training and focus anyone can do most things, it seems unlikely that a person can fundamentally be "bad at math" or a "hopelessly terrible driver." You can see this behaviour in people who say "sorry" all the time, who are also often programming themselves with very limiting thoughts. They say things to themselves like "you can't do it anyway, you shouldn't have tried in the first place" or "you're such an idiot."

The self-talk issue is much deeper than these few examples, but suffice it to say that a person who is smothered in negative self-talk is unlikely to undertake something outside his limited comfort zone. Who knows what that person might accomplish with perseverance and optimism, but the efficient mind avoids spending energy on things it "knows" will fail, so that person's self-talk prevents him from even starting. Even if action gives us only a slim chance of success, inaction gives us 100% chance of failure. Providence assists those who take action. When we take action, many things start to move in our favour. Often, breaking our own cycles of self-talk is all we need to find new ways to solve or peacefully accept a situation.

First Time in the History of the Universe

In all of time, there has never been an unsolvable problem. Every problem that ever existed has been (or is being) solved! There hasn't been a single problem in the history of the Universe that didn't somehow meet its solution and reabsorb into the harmony of the Universe.

You can avert most anger situations by remembering this fact. If you think you have taken on an impossible task, please understand that if this were actually true, you would be the unique and privileged first person ever, in the history of the Universe, to have encountered an unsolvable problem: the unique problem that had no solution.

Of course, we don't always agree with the way things turn out. We may not like or comprehend the solution but believe me every problem does, in fact, have a solution!

If you understand that there is always a way through every situation, that every problem has a solution and that everything in the past has always resolved itself (somehow), you will learn to shift your focus to the possibilities and away from the impossibilities when a problem presents itself. This will stop a possible *amygdala hijack* and its resulting anger reaction from taking hold of your body...

If you want to become angrier, focus on the problem.

If you want to become less angry, focus on finding the solution, there always is one.

Chapter 19 – Anger Escalation in Relationship

When people interact in relationship there may be times of uneven power dynamics. This can lead to conflict and inequality in the relationship. I want to provide you with a new way of thinking about conflict, to give you additional tools for your connections with others. This section deals with the escalation of conflict and what it means. We often get lost in the conflict and spend a great deal of time resisting the forces within the relationship, rather than seeking to understand what is happening during the conflict itself.

Anger

When frustration turns to anger within a relationship, the relationship takes on a predator/victim dynamic. We might at first think that the power shifts towards the predator, but upon further examination it becomes apparent that anger caused by frustration creates a type of escalation that is completely different from the one created by an attack or other aggressive intrusion. Anger that comes from escalation within a relationship is a sign that the aggressor is losing ground to the victim. The victim has stopped responding to the requests of the predator and the predator feels his or her own inability to resolve the situation their way. The predator sees solution options disappear in the adrenaline-induced *amygdala hijack*, which causes the predator to recognize his or her impotence in the situation and feeling their impotence causes their anger reaction.

Threat

What follows this recognition of impotence, the predator feeling poweriess, by displaying anger, threatens the victim. As the gap in the relationship widens, the predator attempts to regain control by threatening to exploit one of the victim's weaknesses. To an external observer it may be obvious at this point that the predator is still the weakest in this situation, for the predator is now using threats to try to regain control. Issuing threats is the outward declaration of inferiority in any situation.

This declaration can be best interpreted as a fear of loss of control, manifesting as a threat. If the victim reacts as if the predator is saying: "I declare myself inferior to the situation" the victim has the power to turn the situation around by investigating the root cause of the predator's fear. Even more progress can be made by discovering how to fulfill the core needs of each person in the conflict. Remember this the next time you feel attacked and threatened as a victim: You have the power to turn this relationship around!

Ultimatum

The next and final threat in an escalation is the ultimatum. Ultimatums have a special place in human interaction and yet they have not been thoroughly studied.

The ultimatum itself is nothing more than a request based in fear. Examining any ultimatum reveals that both the fear (why) and the request (how) can be deducted from the ultimatum. i.e. "I don't want to leave you, but I fear my own inability to control you. This makes me feel unsafe and I fear that I could be violated by agreeing to your demands."

The ultimatum is just as much a sign of weakness as any of the other threats, though as the final threat it is a sign of emotional surrender. You see, if I truly wanted to leave, I would simply leave. But in an ultimatum situation I would threaten to leave if you don't comply with my ultimatum. In doing so, I surrender my power to you and ask _you_ to provide the miracle that will hopefully resolve the situation.

Resolution

It is important to recognise the difference between an Ultimatum and a Resolution. Typically a resolution starts with "I have decided..." while an ultimatum takes the format of "If you don't... then I'll...."

A resolution is a strong decision. While it may still be negotiated, it is not a surrender of power or a request for a miracle veiled as a threat. Resolutions are empowered ways to state your needs and boundaries that are not conditional on the other. They still may refer to another person's behaviour, but there is no intent to force the other person to say or do something, as with an ultimatum.

Chapter 20 – Anxiety

Anxiety is an uncomfortable, over-alert state, where we feel ready to fight or run from the next possible threat, even though we have no idea what might be causing the threat - or if there even is any real danger.

Anxiety is usually triggered by a vague fear of the unknown, or a feeling that we are not up to the task of facing the challenges before us. It can manifest as feeling apprehensive of particular people or situations, or as a general sense of unease. Feeling anxious interferes with our ability to fully participate in life, as we are always anticipating that something unpleasant or dangerous will happen. The lack of engagement, vague worrying and irrational apprehension are symptoms that often lead to the clinical diagnoses of Anxiety or Panic Disorder.

Root Causes

The symptoms of Anxiety and Panic Disorder are often treated with medication, usually chemical neuro-suppressants. Unfortunately, while pharmaceutical treatments such as β-blockers may provide temporary relief or prevent an individual from inflicting self-harm, the root causes of these problems are difficult to address in the context of conventional medicine. Not because doctors don't care, but because most physicians and psychiatrists simply do not have the time or training to explore what is underneath the symptoms and trace those symptoms back to their root causes. Even if following conventional psychotherapy is able to uncover the root causes of anxiety, the solution to ending it usually is not medical. In most cases, ending Anxiety or Panic Disorder requires either learning to interact with triggering situations in healthy ways, or healing the disconnect between the patient's assumptions, beliefs and expectations and his or her actual reality. This work is not something a doctor is able to do for a patient.

*If you are currently taking prescription medication for anxiety, please understand that it is important to keep taking your medication for safety reasons. Many medications create dependency and have debilitating withdrawal symptoms that must be managed appropriately. It can be dangerous to alter a prescribed medication without fully understanding the possible effects of that change. Only ask your doctor to change your prescription **after** you have successfully addressed the root causes of your anxiety.*

You Are Not Alone

Many people are apprehensive about working through their fears to release anxiety because they are worried that this type of processing work will require facing the past. This is a common concern, exacerbated by traditional images of therapists in TV shows and movies, but a largely unwarranted one. The techniques I describe in this book are gentle, permanent and largely concerned with the present and do not ravage your memory or make you depend on drugs to keep you in an artificial good mood.

Discovering the Root Causes

Finding the root causes of your anxiety requires deep self-awareness. You need to be able to look at yourself and understand what creates your anxious reactions in order to stop them. Self-awareness comes from being willing to pay attention to your feelings, thoughts and reactions without judgment or shame- simply observing yourself. One gentle way to boost your self-awareness is to specifically observe how you interact with the people and environments around you.

As you explore the root causes of your anxiety, it is also important to discover if you have any underlying depression. Depression often pushes people to contract what I call their *horizon of awareness;* what they are able to hold in their awareness at any given time. The result of contracting your *horizon of awareness* is that you are only able to see limited aspects of reality and a lot more is left to the unknown, fear and anxiety. Once a contraction occurs, anxiety is a next likely response. It is important to deal with the root causes of your underlying depression to permanently prevent the reoccurring nature of anxiety.

In addition, understanding how and why you react to circumstances gives you insight and mind skills, this is also known as "learning your triggers." Cultivating self-awareness and learning what provokes you, or "what your triggers are" increases your ability to prevent anxiety reactions. Being able to trust that you will respond appropriately in any situation gives you the freedom to re-engage in life and your relationships and ultimately will help you live an empowered, passionate, purposeful and meaningful life.

Understanding Anxiety in a New Way

Embracing the feeling of uncertainty can help us grow. When we have too much orderliness in our lives we tend to seek out adventure and even chaos, sometimes unconsciously. Overcoming uncertainty and learning to face the unknown helps us feel alive and challenged and makes us feel that our contributions matter to the world.

When our uncertainty is manageable we may still feel stress, but this is a type of stress that supports our growth. This "healthy stress" keeps us from feeling apathetic or bored. Even fear can be helpful sometimes, as it alerts us to valuable and potentially life-saving information about our internal and external environments. When our uncertainty becomes unmanageable, however, our bodies go into an anxiety response.

Anxiety is distinctly different from fear. While fear is triggered by sensing an actual threat, anxiety, on the other hand, is a reaction to our fear of POSSIBLE danger, not actual danger. When we feel threatened by something anonymous and intangible we are incapable of actually preparing for it, because we do not know what preparations to make. This sense of helplessness and frustration can squelch our ability to think creatively, solve problems, or function in any kind of rational way. Helplessness and irrational fear ensue and produce stressful discomfort and agitation in the body and confusion and tension in the mind.

The immediate antidote to anxiety is to focus on what is actually happening in the *Here and Now*. This refocuses your attention inside your *horizon of awareness*, which changes your body state in a quick and reliable way. Practicing the following exercise counteracts anxiety reactions and can also calm the underlying irrational fear reaction.

Freedom from Fear and Anxiety

Freeing yourself from the whirlpool of anxiety starts by focusing inside your *horizon of awareness*. Your *horizon of awareness* contains only sensations, feelings and perceptions that are based on reality in the *Here and Now*. Focusing inside your *horizon of awareness* helps keep your attention centered on what is real and present rather than letting your mind stray to imagined possible dangers.

I use the following exercise very successfully with my clients. Its origins are very simple and logical. By having clearly defined the common elements of anxiety, I was able to design an exercise which helps us release our "mind identification" – the belief that what we think is our reality. This exercise has now been adopted by mental health professionals and emergency physicians and can be an effective alternative to avert anxiety for those who are unable or unwilling to reach for anti-anxiety drugs right away.

As with all tools, it only works if you use it. Practice this exercise frequently and it will be easier to return to reality if you find yourself slipping into anxiety.

Exercise: Connecting with Peace - The Three Things Exercise

Moving away from anxiety and fear.

1. Start by taking yourself to an environment where you have fewer sensory inputs. That might mean going into a particular room, or simply closing your eyes for a few moments.
2. Begin to breathe deeply and connect to your senses. Use all your physical senses to become aware of what is "real" in the *Here and Now*. With your eyes closed or open, see, smell, hear, experience the sensations inside your body, taste and touch.
   Now note three sense perceptions, such as, "I see the book," "I hear my breath," or "I can still taste my breakfast". Three things is all it takes. Please use three different senses for this exercise.
3. Next bring three things to mind for which you are grateful– nothing complex, just simple things that spark your gratitude.
   Now note these in your mind also, while still tracking the notes from step 2. State the gratitude positively. Instead of "I'm not hungry" say "I'm feeling satisfied." Use readily available and simple things such as: "I'm grateful for being alive" or "I'm grateful for having a friend." Anything will work for this exercise; it is the mindset that counts.

Chapter 20 – Anxiety

4. Now, still keeping track of the three senses you noted and the three thoughts of gratitude, ask yourself this question: "IN THIS MOMENT, what is missing?"

   Note: The answer that arises from inside yourself at the moment you ask this question will always be "nothing." If you feel that something is missing, then you have allowed your mind to wander to a past or future time, or a place outside of your direct awareness. Refocusing on the *Here and Now* will be facilitated by the fact that your mind is already focusing on awareness and gratitude and paying very little attention to *What Isn't*.

Practicing this exercise frequently will make it easier to return to the *Here and Now* at the times you need it most - when you are in an anxious state.

Why the "Connecting with Peace" Tool Works:

5. When you are aware of the *Here and Now* you stop focusing on the gap between reality and your expectations of reality. If you are aware of *What Is* rather than *What Isn't* you are open and receptive to life as it comes - not caught in your fears of what might happen or even your hopes of what you wish were happening. When you feel most connected to the present moment is when you are in a place of full acceptance.

6. Also, awareness takes the place of thought. And since thought is what causes fear, practicing this exercise also helps to reduce the amount of fear we experience.

7. All fear and worry is about the future. When your awareness is focused on the present you are incapable of thinking about the future. Your fear is not able to take hold of your thoughts when your awareness is rooted in the present moment.

8. Anxiety is a reaction to the possibility of a threat that is outside your awareness. Being present with your primary senses of touch, smell, sight and hearing anchors you within your *horizon of awareness*.

9. Your mind cannot keep track of more than four or five immediate and specific things at the same time. Therefore focusing your mind on six awarenesses at once requires all your concentration and reduces the ability to think about *What Isn't*. This provides a pathway for you to return to peace in the present moment.

Complete Moments

Something interesting that you might notice when using this exercise is that each moment is complete unto itself. The Universe creates and maintains harmony in every moment and every place. It is only outside of the *Here and Now* that imperfection can be constructed, but outside of *Here and Now* is only an illusion. We may not like the current harmony of life and may even wish for something outside the *Here and Now*. But only if we allow ourselves to feel and accept the harmony of the moment can we realise that it is a complete moment.

When concentrating on each item in the exercise, be aware of *What Is* and release *What Isn't*. For example, "I'm grateful that I'm <u>not</u> sick" is focusing on *What Isn't*. Instead, focus on *What Is*, such as "I am grateful I <u>am</u> healthy." You get more of what you focus on and focusing on "not being sick" keeps you more connected to the sickness than health.

Reality of a Moment

There are many moments in our lives when we become aware of a thought. Often our minds simply do not ask if this thought is real or a construction. Being able to identify constructs in our own awareness is very useful when it comes to better understanding the world around us, because understanding if we're dealing with a thought construct or reality inside of us will help us determine if we are projecting our beliefs onto the world outside of us. Being able to recognize and live in reality helps us be less anxious.

There is a simple test you can apply to your own thought awareness to determine the reality of your thoughts. If you are unsure whether a thought you are experiencing is real or an illusion, ask yourself this question: "If I stop believing in the thought I perceive in this moment, will it alter or disappear?"

There are only two possible answers:

If you answer "no" to this question, then the thought is a product of observing actual reality. In this case, you observe that your belief is not required for reality to continue to exist in its current form of perception.

If, however, your thought requires you to hold a particular belief to remain true, then this particular thought is actually an illusion, a construct, or an assumption. Once we understand this thought is not a product of reality, it simply transforms and becomes something that can provoke curiosity rather

Chapter 20 – Anxiety

than assumption. It was your belief that had made the thought a fact and removing the belief has converted the illusory fact into a question!

Reducing our reliance on presumptions and existing in a world filled with more questions than conclusions may take some adjustment, but I can promise you that your lack of prejudice will open you up to becoming much more aware. Living inside the questions will enable you to truly see clearer. Connecting with the world around us in a non-presumptive way brings us more truth, peace, pleasure, more reality and a much, much greater ability to interact with reality. When we truly understand and accept reality then we have more power to influence it, because we are engaging with life as it truly is and not just getting lost in our thought constructs.

Thought Awareness

To illustrate the difference between *thought awareness* and thought construct look at the following example:

Bring your awareness to your left knee. You clearly know that your left knee existed before you had a thought-awareness of it, so this makes for an easy example. Regardless of your awareness of it, your knee existed before you started thinking about it and will continue to exist after you switch your attention to something else. It is simply there, even when you are unaware of it.

Now bring your thought to an assumption you recently made about a person you just met. You may have thought: "This is a nice person" but you made this deduction from an assumption or pattern. In reality, you might have more accurately said: "Based on my habitual interactions with other people I have met in the past, I believe this is a nice stranger."

Had you removed your belief from the equation, all you would have been able to do is think: "In my experiences I have encountered mostly good people, I wonder if this person is nice, too?" The though-awareness becomes a question as soon as we remove our own assumption from the equation.

We make many assumptions in our lives. While these assumptions can be useful as a basis for further deduction, we often rely too much on our own beliefs. These mental constructs then inspire us to make decisions and conclusions based solely on our own assumptions, believing they are part of reality when in fact they could be far from real.

Section 2: Path Within Foundations

Changing the way you observe your own thoughts and choosing to discern between assumption and awareness gives you the ability to alter where you place your focus. This shift in observation brings you closer to reality and makes it easier to navigate your perceptions without getting distracted by thought-constructs that could derail your efforts.

Exercise: The Four Questions and the One Answer

This exercise is drawn from adapting various Cognitive Behavioural Techniques that I have successfully used with my clients. The difference between this exercise and the "Three Things Exercise" is the type of anxiety you might be experiencing. While the "Three Things Exercise" is useful for general feelings of overwhelm and anxiety, this exercise is more suitable for anxiety based on cyclic worry. This worry is often associated with a developing or on-going situation that may be escalating in your thoughts.

Begin by sitting and breathing deeply. Have paper and pen handy to write down answers to the following four questions:

- **What am I worried about? (outside my *horizon of awareness*)**
  Typically this answer is the longest. It is filled with the thought constructs, fears and "what-if" scenarios your mind might concoct, yet still associates with your worrying.
- **What am I not worried about?**

  What is not part of the problem. Be as honest and straight forward as you can and use the *thought awareness* example from above to help you remain clear about *What Is*.
- **What do I KNOW to be true? (about this situation)**
  Write down what facts have already come to light about the situation.
- What DO I NOT know to be true? (and want **to know before I can make a decision about this situation**)
  In the answer to this inquiry lies the solution to your anxiety. Writing about this inquiry will help you know where to place your concentration and can reveal your optimal next steps.

This tool helps structure the thoughts so you can discover a follow-up step that will actually get you closer to inner peace. Instead of filling in the blanks of what could be happening you are creating a sacred, blank space that awaits

its answer from reality as it will come to unfold. Often after a client is lead through this simple four step process he or she calms down and becomes more focused, determined to find the way out of their anxiety trap.

Anxiety is created by our minds when we allow the fear of the unknown to overwhelm our perception of reality. Anxiety can interfere with our ability to fully engage with life and connect to other people but we can overcome anxiety if we are willing to cultivate awareness of the present moment. Practicing these exercises to bring your focus back to what is real in the *Here and Now* can help you release anxiety and begin to accept life as it comes.

Chapter 21 – Depression, Grieving and Sadness

Sadness is a feeling, grieving is a process. Bereavement or mourning is the time and process of grieving for the loss of a loved one.

We all feel down at times. When we are confronted with absence, difficulty, or disappointment, we have a sense of heaviness. Understanding the origins of these feelings allows us to work through them and emerge on the other side. The pain of sadness can be complex. It can seem difficult to overcome or let go of this type of pain, because sadness has a way of sticking to you. More than simply an emotional experience, sadness is a state of being.

Grieving, however, is a process. Sadness is a profound part of this process, but they are not the same thing. Understanding the grieving process can give us new insight into sadness and maybe more importantly, its medical symptom equivalent, depression.

Sadness seems to be a fairly universal feeling. It is associated with periods of loneliness, disappointment and disconnection. Most people feel sad at some point in their lives, some more often than others, but the universality of this feeling gives us clues to unravelling its origins in nature. Due to the revelation that sadness and depression are universal to many species and for the purpose of this book most notably in humans, my approach deviates from the popular medical / pharmaceutical approach of promoting the idea of "treating chemical imbalance."

Sadness and depression have evolved through the ages to be passed down to each and every one of us. We are all capable of sadness and depression and experience both at times. Surely we're not all sick? There must be a good evolutionary reason for our minds to enter such states.

In my view, the mind has natural healing responses to maintain *psychological homeostasis* in much the same way as our bodies do and depression is one of these mental healing responses. The approach of suppressing the depression

Chapter 21 – Depression, Grieving and Sadness

symptoms, in my opinion, slows down the healing response, much like the way taking cold medicine interferes with the body's process of healing from the virus. Pharmaceutical intervention does not support the mind to rebalance itself and re-establish *psychological homeostasis*, because it merely treats the depression symptomatically, without assisting the process of dealing with its root causes.

When you combine the knowledge of nature's insistence on harmony and the use of homeostasis for survival with the universality of triggers of depression, the obvious conclusion is that depression must be a healing response and a process to regain *psychological homeostasis*. And so in my research I concentrate on understanding what the mind might be attempting to restore when we become depressed.

Foundation of Reality

It seems clear to me that a depressed mind is in a battle to regain homeostasis. A mind in homeostasis seems to have a grip on reality, or at least a sense that it can work with its virtual knowledge of reality; its *foundation of reality*. A person's *foundation of reality* is the collection of perceptions forming an internal model of reality; a blueprint of all things we factor into our considerations. A kind of map of the Universe around us held in our virtual minds. We use this virtual map of our Universe as a knowledgebase upon which we draw when we use our *super power* of metacognition to create predictions for our survival. When our *foundation of reality* is contradicted by actual reality we feel out of alignment; our *foundation of reality* is shaken. When our *foundation of reality* no longer reflects reality, our survival is in jeopardy. Our immediate and primary course of action is to heal our *foundation of reality* in order to assure that our virtual mind-reality reflects actual reality to a level whereby we become effective again. Until then, our primary course for survival is to unplug, relearn and re-align our *foundation of reality* with actual reality so that the two are reconciled.

One of our primary needs is having the sense that our world is predictable. Predictability is a key element of our *super power* of intuition. A disturbance in our *foundation of reality* disables our ability to predict the future. Our mind responds with a healing process that restores our functional *foundation of reality* and an acceptable level of predictability. This process is called depression.

While depression and sadness seem closely related and have much in-common, depression has a purpose and a function, whereas sadness is one of the feelings associated with this function.

Depression is the process used to regain *psychological homeostasis*. This process stems from the mind's need to relearn the inevitability of its new reality following *severance*: the separation of our *foundation of reality* from actual reality. We often become acutely aware of this *severance* through the loss of control, the loss of intuited outcomes, the loss of "paths not taken" etc. Depression is the necessary process of realigning with a shift in our perception and internal learning of new awareness: when our *foundation of reality* no longer supports a future we had previously intuited.

In the depression process, our brains re-prioritize and re-allocate additional mind resources to facilitate a more rapid mode of learning through reflection, introspection and active disassociation from the more immediate world around it. During this process, our minds are literally re-processing old *truths* and beliefs and re-evaluating their relevance in our new circumstances or awarenesses. Similarly, this process is also triggered when we make discoveries about our past and when we find new meanings in old memories that require us to re-examine what we had believed to be true in the past. Our minds do this partly by constructing new "what-if" scenarios and calculating alternate futures using the newly acquired knowledge but also by learning how previous knowledge might have been incorrectly constructed. Such a process takes time, focus, energy and resources that are scarce in the brain, which is the instrument of the mind. In the context of grieving it becomes even clearer that depression is not an unhealthy state or chemical imbalance. Depression is a crucial part of a healing process designed to help us regain *psychological homeostasis*.

What Is Grieving

We know the typical circumstances that trigger the grieving process. Typically, we associate grieving with the loss of a loved one, but we may not realize that we grieve throughout our lives, every time we must come to terms with our various unrealised futures. We grieve over the loss of a job or the end of a relationship. We even have a short grieving response when we polish off a nice dinner, at the end of a book, or at the end of a pleasant encounter. The grieving process is also triggered when we transition, even when we transition to something better. Examples are everywhere, pregnancy to post partum, old job to better job, even hostages go through a grieving process when they re-encounter freedom!

While we associate grieving with sadness, we might be better served by viewing grieving as a mind-process associated with *severance*. Grieving is the process the mind goes through to re-allocate the memory of an unlived, constructed future to accepting a new future that is based on new fact presented by actual reality. This process is initiated by *severance* that takes us away from our *foundation of reality* to begin the process of bringing us back in alignment with actual reality. This is where depression proves itself as a well-tuned and highly efficient process of nature that has evolved throughout the ages to facilitate *psychological homeostasis*. Depression is the process that allows us to re-create an internal representation of life that keeps us in the relatively secure knowledge that life, as we see it, is again safely within tolerable predictability.

The Grieving Process: An Overview

As we live our lives, we become aware of the various possibilities of situations to assure more predictability in our future and we tend to project a sense of security alongside this imagined future. We create faith that this future will transpire in the way we are predicting and with this faith we free ourselves to focus on other, changing things in the world around us. Our ability to predict creates a sense of security.

The faith we place in this imagined future is reinforced by repetition and as long as the faith is reinforced we develop trust in our predicted future and use it as a reliable base upon which we can build further. The grieving process starts at the point when this predicted future we had placed trust in suddenly becomes unavailable. We begin to re-examine the faith we had placed in that future, in order to come to terms with its disappearance. We learn to accept that our future path is now forever altered and our future will not be as we had anticipated. There is a disconnect between what we had relied on in our lives and the reality of the situation at hand. The mind loses its senses of harmony and perceived stability; its sense of homeostasis. The more trust we had placed in this predicted future, the more resources are used for the grieving process as we disconnect from the foundation of our predictions of our future. When the mind senses the loss of homeostasis, it begins a process designed to regain *psychological homeostasis*– the process of depression.

Elisabeth Kübler-Ross Model

Psychotherapy has widely adopted the Elisabeth Kübler-Ross model as a means to categorize and understand the various stages of the grieving process. Initially these stages were considered sequential, but later it was recognized that this notion is too rigid to allow further understanding of these states, as they actually have the tendency to present in mixed sequence.

The Kübler-Ross model names 5 stages (states) of grief:

1. Denial
2. Anger
3. Bargaining
4. Depression
5. Acceptance

In studying these stages of grieving for my research on depression, I was able to further understand the "depression as a healing response of the mind" viewpoint that was now becoming obvious to me. In the Kübler-Ross model, the first three states called Denial, Anger and Bargaining are the delusional states, the states where the mind, in its *illusion of control* and entitlement, is in competition with the reality of the situation. The ultimate goal, in the end, is acceptance of the circumstances. And acceptance must come without judgment: it must be a pure awareness of *What Is*. The depression stage is the transition process between the three unrealistic phases and acceptance of reality.

In the first three stages, the mind is still looking for a short-cut to getting its way or resisting change, regardless of the reality of the situation. It's the transition between the unrealistic and the realistic that happens as depression. It seems that the first three stages are interwoven and non-sequential, yet once the transition to depression has started, these stages fade into the background to make way for the final phase. Getting to the depression stage seems, therefore, a priority when assisting the grieving process, regardless of the severity of the loss.

The transformative nature of the depression stage is essential to reaching a new *foundation of reality* upon which we are able to function in the "post loss" acceptance of reality. In fact, it is so essential that it becomes an undeniable priority in people's lives. It takes over our energy and focus. We become preoccupied with the difference between what we believed to be our likely future and the reality of a new future based on a new *foundation of reality*.

The time it takes to go through the depression stage is dependent on many factors, not the least of which are the severity and impact of the change and how different our "post loss" Universe is as a consequence of the loss, but also on how much time, focus and energy we are able to allocate to this process.

Chapter 22 – The Amazing Brain

Our amazing brains have two distinguishable mechanisms for overcoming the realization of unlived futures and a very similar mechanism for re-evaluating old *truths* to experience new realizations.

Understanding Severance

When the path of life changes and we must come to terms with the facts of reality, one of our coping mechanisms is to distance ourselves from the situation and cut-off our association with it. The feelings of "leaving a piece of yourself behind" and "soldiering on" are familiar to all of us in some form or other. A lover leaves and "takes a piece of your heart;" someone dies and "something dies with him." Each of these examples shows the choice of avoiding the work associated with healing, by escaping the pain of *severance*.

Unfortunately, escaping *severance* tends to leave your soul feeling like Swiss cheese. Most of us know a person who has lived through life this way. A person habitually escaping from difficult situations without adequately working through *severance* turns into a "shell of her former self" or seems "hollow inside." These people become reliant on their structured routines to keep them safe from the variety of life. This ability to escape has become a coping mechanism to create predictability in their lives and keep them from feeling their losses, or anything, too deeply.

Processing Severance

Working through the overwhelming thoughts and feelings associated with the loss of an unlived future can be a daunting task. The brain, as an instrument of the mind, requires vast amounts of energy and time to process through seemingly endless options and possibilities. In severe cases, such as

Chapter 22 – The Amazing Brain

the death of a loved one, this process may take years! In simple cases, such as processing a missed appointment, this process may take only a few seconds.

The events leading up to the realization that we need to say goodbye to the unlived future are re-examined and processed through our "what if" circuitry, and associated memories are evaluated for relevance. The process can use so much brain capacity that it often leads us to shut down and disassociate, typical symptoms of depression.

Re-learning

Every day you learn something new. And some days what you learn changes a core value, old belief, or some other profound aspect of your reality. There are moments in our lives that propel us from an old knowledge to a new *truth*. At these times we need to re-evaluate our perceptions about reality and recreate our *foundation of reality* and our identities.

It is difficult to give a solid example of this transformation without going into specifics, so I will tell you a story of a recent client who, for the protection of her anonymity we'll call Janice in this book.

Janice came to me to talk about her inability to relate to men and how she had placed the blame on her father because he had been emotionally unavailable. In recent months she had started to realize that her father had not been able to be physically present in the home for much of her childhood and the two of them had virtually no relationship because they had very little interaction. She had recently gone through a time of financial insecurity and had felt firsthand how much pressure is on a person when there is not enough money to provide for one's family. The period following her personal experience of hardship helped her to understand the pressures and struggles her father must have experienced and she began to re-evaluate the conclusions she had drawn regarding his seeming reluctance to interact with her in her formative years. As she was working through these thoughts she felt herself spiralling into depression, even though she believed that her new realisations were helping her to re-evaluate her relationship with her father in a healthier way.

During her session work, she disclosed that her parents were relatively uneducated and had almost no means to support the three children and their home on the salaries they earned. Mom and Dad had agreed that Mom would work in retail during the day and care for the children when they got home from school. Dad worked two shifts in two different factories and returned home late at night, after Janice's bed time, just to leave the house again early in the morning before she awoke.

Janice realised that, as a child, she had experienced her father's lack of availability to her in a negative way and extrapolated in later years that he was an emotionally unavailable father. It was only when she began to re-evaluate her memories of her father's behaviour and recognized that he was perhaps not to blame for her relationship failures she started to take responsibility for her own interactions with men. Janice went into depression after this realization which was in all other respects a healthier response towards her memories of her father.

So, what caused the depression? The healing mechanism of her mind created a depression response that allocated the additional resources needed to re-learn and heal her old *truths* with her newly discovered truth, and restore her faith in her *foundation of reality*.

The amazing brain combines the mechanisms of processing and "moving on" and through its ability to heal itself, with very little outside guidance, is capable of overcoming the past, processing the loss of an unlived future and predicting a new future.

In this way, depression is not an illness. Sure, it can disrupt our sense of happiness, but depression is the outward sign that results from a healing process. A healing process that can be triggered by a variety of causes and circumstances each rooted in a variety of experiences from trivial to profound. Whatever the cause, depression is ultimately a healing process of the mind.

In my opinion, suppressing depression with drugs and treating it symptomatically as a disease, rather than assisting its function as a healing response, is only a "quick fix" that actually impedes the healing process. Anti-depressants may provide temporary relief, but only as escape mechanisms. When we resort to long-term use of any escape mechanism, we usually exacerbate the underlying problems. In the case of escaping the symptoms of depression, we may experience severe loss of quality of life because we are not allowing ourselves to feel our true emotions. This inability to feel cuts us off from our deeply rooted need to experience our own lives.

Chapter 23 – Sleep and Depression

Many people study sleep and sleep patterns. I am particularly interested in this area as it has provided insight into the mind's learning process and healing responses. I discovered that a variety of studies found similar results, showing profound similarity in sleep purpose when it concerned patterns related to reprocessing of novelty and deduction. Novelty processing occurs when the mind compares recent impressions with previously stored memories and uses these new inputs to augment or repair its *foundation of reality*. Deduction occurs when the mind creates associations and correlations and concludes new possibilities or revised versions of the old *truth*. In both cases the processing takes place during periods of resting and particularly sleep.

Janice from the previous chapter had no problem with sleeping though the night. As we worked through her problem she complained of needing more sleep and feeling more tired. Her mind required extra time to integrate her new conclusions regarding her father into her existing memories and perceptions. Her behaviours and mind patterns were symptomatically similar to a person who is processing *severance* from their *foundation of reality* and is learning to accept a new version of the future, in this case, a better future. As stated before, depression is our mind's response that facilitates the processing of unforeseen circumstances; it is often characterized by periods of wanting more sleep.

Sleep Cycles

Sleep provides the resources to store and sort through impressions. During the night, the mind's new observations, realizations and deductions find a more permanent home in the mind's belief structures.

In a typical night of eight hours of sleep the mind uses the first five hours to process recent impressions based on priority, the more profound the impression, the higher the processing priority. This part of our sleep cycle is crucial for maintaining a solid *foundation of reality*, integrating changes, expanding our comprehension and helping us discover what "familiar" means to us. People who are interrupted during this phase usually report it as dreamless and uneventful.

During the following three hours or so, the mind processes a relatively high number of "what if" scenarios. It constructs in a fluid, non-hierarchical fashion, combining memories and deductions with predictions about potential future situations and possibilities. This sleep phase seems to be related to creativity. The mind uses the brain to correlate pieces in seemingly random fashion in an attempt to find patterns, similarities, correlations and deductions that may support other known *truths*, make sense of new impressions or to allow for the discovery of new possibilities.

While the first phase is crucial for survival, the second phase is necessary for creativity, problem solving, innovation and intuition. People who have but five hours of sleep do function, but are rarely intuitive or creative enough to quickly solve problems in their waking hours. On the other hand, most successful people have at least eight hours of rest during a 24 hour period, even if this is a modified form of relaxation: meditation, running on a treadmill, cat napping, praying, or reverie.

Processing Sleep

Infants and teens are notorious for sleeping and the elderly for their lack of sleep. The correlation contains an easily overlooked clarity: Sleeping is required for processing. But what is being processed?

Studying Sidarta Ribeiro's work on dreaming and Ernest Rossi's work on Ultradian Rhythms and combining that information with my own observations and interviews with clients in deep and interactive hypnotic states, has inspired me to correlate the processing of thought with the phenomenon of depression. I have been able to effectively use this approach with people who had not been able to get through their depression in other ways.

Chapter 23 – Sleep and Depression

I integrate this new approach with the fact that all living systems are attempting to maintain homeostasis, which, as stated before, is a reasonable equilibrium that sustains itself through monitoring and adjustments. The mind is no different. It also monitors and adjusts as a response to the world around it, attempting to maintain homeostasis. In a state of overload or overwhelm, it employs an emergency strategy to maintain a healthy mind. It is also temporary and serves a specific function, accelerating the mind's return to homeostasis. This mind healing response shows symptoms commonly referred to as depression.

Drawing a parallel with the common cold is a great example of our medical approach to depression. Attacking the symptoms doesn't solve the problem, it only serves to disable our ancient healing response. Let's examine the components within the mind-brain co-creation that play a role in depression and compare this to what we already know about cognition to create a newer, healthier approach to working with depression.

Hippocampus

The two seahorse shaped hippocampus regions of the brain are thought to be crucial for the temporary storage of information, such as (partial) thoughts, snippets of specific and non-memory related impressions, constructs and a variety of other temporary information we'll call mind-matter.

Not just new impressions are stored here. Pre-processed images from the visual cortex are combined with pre-processed sounds from the auditory cortex and placed in a previously preened virtual environment; in a conceptual world within the hippocampus. I call this place *the stage of life* as our brain doesn't directly interact with the outside world but relies on this staging area of the brain to observe and maintain a constructed cached copy of "reality." On this stage we place concepts and temporary memories for further processing. We create an entire "personal copy" of our world in this space. Where there are pieces missing, we fill in the blanks. Where there are conclusions to be had, we deduct. We maintain a copy of life to the extent that our minds can work with this virtual reality in comparison to actual reality as it exists at this moment. We're even able to interact with partial, virtual reality when we physically are preoccupied with other matter – a constructed version is often all you need to work with reality on this *stage of life* to navigate onward.

The hippocampus temporarily stores highly volatile new impressions for future processing. This part of our brains might be compared to a scratch pad. We store momentary impressions, concepts and deductions and use them to play out possible "what if" scenarios, like watching a play inside our heads.

The hippocampus is most effective during periods of input scarcity, especially dedicated sleep. While our bodies rest, our subconscious mind reprograms itself and attempts to make sense of what it had learned and what it can deduct from its stored knowledge. This is an effective process of diligently sorting through the brain's library of knowledge, which the brain does to prepare itself for yet another day of life. Without the interruption of stimuli from our five senses, we can most efficiently process the imagery and temporary mind-matter loaded into our hippocampus. We can even augment and embellish our impressions as we process them. Having this scratch or cache memory to work with allows us to manipulate our perceptions. We can quickly compare the impressions we perceive to *"What Is,"* "what could be," *"What Isn't,"* and "what might be if..." - adding and subtracting elements as we process and adjust our perception of reality. Comparing or combining these impressions with what we already know either validates, invalidates, or enriches the knowledge we previously held. All this is processed throughout the day, but most efficiently in times of mental rest: day-dreaming, sleep, reverie, etc.

Revealing Dreams

During sleep we process our new impressions and we run "what if" scenarios against our beliefs and memories. This process sometimes reveals itself to us in dreams. As we sleep, we create these scenarios by playing them out on our hippocampal *stage of life*, which is a way of conducting experiments in a simulated environment. This is a safe way to experience these alternative possibilities because we are in the virtual reality of our minds, far away from the possible real dangers of life. Yet we immerse ourselves wholly in the experience to sense the potential benefit or danger of the imagined experience. If we were to attempt to experience each of these experiments in reality we would quickly run out of time and energy, as we would only be able to live a fraction of the possible combinations that we are able to imagine in rapid succession. And we might not survive some of them! Imagining rather than placing ourselves in potentially dangerous situations is a much safer way to learn. Times when we wake from sleep and are able to recollect dreams through our awareness of this phenomenon are a great demonstration of this eclectic background process.

As we wake from dreams, we are privy to pieces of the imagery and constructs we created during sleep. Our cognitive mind behaves like a storyteller, weaving tales from the impressions it finds on the now quickly fading hippocampal stage. The mind adds a timeline and ascribes meaning to the impressions and a snapshot of bizarre imagery and virtual experiences has been transformed into dream, based in time and meaning.

Overwhelm

How we react to stimuli is not consistent. It fascinates me how, depending on his or her state of mind, the same person will react differently to the same input. People react differently when they are mentally available and present than when they are concentrating on their thoughts or in a state of overwhelm.

Our minds operate differently during times of reverie, day-dreaming, concentration, or overwhelm than when we are aware and present. It is during our "off-line" states that we use our hippocampal *stage of life* as an experimental theatre to learn from improvised scenarios of life. We both observe and direct these little plays.

While in an overwhelmed state, interruptions or new stimuli trigger our defence mechanisms and we may (over)react to the smallest of stimuli, or even disconnect to "shut down" completely. In either case, these responses show an unwillingness or inability to add more input to our already overfull *stage of life*.

When our hippocampal *stage of life* is full, we are unable to add more mind-matter for processing. We feel a need to separate ourselves from reality, shun novelty, or go to sleep to avoid the possibility of receiving additional input. When in this overwhelmed state, we tend to react to offerings of novel input as interruptions to our virtual world in ways that are often strangely out of character. We get upset at loved ones, we get frustrated when faced with small obstacles and we may even close ourselves off from the world.

In the most acute cases of hippocampal overload, we feel overwhelmed or "flooded," and resist anything and everything that might add more stimuli.

We are aggressive to loved ones and, in extreme cases, simply fall asleep, even while driving.

Mind Overload

Imagine a mind that is re-processing reality because its reality has drastically changed. Our anticipated future is no longer going to become real and our *foundation of reality* has become unstable or unreliable as a result. This mind is in a state of insecurity; this mind needs to re-evaluate what is reliable, what is obsolete, where new dangers might lie and what changes might unfold – all based on the *severance* from a previously held *foundation of reality*.

Over the course of human evolution, we have developed extremely efficient minds that prioritize energy usage based on perceived threat. When we find ourselves in situations where the mind is unable to process life's priorities in the allotted times of sleep, daydreaming, reverie and other such input-scarce times, we secure additional resources by becoming depressed during our waking states, effectively disconnecting from distractions that might hinder our efforts to regain our *psychological homeostasis* and *foundation of reality*. Our depressed minds monopolize our hippocampal *stage of life* and our ability to process information, effectively giving us a "short fuse" and rendering novelty, even that of the everyday, unwelcome. Our subconscious minds make us separate from interactions with sources of novelty or low priority issues, especially interactions with unpredictable situations involving others, so we tend to desire more sleep and "zone out" more often. We feel in constant overload and, due to our disconnection with the world around us during these times, we start to add anxiety to the mix of emerging issues.

Creating Separation

Using strategies that match our current circumstances and habits we close ourselves off from the world. Typically, we separate ourselves by hiding in our homes or bedrooms. Playing music on headphones is a form of separation, so is anti-social behaviour such as fighting and criticizing, frequent partaking of mind-altering substances and giving into addictions like alcohol, drugs, sex, TV and food are forms of separation. We separate ourselves from our peer groups or tribes while we "find ourselves." At these times we usually feel misunderstood, but we make no attempts at inviting our loved ones to understand us, because likely we no longer understand ourselves.

Chapter 23 – Sleep and Depression

In more acute cases, for instance in a case of hippocampal overwhelm, our minds may force us completely inward and we may cry, wallow in self-pity or, at times even use aggressive behaviour to create separation. We may even shut down completely and go to sleep when we come near to our capacity to deal with additional input. These behaviours can become chronic if we push ourselves to overcome our own healing responses too rapidly, or if we repeatedly separate ourselves from and effectively ignore, the underlying issues that have destabilized our *foundation of reality*.

Imagine going home from a full day at the office. Your mind has many things to process and may even feel "full." You're driving on the highway and feel yourself falling asleep at the wheel. The reason for this is hippocampus overload. Your hippocampus is filled with unprocessed impressions from the prior hours at the office and is constantly being filled with the impressions of city driving (on the other hand, familiar or empty country roads is a perfect setting for the relaxed mind to process "what-if" scenarios). In this case, as you cannot add more water to a full sponge, you cannot add new impressions to a full hippocampus. Your brain loses its ability to process more data and attempts to force you off-line to maintain *psychological homeostasis* by integrating all of these impressions and you start to fall asleep.

Similarly, imagine working on a project or spending concentrated effort on a problem or issue. Your hippocampus is filled with possible combinations and constructs and is keeping track of every non-permanent idea that may be useful to solving this problem. Now is not the time to be interrupted. Interrupt a person in this mode and they will act irritated, even aggressive and quite primitive about the interruption. What is happening?

Clearing the Cache

When the hippocampus is full, either from external input or from internal staging of "what-if" scenarios, the brain requires time to regenerate and clear the mind-space of the brain cache. The mind needs to free up capacity on the *stage of life* so that it has room to process the next impressions and thought-constructs that continuously present themselves in a never-ending stream of reality and awareness.

When the hippocampus runs low on temporary storage capacity and approaches its limits, we need time to process our impressions to regain a solid *foundation of reality*. This is when we go into a depressive state. We force separation from the outside world to retreat to our internal world and work through our depression in private. This gives us the sorely needed space to do the processing required to create a working model of our reality. Once we return to the peace that comes from knowing that we can maintain ourselves in the future, we are able to relax again into our ever changing environment.

Taking time to clear the cache gives us that capacity. At times of personal growth, realizations, revelations, new directions, *severance* and grieving, we need to allocate additional time for processing, sleeping, day-dreaming, reverie, meditation, prayer and stillness.

The self-healing mind needs this time in depression to allow it to catch up to reality. It is like a highway under construction. For a while the construction creates additional congestion, but after the construction is completed, the highway can accommodate more traffic at heightened efficiency.

Chapter 24 – Strategies for Effective Depression

Attempting to shed light on the subject of depression, in a way that is radically different from the popular conception that depression is to be seen as an unwanted disease, can be a proverbial "can of worms." There are so many forces at play, notwithstanding the undeniable profits that are to be made by categorizing depression as a disease. This book will be useful to those who truly want to work with their personal interactions with life and who are willing to work through and understand their depression, anxiety, anger and other negative or self-destructive states and behaviours and see them for what they really are, self-preserving mechanisms that are rooted in our nature. Understanding these parts of ourselves better will allow us to make new choices that serve us rather than harm us in the long run.

Except in extreme rare cases, slowing down the mind's natural healing response with medication has never been proven to address the actual root causes of the symptoms. This is not to say that we should collectively discard all our medications. There are clear indications that temporary relief from our anxieties and depression symptoms can be beneficial and restorative to our physical health. Unfortunately, it seems that this approach is being adopted as a long term strategy and as a way to address our mental health. Is this for lack of alternatives or lack of foresight? Or is there simply no cure-all for dysphoria other than short-term escape? Maybe it's too complicated to devise steps that would work in most non life-threatening cases? Or is it simply that these steps would undermine the profitability of prescription medication? Personally, I am still pondering this very question. Which leads me to the next question, how can we effectively assist the healing response of the mind?

Reduce Input

The mind has a tendency to start the self-healing process without much assistance from its owner. The very first response that can clearly be noticed is a tendency to segregate oneself from others. Isolation behaviours include an unwillingness to socialize, increased irritability and irrational anger as ways to alienate oneself from others.

To assist the healing response of the mind, starting immediately, schedule times of structured input-scarcity. You don't have to sit still in a dark room. Less input is certainly better, but physical activities that help free the mind have similar beneficial effects and often assist the subconscious healing process. This includes getting more sleep, taking long baths, going for walks in nature, even taking drives in the country, (though not in traffic or between urban intersections in the city), working out or participating in sports, which provide the added benefits of physical fitness and pleasure, practicing meditation and participating in activities such as yoga, dance, group meditation, prayer, or adult education classes.

We are likely to believe that when our bodies are resting, our minds are resting as well. This is not necessarily the case. There are many ways that we can be physically at rest but still using a lot of mental energy. For example, browsing the internet or watching TV exposes you to many purposely placed messages that constantly compete for your attention and mind-space, leaving you very little energy for processing healing.

Sleeping in and long Sunday morning walks with the dog are really some of the most effective ways of creating structured input-scarcity.

Sleeping Pills and Drugs

Please understand the difference between a working, sleeping mind and a drugged brain. Both states are categorized as sleep, but only a working, sleeping mind is healing. A drugged brain is escaping, which does nothing to regain *psychological homeostasis* to effectively work through its depression.

Set a Reasonable Time

Both the disappointment of a missed appointment and the loss of a loved one require grieving time. Clearly they each require different amounts of time and different people react faster or slower in their healing responses. Having a reasonable understanding of the time each of us personally require for our grieving allows us to allocate realistic time for this process when it becomes our time to heal through depression. Set this time limit. Set it without drama and in all reasonability. Then monitor your healing process and adjust the time you anticipate it will take to complete the process. The idea is to be reasonable and realistic with your own internal processes. It doesn't take forever to get over the loss of a loved one, but it can be as long as 18 months before you reasonably assume all your previous responsibilities again and plan your future. The disappointment of a missed encounter might take as long as 3 minutes, or up to an hour. In all cases, you can set a time limit and adjust it later. Just set a time limit as soon as possible. You want to avoid putting off your grieving or getting comfortable in a depressed state, but certainly don't ignore the health of your mind by allocating unreasonably short periods of time. The purpose of setting a reasonable time limit is to learn to understand yourself as a healing-self.

Find a Guide

It is helpful to find a therapist, a friend, or an elder to talk to, but understand that person's role is not to "fix you." His or her main roles are to interject the conversation with logic, help you identify patterns of repeating old stories, point out attempts to derive secondary gain such as significance, pity and attention from your stories; identify when you use negative language, talking about *What Isn't* instead of *What Is*; and refocus you on what you want to experience. Be honest and avoid using this as an excuse to latch on to a well-meaning soul to suck their energy.

Having a guide is quite valuable, as that person can help you in two important ways:

- Once you decide together how long the processing of *severance* should take in each case, given the severity of the situation, they can then hold you accountable to the agreement about the timeline.
- Keep you focused on speaking about *What Is* and "what you want "rather than focusing on negatives.

If you cannot find or afford a guide, at least find a monitor. A real person who will remind you to eat, who will walk into your bedroom after three days, open the curtains and drag you into the shower, who will put a plate of your favourite breakfast in front of you (even in the afternoon) and drag you to the park for a walk. At the very least, if you don't have someone else to do this for you, be honest with yourself and make an honest, if at first mechanical effort on your own behalf to engage in these tasks of self-care; literally set your alarm to periodically remind you to do these things.

Tell this person to do this two times a week for a reasonable period of time. Then, when the "reasonable" period of time has passed, re-evaluate your situation with the clear goal to work towards resuming your life, pick up the pieces and start from reality.

Feed Your Mind

This one is easy. When you feel depressed, you have a tendency to eat. Mostly because your thought processes requires a great deal of energy, but also to fill a sense of emptiness.

If you indulge in your cravings with junk food you'll gain weight and usually this is not conducive to feeling better about yourself.

Eating the right carbs feeds your brain, without causing you to gain weight. The brain requires readily available glucose. Glucose based foods such as complex carbohydrates (typically starches) and fresh fruits and vegetables are an excellent source of brain food. Avoid oils, proteins and refined foods that contain oils, fructose (including refined sugars), or alcohols. These foods aren't metabolised well by sedentary bodies.

It is not a good idea to be on a diet while in the process of depression. Diets are mostly based on depriving the body of energy, which it must then obtain by converting its own fat stores. During diets the glucose levels of the body are deliberately low and the brain, which is already low on resources, has difficulty processing the depression.

Curb Escapes

Escaping can be healthy, but avoid excessive (chronic) escape strategies. Set a limit to your escapes and choose escapes that support your healing.

Do not confuse times of reduced input with escapes. Times of reduced input are typically quiet times for the mind, while escapes usually provide many inputs such as internet browsing. Other escapes involve dulling the mind such as the overuse of alcohol, drugs and sex. While there is no moral message to this advice, in my opinion it is much better to allocate time to quiet activities filled with relaxing input, which allows the mind to do the background work required to get through the depression, than to be entertained by input-rich escapes that prevent the mind from doing its work.

Find patterned-based activities that require some attention but do not require very much learning to take place. Creating a meal (yes, just for yourself,) washing the dishes, knitting, playing a familiar tune on an instrument, taking a dance lesson are excellent examples of patterned, input-scarce activities.

Don't Hope for Miracles - Participate in Creating Your Own

This message is simple. Hope is idle. Hope is waiting. Hope doesn't participate in its own solution. Hope externalizes the problem.

Even when life is messy, start creating something. Anything! Even if it's clumsy or unrelated, just start. Working with the reality of a messy life is more rewarding than attempting to apply your "perfect" thought illusions to a universe that won't budge. What you choose to do need not be big or significant. Just get on with it.

Find Your Own Normal

Observing your own behaviours and thoughts without judgment gives you great insight into your stories and helps you see what has shaped you into your unique self. Avoid mimicking or complying with what others consider normal as much as possible. Be curious about your own uniqueness and don't expend too much energy worrying about what others might think of it. Most people go to great lengths to get you to join them in the belief systems that they themselves have yet to examine; this will not serve you in the end. These people have not yet broken free from their original programming and hope that you will validate their belief systems with your behaviours. Just create your own belief systems.

Fall Back on Rhythms and Tradition

We feel safe when the world around us is predictable. This is a simple fact of nature. Unpredictability is not a welcome feeling to a person who is allocating their remaining mind-energy to creating a stable *foundation of reality*. If you want to create a sense of wellness, finding rhythms and patterns in your life can be very supportive.

Section 2: Path Within Foundations

Following patterns, rhythms and traditions could be as simple as getting up at the same time every day, eating the same foods on Wednesdays, or driving the same route to work every day. When my daughter behaves in a way that indicates she is processing something, we go to the restaurant we "always go to," sit in the same booth if possible and order the same food. It's a very simple but highly effective way to bring some predictability and safety into her reality.

Remember, depression is a natural healing response of the mind, let it heal you by supporting yourself as much as possible.

Section 3: Path Within Sessions

The following chapters outline the main ingredients and practical aspects of The Path Within as provided in session with clients in my office. Interwoven into the fabric of its logic and philosophies, these Path Within sessions outline real, everyday skills that can be easily integrated into one's life to help you benefit from your own experiences and beliefs.

This is not all new material. I'm sure that many practitioners and authors claim to be the originators of various methods. But instead of trying to make a new system, in this book I demonstrate in practical terms how to integrate the Path Within philosophies as coupled with widely accepted approaches into daily life. I want to provide examples of how this work can help ease anxieties and challenges. The practical side of The Path Within helps you see major aspects of the universe in a way that is potentially and constructively different from how you may have perceived them before.

Please do not be in a hurry to read through this section. I recommend that you allow enough time after you read a chapter for the seeded changes to grow within your own subconscious and reality before embarking on the next chapter in the book. Reading too quickly, only leads to the acquisition of more knowledge, not an integrated know*ing* and understanding through experience.

The Path Within is experiential and immersive. Allow the concepts to sink in. The homework assignments are purposely designed in a way that will stimulate your conscious and subconscious mind. Even if you think they don't seem pertinent, do them and let the realisations become breakthroughs and discoveries. There's no need to change what you believe or your religion, just integrate the concepts into your own *truth*.

Change happens by applying sustained effort; by <u>doing</u> the change. Introducing new thought and awareness can create an enormous shift but no

Section 3: Path Within Sessions

pill, ritual or book is a onetime easy fix. Doing the "Three Things Exercise" from the previous section <u>once</u> is not going to make all your anxiety just go away. You can't just think about how you should do it. You <u>do it</u>. You place your priority and attention to peace and healing in the *Here and Now* on a regular basis. Five minutes of trying to meditate one evening will not solve your ongoing sleeping problem. Prioritizing sustained effort is what moves you towards your goals. Do the exercises, apply yourself to your goals.

The Path Within Program is a holistic approach to transformation, it comprises of three progressively presented thresholds. Once they are assimilated, these thresholds can help you to create integrated results.

First Threshold: Understand

In the first of three thresholds, we explore ways to integrate The Path Within Foundations into understanding ourselves and others. We learn through observation how to better interact with our Universe.

The first threshold helps to create an understanding of the world. A world that is free of externally imposed belief systems that try to own and police our nature. This world includes a candid and more primal look at our behaviours and interactions and lacks the domestications imposed on us by our tribes. Once we understand this fresh way to approach subjects such as shame, blame, guilt and regret, we can begin to re-examine our deepest realities. We will be able to define new boundaries between reality, illusion and constructed thought.

Such realizations become basic tools we will use later as resources to help us to thrive within the harmonious Universe and to navigate our own needs, desires and motivations

Second Threshold: Embody

In the second threshold we pilot through the process of becoming aware of our authentic selves within a world of influences. Becoming and embodying our own, sovereign beings can be accomplished through deeply and honestly interacting with our *core Self*. This authentic interaction with our *core Self* leads us to insights and realizations about our own thoughts and behaviours. We then become the designers and creators of our own awareness; the true navigators for our actions – we become the paths to our destinies.

The second threshold opens the door to free our minds; to create our own thoughts and opinions, free from habits and doctrines imposed on us by society, our predecessors and caregivers. This new freedom provides new opportunities and the space to make new choices in the journeys of our lives.

To embody this knowledge, we must fully engage with the process and begin to understand our own roles, responsibilities, behaviours and above all our influence upon the world in which we live. Then we are able to connect to our *higher purpose* and begin to create a reverent relationship with our *authentic core being*.

Third Threshold: Relate

The third threshold is how we learn to interact with the world. It is about finding that perfect harmony that allows us to assert ourselves and work with "flow" while simultaneously being able to surrender to the awareness that we are but a drop in the wholeness of the Universe. We begin to recognize that we are essential parts of the Universe, yet no more essential than others. We are individual drops in the ocean and we are the ocean. Without drops in collaboration, the ocean wouldn't exist. We move the wave; we are the wave and concurrently we move within the wave while the wave moves us.

Working with the more practical applications of the third threshold shows us our awesomeness and our humbleness simultaneously. We let go of our judgments and entitlements, which are at the root of our unhappiness, while aspiring to collaborate in the co-creation of the Universe. This co-creation starts from the inside out and enables us to live and grow inside of the deepest, most fulfilling connection with our own *highest purpose*.

First Threshold – Understand

In my interviews with potential clients, I often note that they refer to themselves in third person singular tense, as if they were observers in their lives, not the main characters and most active participants.

Many interviews are narrated as a story, complete with comments and sidenotes that seem to originate from an external commenting voice. How is it possible that so many people see themselves as victims of the world, helplessly tossed among the fangs of reality and continuously experiencing one state of violation or another? Who is causing all this suffering? All this pain? Who is responsible? More importantly, who can do something about this? When does this victim finally stand up and say "enough is enough!" and take responsibility for his or her life? Surely these victims are not to blame for their hardships, or are they? They were victims, their pain was inflicted upon them! Or is there a possibility that they are accepting this pain, or worse, perpetuating it? Are they causing their own violations?

Maybe so, maybe not. Surely there's justice in finding the violators and making them pay for what they've done, but does this lead to a solution, empowerment, or peace?

Chapter 25 – Accepting Responsibility

The moment of Awareness is the moment of Responsibility.

Many people are constantly externalizing the causes of their feelings and circumstances.

We claim that some things <u>make</u> us feel bad and that the world conspires against us to create circumstances we are forced to endure. We even claim unfairness when something happens to us that disagrees with our perceived right to experience happiness. We externalize responsibility for our own path in life and deny accountability for the actions we take, operating under the belief that these actions were taken as a result of circumstances outside of our control.

As children we naturally wanted to constantly experiment with reality. Children don't understand consequence in the same way as adults do. They want to find out for themselves if they are able to overcome obstacles and difficulties. Unfortunately, parents and teachers, in their self-declared responsibilities and their well-intentioned attempts to save children from harm, over-assist and prevent the child from making the attempt or take over before the child has a chance to complete the experiment. These efforts might seem like acts of rescue, to keep the child safe from the possibility of failure and harm, but in the absence of real danger, they only stifle the child's ability to learn how to navigate the world for themselves.

I recall a seven year old client with whom I worked. I asked her what she did to cheer herself up. She responded that she simply tells herself "Yay, you're number 1!" When I asked her if this method was useful, she explained that pretending by repeating a silly and untrue statement to feel better didn't work for her. The way we teach our children to fake their feelings denies them their ability to learn and forces a false sense of self-confidence upon them. We rob them of the authentic independent experience of discovering

First Threshold – Understand

their abilities in relationship to their environment. Authentic independent experience is the only root to self-reliance - the true source of self-esteem. The denial of authentic independent experience becomes the primary factor in the unwillingness to take responsibility later in life.

The other primary factor in externalizing responsibility is using punishment and reward to train our children. Most people have a deep, child-like, primal understanding, reinforced by their parents, that once they've been found responsible for or guilty of something, they will be punished for it. Children who are punished for their "negative" outcomes associate responsibility with pain.

Regardless of our intent, we are punished for the "negative" outcomes of our actions when we are children and so we disassociate for fear of punishment. We are held accountable for every action and subsequent actions to which our actions may have contributed. As children we learn that taking ownership of an action comes with a price we are not willing to pay and as adults we simply avoid responsibility or accountability for anything, if we can avoid it.

And so as adults we externalize responsibility and thus accountability to avoid the pain it is associated with.

Homework:
Recognise that each and every time you recall a story, you can use it to justify your inabilities or you can use it to show how the situation made you stronger and more capable of living your life in a better way. Spend some time with the stories you tell yourself and others. Listen carefully when you say: "well, that's because....," "so now..." or "I just..." it takes some time to catch yourself externalizing responsibility. What are you unwilling to take responsibility for in your life, to avoid the pain associated with possible negative outcomes?...

Most Complex Life

I often ask my clients directly: "In your view and experience, who has the most complex life?"

The answers I get are varied but consistent in one regard. Most people I interview honestly scrutinize this question and answer something similar to: The President of the United States, or the CEO of a large corporation.

Chapter 25 – Accepting Responsibility

The truth is that "in your experience" <u>you</u> have the most complex life, because you are the only person who is able to actually experience your life. This, of course, is the exact same for everyone. Just as no one else can imagine the complexities in your life, you are unable to imagine the complexities in someone else's life.

Others' lives are not experienced by you and therefore can't be truly perceived as complex. Your life, however, is experienced by you. Your awareness, your perceptions, your thoughts and your mind-constructs are all uniquely experienced by you. You are the only one who can experience every nuance of your life.

This brings up an interesting point: Who cares?

In all honesty, who on earth actually cares for you more than you do? Nobody. The truth of the matter is that no one cares enough about your life to take a high level of responsibility for it. Often we'd like to abdicate responsibility and even blame others, especially the people who trained us into our current ways of thinking, feeling and behaving, but the truth remains that once we become aware of our behaviours, we become responsible for them, regardless of their origin.

Who is Responsible? Externalizing vs. Internalizing

Who is responsible for your life, for resolving the problems in it and creating the best experience for you possible? You are!

We must be aware that the brain is always looking for ways to economize, to use as little energy as possible, to be efficient. It makes perfect sense to delegate the responsibility of your life experiences and happiness to others. This would be the smart and efficient thing to do, if it weren't for a small problem. There is no one who would want such a responsibility; everyone else is too busy taking care of their own lives!

In our modern-day culture we have a tendency to look outside ourselves for solutions. In our minds we blame others for our issues and hold our doctors responsible for making us healthy again after contracting illness. Advertising and marketing contribute to the sense that we are entitled to externalize responsibility, but eventually it is up to us to resist the temptation to abdicate our responsibility for our own lives. This temptation is hard to resist as it is ubiquitously granted by church, state and commercial enterprise. In addition to enabling us to blame others for our circumstances, this conditioning causes us to become addicted to externally available escapes from our conditions. Those same church, state and commercial enterprises are likely to suggest which externally available escapes might be appropriate choices for you. And did I mention who would actually stand to you gain from you participating in those escapes?

The Path Within Program requires that you commit to a deep and absolute understanding that no external person or organization is responsible for our individual wellbeing and that our healing must come from our own abilities and awareness.

Take care of yourself and be assertive! You are responsible for your life, even the parts that don't go your way. You are also the beneficiary of your life, both the good and the bad. When you are assertive in your life, you lean it towards the direction you want it to go. This assertion keeps you present in each moment.

Homework:
Self-care. Reading this book is a good start. Take time to replenish yourself. Physically, Mentally and Spiritually. Stop doing what is expected of you all the time, turn off the TV, spend time alone or in quiet discussion with friends, join a weekly group, take a bath, go for a spa treatment, hug a friend, eat nutritious food and spend time preparing it, pet your dog or cat or friend, be good to yourself. On a regular, ongoing basis.

Chapter 26 – Happiness

In my search to simplify happiness I discovered and realized that in order to understand happiness better, I would need to study unhappiness as well. It was noteworthy that <u>un</u>happiness seemed more thoroughly defined. More people seemed to be better at describing their unhappy tendencies and triggers than how they were able to find their moments of happiness.

We understand happiness in our core. Happiness is often difficult to describe, because we have never really thought of happiness in definable, describable terms. Yet we feel happiness, we remember happiness, we long for happiness.

So many books and sayings tell us that happiness cannot be bought, yet when we buy things we experience moments of happiness. Many other books and sayings tell us that happiness comes from the inside and countless people go searching within for that elusive, isolating escape of mind that might bring them the Holy Grail.

In the next few pages you will learn what happiness is, how to describe it, how to find it and that it doesn't come from the outside nor the inside. Happiness springs from the perceived interaction between the outside world and ourselves. Even people who explore meditative states in order to find happiness are still interacting with a virtual "other" world. While this escape is advocated as the solace or cure for our ails, it is still a form of mental masturbation and escape from reality. True happiness is when we remain content within, or even derive pleasure from full participation in reality; without the need to escape it or enhance it.

Let's get to work...

Unhappiness by Design

Why are so many people unhappy? Why does this number seem to increase all the time? There's a clear correlation between the wealth of a nation and the numbers of unhappy people in that very state. Is there a correlation between unhappiness and wealth?

The answer is clear. There *is* a correlation between wealthy nations and unhappiness, but it isn't a direct correlation. As I studied this question I came to a curious and more obvious answer: there seems to be a clear and direct correlation between unhappiness and exposure to advertising and/or propaganda. Advertisers are interested in people with discretionary income. The leverage in advertising is desire, or want. If the advertiser can awaken a desire in a person, that person is likely to spend money on obtaining the desired item or service. This part of advertising is called "driving the want."

It's true that you can't want something about which you have no knowledge, so classical "Informative Advertising" has some impact. Clearly, if you don't know what a pizza is, how can you desire one? Showing images of people enjoying a pizza is a great way of letting people know that eating a pizza can be a satisfying way to relieve hunger and yet this is no longer the main driver in advertising. There's simply not enough return on investment in "Informative Advertising."

The next level in advertising is to tell people what feature the product or service has and what it can do for them. Highlighting the personal benefits of a product or service is a great way of connecting to people's desires, but it doesn't stop there. Unfortunately, advertising has taken the next step in "driving the want," it's called "stirring the hurt."

"Stirring the hurt" reminds people of their personal suffering, their pains and their perceived inadequacies. Advertisers are quick to point out your issues, to subtly remind you that you, too, are flawed and perfectible. By connecting us to our personal wounds and promising relief of the hurt we feel as a result of being reminded of our pain, advertising reaches deep into our egos and makes it seem that the offered product will feed our primary needs to be safe, loved, significant, etc. Connecting with our feelings of lack is what drives us to reach deep into our wallets and spend our money on items and services that promise relief. And as we are constantly reminded of our lacks, pains and anxieties, we feel unhappy, unfulfilled and removed from the things that bring us contentment and happiness in our lives.

Advertisers aren't concerned with the emotional cost that drives us to seek relief. They are interested in our desire to seek relief from pain, which drives us to spend our money on their products or services. The simple truth is that a contented individual is not looking for relief. It is the discontented individual who finds ways to better his or her situation and seek relief through proposed action.

Action Is Profitable

It is the action that generates profits. If channeled well, the action generates profit for the individual searching to fill the implied "void," the company that is marketing the product and additionally, the company which that person works for. As long as the individual continues to work and remains connected to the economy while searching for the means prosper that individual generates profit. Unhappy individuals seek to better themselves. Unhappy individuals are more profitable than happy ones.

Our Economy Depends on Your Unhappiness

Modern economies are based on monetary growth. Entire nations are dependent on taxable growth. This growth comes from commerce; the exchange of goods and services for money. The problem is that happy people don't buy much.

It's the unhappy people who, in the attempt to escape their situations, pay for the economy, the economic growth, corporate profit, taxes, bank fees, etc. If everyone were happy, no-one would need anything. The economy, the way it is, would stop. So to drive the economy, the big influencers (church, state and commercial enterprise) highlight your faults and weaknesses and offer comfort, in exchange for your effort, energy or money. Unhappy is big business!

Unhappiness Is Big Business

Our happiness is monitored and influenced constantly. Maybe not directly in an attempt to generate unhappiness, but Organized Religion, State and Commercial Enterprise are well aware of what their marketing or propaganda departments are doing. They compete to maintain a level of profitability, without any concern for the unhappiness they cause as collateral damage.

First Threshold – Understand

It's a simple fact: Happy individuals are commercial nightmares. They don't buy anything, they don't seek to better themselves, they don't pay for relief, solace, support or salvation; they don't need anything! Happy individuals are content unto themselves.

In order to be motivated to earn more and then to part with their hard earned money, people need to be made aware of what they can do better, what they deserve, what they don't have and what they could be - if only they buy the products or services that insinuate this relief from the lack or hurt they feel.

"Big business" wants you to believe that you can get happiness through the purchase of a new toy but the truth is more sinister. Modern commerce "drives the want" by showing you <u>more entitlements</u> – and as such, increases the gap between your reality and your perceived entitlements (expectations). In highlighting your shortcomings and convincing you that you're entitled to their product, they help cultivate your sense of unhappiness and present you with their product as the cure.

The negative side effect of all this marketing is that we are constantly bombarded with messages that attempt to convince us that we're not good enough. Or, at least that we are not as good as we could be and that we deserve a better life than we are currently living. Happiness itself is simply not very profitable. Selling the promise of happiness is highly profitable, but it requires each individual to be convinced that they are not happy yet.

The American constitution is very clear; it promises the right for every individual to Life, Liberty and the <u>Pursuit</u> of Happiness. It could have easily read "Life, Liberty and Happiness," but the intention becomes clear when one reads this phrase with fresh eyes. What drives a country and currently the entire western world, is NOT happiness, but the pursuit of happiness. It is the pursuit that makes profit. If we were all happy, we would simply stop spending money on the pursuit of happiness.

Homework:
1. *Examine the commercial messages you see and hear each day in web sites, radio shows, TV shows. Find the hidden message that "stirs your hurt." At some point you're being told that you're not good enough in some way that you can be improved upon. Or that you might "belong" to the group you've always wanted to be part of. These messages are hidden, because they are often not directly related to the product or service that's being sold.*

2. *Stop buying. Be fanatically frugal for a week. Ask yourself the question, "do I need this item or service, or may I be in the pursuit of improving my perceived status in some way." Really attempt to stop buying altogether for a week. See how resourceful you can be with the things you already have. You'll find this easier than you may have initially thought possible.*

The Origin of Happiness

I believe it is important to define happiness before learning how to find it. After all, it would be futile to seek for something we're unable to recognise.

First, I want to be clear. Happiness and unhappiness are both states of being. For the linguists, the ending 'iness' means just that – a "state of being." These states are created in our bodies as reactions to interactions with the world around us or perceived worlds we imagine. These states are not caused by external forces (as in "you can't buy happiness") nor internal forces (as in "happiness comes from within"). Happiness is a reaction to the meaning we attribute to an interaction between us and the world. We're always happy about or as a result of an <u>interaction</u>.

When I'm in my office explaining the definition of happiness to a student, I find the quickest route to defining happiness is actually defining unhappiness first, then to explore the definition of happiness by looking at the word "Happiness" itself.

Defining Unhappiness

The definition of Unhappiness is: "When reality doesn't meet with our expectations of it."

It really is that simple. Unhappiness is the feeling that reality should be different than it is! This is also known as "being entitled." What is most interesting to me is that this definition can be universally applied and that it contains much of the answer to avoiding unhappiness. For example: "We expected to be safe, yet we found ourselves in an accident." Other typical examples:

- I was hoping for better grades
- No matter how hard I try, I can't make any friends
- I'm always running into "Murphy's Law "
- My life sucks right now

First Threshold – Understand

All of these examples show an implied expectation that isn't being met. Interestingly, an outsider can spot the entitlement right away. The unhappy individual, however, is subconsciously hoping that the world will change and that person becomes attached to particular expectations of the world. Expecting fairness is a big issue in the battle for happiness. Once we learn that the world <u>ought</u> to be fair, we find it difficult to understand the harmony in all things and we start to expect fairness. Not from a holistic, universal perspective, but from our own, tiny reality that wants the Universe to bend in our favours.

And therein lies the rub. Unhappiness is when the Universe is different than our expectations of it. Clearly the situation will solve itself when the Universe and our expectations are aligned. Is it realistic to expect the Universe to change course to meet our expectations, or would it be simpler to align ourselves with reality?

Therefore, again:

> *Unhappiness: Reality doesn't match your expectations of it.*

More technically this means that reality doesn't provide us with what we feel entitled to. I use the word entitlements, as unhappiness is purely a matter of viewpoint. An individual who believes they're entitled to $100 and receives $101 is happy. If they receive $99 they're unhappy. So check in with yourself. Do you feel entitled to that amazing job, to the wonderful spouse, to an easy lifestyle? Your entitlement must match your reality, or you won't be happy.

There is a growth element to happiness, so "wanting more" is part of feeling capable and growing as an individual. There will be more about this growth element later in the book when we talk about asserting your desires upon reality.

The Basic Rules of Happiness

Here are some of the most basic truths about happiness. While the theory is relatively simple, understanding how to integrate these rules into your life may require more than a little thought.

3. You can only make yourself happy
4. You are responsible for your own happiness
5. Happiness comes from within you, through interaction with your reality.

In more detail:

You Can Only Make Yourself Happy - You Cannot Make Someone Else Happy

There's a strange myth many of us believe: that we cause feelings in others. This actually isn't true at all. We might be able to behave in ways that allow others to accept (like) or reject (dislike) our behaviour, but we cannot create feelings in others.

Likewise, no one actually <u>causes</u> or <u>makes</u> you feel anything. The reality is that you and only you, can actually generate the feelings created in your body and brain. You react to your environment. When another person does something, you may or may not have a certain reaction to this behaviour; often you will react differently to the same behaviour depending on your state and interpretation of events. With longer term relationships, once people know each other better, they are able to learn what triggers cause the other to react in certain ways. But even then, feeling isn't transferred; it is separately generated in each individual.

YOU Are Responsible for Your Own Happiness– You Cannot Look to Anyone Other than Yourself for Happiness

It is true that a life shared is a happier life. But this is due to <u>interaction with</u>, not <u>caused by</u>, the people you're sharing with. While other people can contribute to your sense of wellbeing, even create situations and hence feelings that are very pleasant, those people are NOT responsible for your happiness! You are.

Never assume others can read your mind or understand what you need to feel better. Communicate! People LOVE to help. They really do want to contribute, but if they don't know how, they will be denied that pleasure. So communicate your needs and take responsibility for your own happiness.

Happiness Comes from within You as You Interact

Happiness is a result of your interaction with your reality – not from any external influence, but by the meaning you give to the external influence. We filter reality, then give meaning to this filtered reality and this meaning is what makes us feel happiness.

First Threshold – Understand

The Meaning of Happiness

It still amazes me how many times clients and students tell me that they are in pursuit of happiness, but are unable to provide an accurate description of what they are seeking.

Without a reasonable understanding of what we're seeking we won't know the direction to go and worse, we won't be able to recognise it when we get close! You may be closer than you think. You may have surpassed it, or you may even be going in the wrong direction.

Let's start with the word *happiness* itself and then look at the experience of happiness.

The Word Happiness

The word happiness has three distinct parts "hap," "i" or "y," and "ness."

Look at the words happen (occur), happening (occurrence) and happenstance (co-incidence – multiple events occurring simultaneously) for the common meaning of "hap."

"Hap" (occurrence,) in the verb means "come about" or "come into being". The rest of the word happiness is straight forward English. "i" or "y" means "being full of" or "characterised by." Adding "i" or "y" to a word changes the word into an adjective. For example, greedy means full of greed.

"Ness" indicates "state of." So for example, greediness is the state of being full of greed.

So as we seek to attain a functional definition of happiness, happiness is the state of being full of occurrence; being *Here* and *Now*; being in creation.

Happiness is being in creation.

Wordplay is by no means supposed to convince you of this definition. Do that for yourself. Reflect on times when you're moping on the couch or when you're actively participating in an engaging pursuit. You will not just see for yourself, you will <u>experience</u> happiness.

The Happiness Experience

We experience happiness on a spectrum that goes from Contentment to Ecstasy. There is no happiness below Contentment nor above Ecstasy; these two feelings set the outward limits for our study of happiness.

Contentment is defined as a sense of wholeness, Ecstasy refers to being out of state or beside oneself.

While the word Ecstasy truly describes our experience of extreme happiness, "Bliss" provides us with a description of the feeling associated with the experience of Ecstasy, so I will instead call this up-most level of happiness "Bliss." I would further like to note that happiness and bliss do not subscribe to the neo-hedonistic idea that you must "like" or "enjoy" the moment as a prerequisite to happiness. We're often happiest when we are overcoming obstacles and making progress through difficulties. Once we have overcome all current obstacles and difficulties, we seek new ones! No, there is no correlation between liking the circumstances and being happy, but there is a correlation between our expectations of a moment and our ability to experience happiness.

Earlier we defined unhappiness as the gap between reality and our expectation of reality. What is the cure for unhappiness? Is the lack of happiness enough to make us feel happy? Let's examine the two extremes of happiness. Contentment is when we're "not unhappy" and reality is meeting our expectations. Bliss is when reality nourishes our soul.

Contentment

As said above, contentment is understood a sense of wholeness. I have developed a more specific definition of contentment that I will explain in detail below.

Contentment is Understanding and Accepting What Is

I identify three elements in the definition of contentment:

1. *What Is*
2. *Understanding*
3. *Accepting*

Let's explore them individually and learn how to work with them in harmony.

What Is
Reality, the World, the Universe. From my viewpoint these are best summed up as *What Is*. Working with reality may seem more energy consuming than working inside an illusion, but working with the true nature of the Universe is the only way we might experience success or growth in any endeavour, materialistically or spiritually. Unfortunately it is often easier to simply make assumptions when we experience a lack of time, lack of resources, or inability to explore things beyond our reach and we drift off into illusion.

The simple truth is that being with reality is the only way to be truly happy. Anything else is an attempt to escape through illusion or temporary distraction. Our minds have a tendency to augment and filter reality in an attempt to complete the picture. We feel safer when there are fewer unknown factors in our realities, so we simply make up the difference. The more we use our illusions, assumptions and filters, the bigger the distance between reality and our expectation of it.

Leave a little space for questions. Not everything needs to be understood by you. Which brings us to the next element in the definition of contentment: Understanding.

Understanding
An understanding of *What Is* is not strictly required for contentment, but it is the prerequisite for participation. Without understanding, one cannot participate; without definition, it is difficult to even observe reality. It's impossible to interact with something about which you have no understanding. Interestingly, we need not have a deep understanding of most of our reality. Understanding that something simply *is*, is often understanding enough.

Having a rudimentary awareness of something and accepting that we don't know everything about everything, is the beginning of understanding. Having the awareness required to meet a basic level of understanding, with only minimal interest in the details of things, provides us enough understanding to take contentment all the way to bliss. There's a widespread tendency to confuse "wanting to know everything" out of interest and "needing to know everything" out of the fear of loss of control. If curiosity is driven by a fear of loss of control, we will become judgmental and discontented.

Chapter 26 – Happiness

The Magic Ingredient

You don't know what you don't know. You often don't even know what you DO know. Furthermore, the more you learn, the more you learn that there is always more detail, more nuance. And the trick is not to dig deeper into the rabbit hole than is necessary; to allow ourselves to be curious and interested, but to know when to stop. To recognise that we don't need to know everything and that we can assign the remainder to mystery; to simply stop digging for knowledge or deeper meaning as soon as the information becomes useful rather than exhausting all information. Just look at things and events in their simplest form. The rest can be considered magic.

Our minds dislike the unknown. After all, what you don't know might harm you. But the problem with knowing too much is that we assume a position of judgment. As we accumulate knowledge we create an illusion of superiority and we begin to feel entitled to judging the subjects of our studies. We assume and believe where we ought to ask more questions in order to gain a deeper understanding of our subjects.

Do you really feel safer when you think you know everything about a subject or situation? You assume that knowledge alone gives you the capacity to be ready for any situation. Focusing on accumulating all available knowledge makes you believe that your knowledge entitles you to more control and judgment over the world. In addition, accumulating more knowledge prevents you from participating; actually "doing" rather than insisting on learning from the sidelines.

Think about it for a moment. Would you actually be safer knowing what you believe to be everything if the deeper understanding you have created is actually constructed from illusion?

This chapter is about our ability to experience happiness. I invite you to simply experience allowing questions to remain unanswered and assign the lack of detail to "magic" or mystery. Experience for yourself how this changes your interaction and relationship with the world around you for the better. Improving the way we react to the world begins with how we interpret our interactive experience. Allowing magic as a valid contributor to what we experience simplifies our interactions to allow us to release the need to control and focus more on the experience of a moment.

First Threshold – Understand

Homework:
Start looking at things as "magic." Stop spending time and energy defining everything and understanding everything. Stop using the lack of understanding of something as an obstacle/excuse to moving you forward. Start calling things 'magic' or 'magical' as most things have many mysterious and magical things in them.

Accepting
Accepting reality can be difficult especially when we have an illusion that we're entitled to the manifestation of <u>our</u> version of the Universe. Having our illusion of entitlement reinforced over and over again by commercials, politicians and religious leaders has caused much unhappiness and disillusionment in those who have looked to others for direction. Realising <u>that we are not</u> entitled to the Universe unfolding in the ways we want can be difficult to accept.

Now think about the alternatives. Contemplate changing the way you think about the world. Decide if you'd rather be unhappy that the world doesn't behave the way you want or if you'd prefer to be happy by learning to accept the reality of the world. It really sounds simple doesn't it?

Accepting *What Is* means letting go of unhappiness and disillusionment.

Accepting *What Is* means being close enough to reality to be able to affect the future through participation and change – considering that change only happens in reality, not in illusion.

Accepting *What Is* means being with reality.

Accepting *What Is* leads to being able to accept opportunities as they present themselves and foregoing endeavours that don't serve you.

Without Judgment
Unfortunately, most of us have learned from our parents, caregivers and societal influences that before we are able to accept something, we must first like it. We often confuse the judgment of "being acceptable [to me]" with the more pure, non judgmental "being in acceptance with."

It seems that it's easier to accept something when you like it first. We feel entitled to judge reality and then to accept or reject it based on our judgments. Are we so deeply connected to our illusions that we don't see reality for what it is? Sure we can dislike reality, but to think that reality would simply comply with those who dislike it is wishful thinking. Reality continues on indefinitely, seemingly indifferent to those who dislike it and barely influenced by those who exert energy upon it.

Accepting only the parts of reality that meet with your approval can be a hard habit to break. But as long as we disapprove or even approve of reality, we remain on a direct route to unhappiness. It is also a big waste of energy to be upset when reality does not meet with your expectations of it. Reality is simply not going to reverse time and change something and then re-present it to you for your approval. Once we start to accept reality as it is, observing it as it behaves according to the laws of the Universe, we remove the largest barriers to happiness. Subsequently, we can let others be themselves according to their own laws, habits and values. When we accept "the way it is," we move directly towards contentment.

Illusion of Superiority
In order to judge something, we assume a position of superiority over what we judge. We can't judge anything without first observing it from our superior position, assuming permission and authority to judge. This is not only true for things we dislike, liking something is also judging. When we refuse to accept reality for what it is, or decide to like or dislike something, we assume an elevated position of superiority. Of course this feeling of superiority is itself a delusion: our opinions about reality don't actually affect reality. In our delusions we actually consider ourselves superior to reality, but reality already "is" and our judgments of it are futile attempts to compete with the Universe.

Effecting Change
Keeping our judgments of the Universe separate from the acceptance of it allows us to better effect change, whatever opinion we might have about the Universe. This is not to say that we must like everything. Understand that our judgments of *What Is* and our acceptance of it are completely separate. Acceptance of *What Is* brings us back into reality and away from the illusion of what we believe should be true. Being in acceptance is a key ingredient of contentment. Accepting the Universe, as it is, brings us closer to it; helps us move away from the energy-consuming illusions of *What Isn't*. Moving closer to *What Is* allows us to more successfully assert our desires upon

reality instead of wasting our time in the futile endeavour of asserting our desires upon what we believe "should be reality."

Contentment doesn't happen to you, it's a skill you master by practicing acceptance exclusive of judgement. You don't have to like something to accept it, but you must understand it. Understanding can be as simple as seeing reality as containing various layers of magic.

Homework:
Observe your surroundings, your circumstances and the people you are in relationship with and accept them without judgment (good or bad), just accept. Look for situations where you think "you know better" and practice accepting these situations as equally valid. This doesn't mean that you have to like everything. Once you accept, if you still desire change, you have the opportunity to contribute your desires to reality by focusing your energy towards the desired change. But you can only begin this endeavour once you have accepted the person or situation, the way it is now. For now, simply practice accepting What Is.

Bliss

Contentment is the entry point for happiness, ecstasy or bliss is its highest form.

Bliss is Participating in What Is

Participation
Participating in *What Is* takes us directly to bliss. Merely Understanding and Accepting *What Is* makes us observers of Creation and brings us to contentment, but participation elevates us to being in the act of creation itself: being the Creator. As we become participants in the process of Creation itself, we transform the conceptual to the real. By contributing our Desire to *What Is*, we Create! We manifest *What Is* from Potential. Participation in (the process of) Creation is where we feel most alive. We intrinsically understand how action and intimate participation in creation elevates our experience of life from contentment to pure bliss.

Many of us have been influenced by the fear of harm, fear of failure, the discomfort of the unknown, or the responsibility of that which we created. These fears hold us back and we allow them to keep us from the exhilaration of intimate connection to and full participation in *What Is*– "As it is," and the subsequent feeling of bliss that comes from it.

We justify our fears and lack of participation with the idea that real ecstasy can only be felt in the absence of discomfort. This is simply not true. Any mother who knows the bliss of being in creation, any man who knows the feeling of a job well done and any person who knows the joy of being in the midst of passionate acts of creation knows that the creative force that sources our ecstatic experience is unrelated to pain. Some acts of blissful creation include copious amounts of pain and discomfort and we still passionately participate in those experiences. There are people who still continue to insist on the notion that they can't do anything about their happiness because they feel pain but in fact their lack of engagement with reality is the source of their unhappiness.

Ban the notion that real happiness is dependent on the absence of pain. Don't fear active participation in reality for fear of getting hurt. Follow your bliss.

Being Happy

As said before, happiness is being in creation. Both contentment and bliss fall within this general statement but there is one very important distinction.

Contentment is: "Being in Creation." Bliss is: "Being in Creation." At face value they appear exactly the same but in the definition of contentment, "Creation" is a noun; simply being a part of the Universe of *What Is*. In Bliss "Creation" is a verb; denoting action and participation. The transition on the spectrum goes from passive observer to active participant. Participation in reality first requires contentment, but once contentment is reached, upgrading to bliss is quite an easy transition.

Before we continue to the next chapter, I'd like to address a question I often get asked: "Do we need to follow our bliss all the time?" The simplest and most accurate answer is that we always naturally do follow our bliss. When we're living we grow; we assert our desires upon reality. Even when we choose to be in contentment, we're participating in some way. The only time we're not experiencing bliss is when we shift our awareness to fear or judgment. The experience of bliss originates from our non-judgmental, fearless awareness. When, however, we are not understanding or accepting *What Is*, or not in reality, we are unable to elevate our awareness to bliss and our true nature.

First Threshold – Understand

To summarize:

As we live, we're always in some form of participation (inter-action) with the Universe– therefore in bliss. But we don't always experience our bliss. Non-judgmental awareness of our participation in Creation is required to experience Bliss. Our experience of Bliss can be obscured by:

- Liking or disliking (judgment) our experiences.
  Judging the Universe requires us to assume a superior position. We are unable to experience something if we're not "on par" with it. Both liking and disliking have the same detrimental effect on the experience of Bliss.
- Wanting to understand every part of our experience, analysing it rather than being in it, as this means we are attempting to control or own it.
  We could simplify our need to understand by declaring the parts we don't understand as "Magic." Our need to understand is our wish to manipulate, control and possess our experiences. The experience of Bliss cannot be controlled or owned. Happiness is simply being in a moment without having to own it.
- Being in illusion, either by choice (competition/superiority with the Universe) or through misunderstanding (our belief systems override or filter *What Is*).

The Universe doesn't engage in competition, it is always in completeness and harmony. Deep down we understand this. The real threat to our ability to experience Bliss is the illusion that we already know something about the reality we're in. We call this our belief systems. Understanding that we filter reality through our Belief Systems is the first step to reacquainting ourselves with reality and the Universe, disconnecting from our "shoulds and ought-tos," and becoming familiar with *What Is*. Our reward is "the experience of Bliss."

We sometimes attempt to avoid (inter) action with the Universe out of fear of consequences, or to avoid discomfort. The experience of bliss is exclusive of this discomfort; we can't help but interact with our Universe. Sometimes bliss is painless, sometimes it hurts; creation often goes hand-in-hand with friction and resistance and comes to being in cataclysmic events. Fear itself doesn't remove us from our experience. This doesn't actually change the fact that we remain in creation, both as a verb and a noun. Fear conjures up

Chapter 26 – Happiness

a secondary block, such as judgment, control, and illusion. Allowing fear-filtered perceptions to infiltrate our experience of reality takes us away from the happiness experience.

Homework:
Do something – anything! Find something to which you can contribute your action, participation and attention. Possibly something you've never done before. A behaviour that serves you or a physical contribution to others. For the time that you participate, contribute your full attention and all available energy. Be in the thick of the action, be present. Experience bliss.

Chapter 27 – Laws of Self-Preservation

Nature has miraculous abilities to survive and thrive. We can see the results of this mechanism of the propensity to thrive, but how does nature do this? How is this accomplished? Natural systems survive and thrive by adopting and fine-tuning an evolved set of rules. Nature survives through evolution and by following the *laws of self-preservation*.

We are all born with a primal desire to participate in evolution. Nature's rules of survival form our most basic rules; we are nature. These rules ensure that we continue to participate in evolution. While the interpretation and execution of the *laws of self-preservation* have evolved to include our increasingly complex modern world, the most basic rules have survived the test of time. Understanding how we live within the *laws of self-preservation* helps us understand how we are all part of nature itself.

Every living thing is born with basic *laws of self-preservation* already in place. Most of our minds are open to being influenced, but some parts of our awareness are already in place as we enter this world. If we were computers these basic instructions might be considered the BIOS that is loaded as the start-up or boot sequence of the device.

Our evolutionary heritage requires that we begin life with these basic instructions and directives. These basic rules give us the ability to survive and participate in evolution itself. All things alive participate in the same basic rules; therefore, I call them laws. Life itself has originated and reinforces these laws. While mutations and experiments are relatively common in nature, these basic laws still prevail. Any anomaly that overrides or disregards these laws is eliminated from further participation with evolution: the experiment ends. On the other hand, every natural experiment that participates in these basic *laws of self-preservation* survives beyond its own generation to become part of evolution.

Chapter 27 – Laws of Self-Preservation

Discovering these basic *laws of self-preservation* is the pathway to freedom for anyone who cares to examine them. Freedom from doctrine. Freedom from control, expectations, fairness and entitlements. Freedom from organized religion and belief systems. Freedom from imposed agreements with society, our parents, our peers and our self-deprecating identities.

1st Law of Self-Preservation

How does nature know how to proceed? How do you know how to proceed? Which course of action to take? Humans are not exempt from natural laws. Life is fueled from desire and manifests through intent.

Have you ever made a bad decision? Think about this for a moment, seriously.

Many people contemplating this answer find themselves in one of three camps:

1. Of course I've made bad decisions.
2. I must have made some bad decisions, doesn't everyone?
3. I was told many times as a child that I was bad, so I must have been.

Think about the moment of decision. In that moment, what decision did you make? Did you make the best decision you could under the circumstances, or did you choose an option that you knew was not the best choice?

In hindsight, your decision may have unintended outcome. Looking back you may have made a better choice if you knew then what you know now. Or a person in authority judged your decision as bad and may have even judged you, as well. All of these scenarios may influence your conclusions, but they are not valid when it comes to evaluating the decision in the moment and context it was made. Every decision is made based on *intended* outcome, not on the outcome itself. Society teaches us that we are responsible for the outcomes of our decisions. This may be so, but should we be morally judged for outcomes? Morally, we can only be judged for our intentions.

The truth of the matter is that you are incapable of actually making a bad decision!

In many circumstances you might make a decision that has an undesirable outcome, but this can only be assessed after the outcome becomes apparent. The intent that accompanied the choice is purely based on what was known at the time of decision. And the decision is always based on selecting your

First Threshold – Understand

best choice at that time, even if your choice is to abstain from choosing! This is an important fact to note. You only made the best choices you can, at any given time. In each moment you chose the path that, within your awareness at the time, would have provided you the best chance at the best outcome.

As *your best* is a value judgment, we'll explore making choices using values and beliefs.

1st *Law of Self-Preservation*: I am incapable of making a bad decision.

Please understand the timing of this law when contemplating it. IN THE MOMENT of decision, you always choose what you believe is the best available option. Even if you have to pick from two bad choices, you always choose the better of the available choices - based on what you know, value and believe in the moment.

When you look back on your decision, you might see that you could have taken another path, but in hindsight you have more information, as well as the knowledge of the consequences, with which to evaluate your choice. In the moment of decision you simply didn't have the luxury of information that hindsight provides and you needed to make a decision in the moment. In the next chapters we'll examine the internal process of creating a decision, the process of choice itself.

As the *laws of self-preservation* apply to all living things, this law applies to everyone! No one is capable of making any choice other than the best one, in the moment, based on the available choices and that person's values. Does this mean that everyone does their best? It certainly does!

You might ask: What about suicide bombers, serial killers, evil dictators and other people who have caused harm? Yes, those people also. When we properly examine those people's actions from their viewpoints, their values and their intents, we can see that they too operated within the same *laws of self-preservation* and therefore did their best. Popular ignorance and quick judgment may help us distance ourselves from their acts, but once we understand the circumstances and choices that led up to the decisions they made, we can realize that they, too, acted within the same laws and directives with which we are born. Taking a moral high ground and the assumption of judgment may provide an illusion of superiority. But the truth is that with the same knowledge, upbringing, belief systems and values, we would have made the exact same decisions that brought about the events and outcomes upon which we are now frowning. We'd rather believe that others are evil than acknowledge their humanity and understand the true narrowness of the decision path.

You Always Select Your Rather
In our moment of choice, we always select what we believe to be the best choice. I generally dislike the use of absolutes, but in this case I must use the word "Always" in context with choice. You always select your *rather* - the preferred choice - in any moment. Always.

By understanding that "best" is from the viewpoint of each chooser, we avoid the pitfall of judging others for their choices. We have a tendency to judge the outcome of a choice rather than the intent of it. I invite you to learn another perspective: evaluate a choice based on the intention of the person who made the choice, not the outcome. Base this evaluation on what that person knows, believes and values; not on "what you would have done" or with the hindsight of knowing the outcome and the consequences.

Once you evaluate based on the chooser's intent, you'll understand that each person mechanically selects the best available choice. Yes, mechanically. Choice is a mechanism. As much as we were taught by our caregivers and leaders that choice is free, the truth is that choice is based on a set of fixed criteria. In the moment of choice, you must work with a finite set of criteria. And you always select your *rather* the option that, from your limited viewpoint, will benefit you the most and create the least potential harm.

Every living thing on this planet adheres to the same, deeply embedded self-preservation laws. All living things evaluate their options as best they can from their viewpoints and each living thing intends the best outcome based on the values and beliefs that are assimilated as part of the *core being* of that creature.

Choice or No Choice?
So much is dependent on how we choose. Re-evaluation of our approach to choice would create a whole new understanding of the way we interact with our world and navigate our observations. The implications of a new paradigm on choice are far reaching. We would start to create a better understanding of each other and we would begin to re-evaluate how we judge one another. For example, if a person is incapable of selecting anything

other than the best option available at the time of choice, how can we say that we have a free will? We clearly adhere to a mechanism of selecting the best available choice in each instance; how is that a free will? It isn't. It's a mechanism. Choice is a mechanism.

Understanding the *1st law of self-preservation* fully means recognizing that since everyone selects the best available options, in their viewpoints, we cannot say that evil exists. How could we judge others to have evil intent when we know that they, too, select their best from available choices? When a person makes a choice that has a negative impact on us, we are quick to judge that this person meant harm or may assume this person is possessed by evil. But this judgment implies that we have failed to do our research and due diligence. We simply distance ourselves by assuming our personal or collective superiority and declare the other person evil for the sake of superficial clarity and solution.

Now, I fully agree with the idea that an outcome is owned by the person who turned his or her intent into action, but to declare that a person's intent is bad is to declare that this person's existence, from birth to the moment of the action, is invalid! All your best choices got you where you are today. All their best choices got them to take their actions. Are you or they evil? It's way too simple to judge another person as evil when the intent was good, or at least the best available option, based on their belief systems, values and knowledge. Sometimes I'm grateful that I don't have to choose between some horrific act and its next best thing. Some people do; some people are faced with such decisions.

Please don't forget that choices are made in each and every moment. Each choice, once made, is permanent and cumulative. Being permanent doesn't mean you cannot choose again, it only means that a choice, once made, cannot be replaced by another choice in the same context and moment. Later we'll examine *re-choice*, making a new choice after a previous choice begins to reveal an outcome we no longer desire. In the natural flow of life, choices are made upon the foundation of previous choices, in sequence. You cannot go back and "fix" an old choice. All your previous best choices are now a permanent part and foundation upon which you build your future.

I sometimes imagine the societal impact of widespread knowledge of the *1st law of self-preservation*. Imagine people, no longer morally judged, but understood and assisted to make choices that would impact others in less severe ways. This doesn't mean that people can separate themselves from the impact of their choices, or that they don't own the consequences of their actions. Sure they do, but instead of judging them as evil, people who hurt others can be made to compensate; give restitution as best they can rather than receiving punishment for their "bad" behaviour.

Shameless
The *1st law of self-preservation* deeply impacts everything we do. To understand this impact, we must feel this truth deeply: "I am incapable of making bad decisions and I live in the mechanism of choice, always selecting my *rather*." This *rather* is based on values, beliefs and knowledge at the time of decision. This *1st law* eliminates the validity of shame.

While reality presents us with a finite choice, our beliefs are based on what we actually know and not what we should have known. We always make the best decisions we are able to, in the moments we make them, therefore, there is no valid basis for shame. The very definition of shame is, "you should have known better." And yet, in each instance the truth is simply that had you known better, you would have chosen the better option. The *1st law of self-preservation* is omnipresent and an infallible ally in evolution, without shame. Let go of shame. Shame is based on the impossibility of providing our past-selves with more knowledge about our future outcomes. Give up your attempts at altering the past, you don't have that power. Shame can't exist in reality; it is a construct of parents, caregivers and others in positions of power. It is designed to emphasize the misconception that we are somehow flawed and should be improved. Believing in shame implies that we miss an ingredient that any other person in similar circumstances would have possessed, that would have allowed us to effect a better outcome - whatever "better" represents in this context.

No one else was (or could possibly have been) in that situation other than you, with the knowledge you had at the time. The past cannot be changed to create a "better" outcome.

No Sorry Either?
When people say they're sorry for particular choices, they usually mean well, but they are referring to feeling remorse for a decision at the time the decision was made. It must be clear now that another choice was simply

First Threshold – Understand

impossible and that saying sorry for making the decision is actually quite incorrect.

Sorry may be seen as recognition that a choice you made with the best intentions impacted another negatively, or you may still be sorry for the way your decision played out: its outcome. The expression of "sorry" is not remorse, however, but recognition that your well-intended choice had a negative outcome or side effect – still with the best intentions.

Please understand that everyone constantly makes their best decisions. This means that regardless of the impact of their decisions (the outcomes) their intents are <u>always</u> to make the best decisions they are able to make! In the 2nd *law* we continue on this subject to better understand the impact the 1st *law* has on our interactions with each other.

How We Make Motivated Decisions

Now that we understand our mechanism of choice – that we always make the best available decisions, based on the values, beliefs and knowledge we posses at the time of making them – maybe we should further examine how our minds actually come to decisions. Then we will be able to empower ourselves with the skill to make better choices, within the limits of the mechanism of choice and the *1st law of self-preservation*.

There are various methods we use to come to a decision. The factors of choice are finite: Our values, our knowledge and our beliefs. The way these factors influence us, ultimately determines how we decide.

When faced with a decision, we begin our decision making process by projecting ourselves into the future. We intuit a few most likely outcomes and then judge the decision at hand as being "good" or "bad" based on those projected outcomes. We actually imagine the impact of the decision in the (near) future and make a choice based on our most desired outcome. Interestingly, we often evaluate multiple future impacts from the same decision.

For example: We're faced with the decision of whether or not to consume a piece of cheesecake. We quickly project ourselves a few minutes into the future and imagine how we will feel when we're enjoying delicious cake. Our conclusion: Good decision. Then we project ourselves forward a few months to remind ourselves of our goal of losing weight. Our conclusion: Eating this piece of cheesecake is not in our best interest.

Chapter 27 – Laws of Self-Preservation

In the previous example, we weigh the two feelings and make a decision based on what we perceive is our most desired feeling. Not what ultimately is best for us (as decided by us), but how we imagine we will feel. Unfortunately, this way of deciding is subject to the *perspective of returns* and we may likely be more influenced by the more immediate return. We'll examine the *perspective of returns* in the following pages, but first I would like to discuss the evaluation process itself.

A Pot of Gold

In the previous sections I described choice as a mechanism of evaluation. In this section I'd like to examine this evaluation process as a mind process.

When you have two directions from which to choose, you always have three main options: Go one way, go the other way or take no further action. As per the *1st law of self-preservation*, you always select the best option from your viewpoint, with the knowledge you possess in the moment, the values you have and the beliefs you hold. Knowing these factors makes it possible to predict all choices we might make.

Question: What would you rather choose? A *pot of gold* or a pile of manure?

I'm sure you picked the *pot of gold*. In fact, everyone has a very similar reaction. So, let me ask you to answer a few questions. From the following list, which would you choose?

- Something good or something bad?
- Something good or something better?
- Something really good or something even better?
- Something bad or something worse?
- Something truly horrible or something even worse than that?

Do you notice that your answers are repeatable and predictable? You always select your *rather*, the better option.

So let's change the circumstances and see how the *pot of gold* holds up. Imagine you're alone on a deserted island with no prospect of rescue any time soon and you hold plant seeds in your hand. Now ask yourself the exact same question: what would you rather choose? The *pot of gold* that no one will purchase from you or the pile of manure that will help you grow your seed into food? Of course you will likely choose the pile of manure. It has more value in this situation. You see, your *perspective of returns* determines the value of each option and ultimately determines what your decision becomes. When you understand the knowledge, values and beliefs of the circumstance within which the decision is being made, the evaluation of options still remains nothing more than a mechanical exercise.

It seems we're always moving towards a perceived benefit or moving away from a disadvantage or fear. This mechanism cannot be overridden. This is a built-in process; a process proven over time and reinforced through evolution itself.

Two Types of People - Moving Away vs. Moving Towards
This is a popular concept in psychology. All actions are motivated by moving away from a pain and moving towards gain. Different people decide in different ways but by far most people are "moving away" – type people, where decisions are more influenced by moving away from pain.

Moving away from poverty and moving towards wealth sound almost the same. Yet when you look at the decision weight of each statement, you're more likely to respond to "moving away from poverty" than to "moving towards wealth." We simply react more to the fear of pain than the benefit of gain. Keep this in mind when making decisions. Avoiding pain or fear may be the motivation behind your first responses, but don't react too quickly. You may be sabotaging a wonderful long-term gain by simply avoiding a short-term pain.

Perspective of Returns
A benefit now is worth much more than a benefit later, even if that benefit is much greater. The numbers might be different for each person, but a million dollars right now seems worth much more than three million dollars in three years, even though it would be difficult to turn the million dollars into three million in the same period of time.

If you were offered a suitcase with one million dollars in it, or a certified bank draft for three million dollars, post dated for three years from now, which one would you take? Most people understand that gratification is influenced by both distance and time proximity. Anything that's closer to us seems "more real" to us and has a disproportionately larger influence on how we measure its value.

Avoiding a Loss Is More Motivating than Obtaining a Gain
What would you do?

As an experiment I conducted with dozens of clients over time, I asked them how much money I would need to pay them to run into the street in their underwear and the results became extremely predictable.

For example, when I asked a man to name his price, I had to offer him one hundred thousand dollars before he would do it. I negotiated him down to eighty five thousand, but he refused to accept less.

I reversed the question and got a completely different result. "I have your wallet with your last two thousand dollars in it. I will return your wallet after you run into the street in your underwear." And he responded affirmative!

I found that women negotiated a higher price (a million dollars is not uncommon) and men often agree to, in comparison, a mere thousand to go out into the street in their underwear. Yet every time I reversed the proposition and turned it from gaining new wealth to losing their last money, each of the test subjects were willing to negotiate significantly lower. Typically about 10% of the value they would have accepted as gain for women and down to as little as 2% for men.

We choose differently when the projected outcome of a potential choice is stated negatively or positively. We have a tendency to evaluate the benefit of obtaining a gain as less motivating than the benefit of moving away from loss.

Using the cheesecake example from the previous section, we make a choice whether to eat the cheesecake based on how we will feel in a few minutes vs. how we'll feel in 6 months. At first we seem more motivated by the immediate gratification than by the long term benefits of being slimmer. But reversing the question gives us more information we can use in our evaluation as we are now evaluating the immediate loss of the cheesecake vs the benefit of not getting fat. All options considered, not getting fat is the option that most motivates us in how we choose the action that follows.

Strategy: Creating More Choice Options
Because a positive future has less impact on a decision than a negative one, comparing the consequences from the two opposite scenarios (not having cheesecake now vs having cheesecake later) gives rise to new choice options.

First Threshold – Understand

Looking at the choice from the opposite view may swing the balance in the other direction. Say to yourself: "What if I don't? What if I don't eat that cheesecake?" but still compare that against the consequence of "What if I do?" (the negative future of being fat) In the near future you don't get to have the cheesecake and in the long term you are thinking of the negative future of being fat

No longer am I evaluating a piece of cheesecake versus a slimmer, trimmer future me, I am evaluating having no cheesecake against the prospect of an overweight or obese future me. The possibility of an obese outcome makes our choice much clearer and we feel enough motivation to forego the cheesecake.

A benefit in the future is perceived with diminishing value, depending on how far into the future the projected outcome is expected to occur. A disadvantage in the future does diminish in value, but not nearly as quickly as a benefit does. Stating the question in terms of how I will lose rather than how I will benefit, especially in the future, presents the choice in a different light using the prospect of loss to influence our motivation right now.

Making Decisions That Count
Do you find yourself wondering if you're making the right choices in your life? How do you decide how to proceed without knowing which options are wasted efforts in the long run? There are so many options; it can be difficult to decide what choices will work out for you in the future. We don't know the future, so the answer to this question isn't black and white. But there's a lot we can do to help us make choices which will support our future outcomes.

We often choose the easiest route forward; we choose easy over difficult. But making choices based on a low level of difficulty leads to boredom and lack of motivation when it comes to taking action and staying focused on our goals along the way. Choosing more complex routes to achieving our goals isn't motivating either as our mind, given the choice, wants to pursue the most efficient route.

So how do you choose from the many possible routes you can take and not lose your motivation along the way? The answer is quite simple. Choose options that are either Interesting, Important or Fun. Choices based on interest, importance or the reward of joy remain engaging throughout. They keep you highly motivated, focused, challenged and participating regardless of how difficult the execution is.

A few years ago, I was assisting a university student to choose the courses he wanted to invest his time and energy in. He was frustrated that his previous year was marred in procrastination. He had difficulty finishing any task, however small and had no motivation to stay on track. His choices were made difficult by the fact that he wasn't sure what career he was going to pursue and without a clear image of his future, he became reluctant in his choices. He started selecting courses that sounded easy to complete; some because he already knew the subject matter and others because his friends were taking these courses as well. He was already predicting another year of unrewarding work that he would find difficult to overcome without motivation to finish the course.

When I asked him to highlight the courses which were Important, Interesting or Fun in different coloured highlighters, he was surprised to find a clear overlap in course material. This little exercise helped him choose courses which kept his focus and motivation, even through tough times. As the year progressed, he remained motivated and in the following year he found a niche in the financial industry which had previously been obscure to him. He was able to connect with his personal reasons for wanting to finish the courses and became so focused on what he wanted it accelerated his progress.

Strategy: What, Why, What Else, How

We feel a desire; we want something. Yet we find it difficult to get started or motivated. Often we don't know how to get from where we are to where we want to be.

This is a recipe for disaster. When we focus on HOW we're going to get there, we're focusing on the wrong aspect of the desire. We feel inadequately prepared for any part of the task ahead. We're unable to predict the many ways and diversions the journey to our desired outcome may take us and the complexity leads us into overwhelm and paralysis. In attempting to prepare for each unknown we procrastinate and become discouraged. We're unable to understand the details of each step until we get closer to the step. We must trust that as we take each step, we will be skilful, curious or determined enough to overcome each obstacle along the way.

First Threshold – Understand

Understanding the reason we want the things we want is more than enough to start the journey. Waiting until we've understood and researched every possibility prepares us for nothing. It's just an excuse for getting started.

So here's an exercise that will help you to connect with your direction and drive and improve your motivation to fuel your desires.

- First, focus on WHAT you want.
- Second, understand your reason: WHY you want it.
- Third, think of WHAT ELSE: all the other ways in which you might fulfil your reason.
- Fourth, working from your WHY look at the FIRST, NEXT step to achieving your goal and stay focused on the reason.

What

What is it that you want? Often we notice a need only after we notice our desire for something. It seems as if we want something, but is this true? Do we really want a particular something, or are we seeking a feeling or to fulfill an underlying basic human need?

The first step is, therefore, to understand WHAT we want. Would we get the same feeling if we got something else, something other than what we believe we want? Really identify the feelings associated with the thing you want and soon you'll sense why you want it, the reason behind your choice.

Why

You want something because of the feeling you believe it will bring you, likely a feeling deriving from one of the basic human needs (discussed later in more detail) or prime directives of the mind:

- Do you want it because it will give you a better sense of stability?
- Do you want it because it promises a sense of variety or vitality?
- Do you want it to feel more important, or because it gives you a sense of purpose?
- Do you want it to help you feel more connected or less lonely?
- Maybe you want it to prove you have the ability to get it?
- Maybe you want it to be better than something, someone, or your former self?
- Maybe you want it as a means to accomplishing some other goal, or as leverage?

Chapter 27 – Laws of Self-Preservation

Check in with your feelings. Find the reason, the WHY for your desires. Understanding your reasons will keep you motivated. Your desires are the fuel for life, the motivation to keep you focused on your path even when times get tough.

What Else
Be real. Be reasonable. Once you know your reasons, your WHY, you'll be able to think of a few alternative ways to achieve these feelings. Is it fair to say that you could experience a very similar feeling in a less expensive and less lofty way? Evaluate carefully, you may find it easier to reach for the low hanging fruit at first before upgrading to more difficult options. What if you realise that you can reach your desired feelings by other means? What if you don't need what "they" sold you? What if you're able to create these feelings in a more efficient way, or with fewer resources?

How
Focus on your upcoming next step. Don't bother going over the entire plan with a fine tooth comb. Don't allow the desire and associated rewards to slip your mind. Trust yourself to make each decision when needed, with the desired outcome in mind and literally accelerate towards your goals.

Planning the HOW causes inflexibility and may cause delays when you are faced with obstacles and adversity on your journey. Staying focused on your WHY for achieving your outcomes forces you to be agile do whatever it takes to get to your goals. in favour of the Be willing to change your course quickly and discard your old HOW when needed. You keep your energy focused, you leap and duck when needed, you stay alert and present and capable of reacting in time to anything that comes between you and your goals or that might divert you from your path.

Your ability to make decisions and act in a timely manner to effect change that is congruent with your goals is a direct function of how clearly and honestly you are aligned with your desires. The ability to reach your goals and remain on track is based on how deeply you embody your desire. But staying focused on what you want is not always enough to ensure that you follow through and make the progress you want. Adding reason to your focus keeps your mind from being distracted by the details of the HOW and this separation gives you agility when you need it and resourcefulness when

First Threshold – Understand

you're looking for solutions. The resulting success and progress will help you hold on to your faith and make it through the obstacles in your way. Your WHY is more important than your HOW will ever be. It's amazing the way the HOW can create obstacles and excuses that interfere with achieving your desires. HOW is useful in hindsight only, WHY fuels the focus, faith and motivation to make it happen.

Looking Ahead
Imagine that you're driving to a far away destination. You have a general direction and you've made a plan. You know why you want to go there and you've decided to start on your journey.

The journey is long and you can only see from the top of each hillcrest to the next. You can't see beyond the next hill. You don't know what's beyond the next bend in the road. You can't see your destination and you know that your journey will be filled with obstacles and challenges that will add to your skills and knowledge of life itself. Deep inside, you crave the destination yet simultanously you understand that the challenges along the way will make you stronger and fulfil your deepest human needs.

And while you feel the destination and you can even imagine the outcome, you can't yet see it. You cannot plan each step, nor prepare for each obstacle. And still you move forward, seeing only one part of the path ahead, the approaching part.

Being present, staying focused on your reasons and being stubborn will move you closer and closer while mastering the challenges along the way.

Action Speaks Louder
Start! Don't prepare, START!

Eventually preparation will act as a force against you. It will act as an excuse. You will never be prepared enough to start, so start.

Once you know what you want, take a step, any step. It doesn't matter if it's in the right direction. Take action first, then use the movement to steer your choices. A vehicle must first move before it will change directions. No matter how much you turn the steering wheel, you must first move the vehicle before it will turn. Action first, then adjust the direction of your action. Create some tiny progress right away. Get yourself in gear, do it right away.

Not tomorrow, not even in an hour. Do something now, then continue to read this book.

Any movement is progress towards success. Achieve any success, however small, then move ahead and find milestones, but take action first! NOW !

What's Left of Choice?
No wonder our lives seem to be guided by an external force. No wonder we feel so insignificant against the forces of nature, when we were taught to believe that we have free will, yet have nowhere to exert this true freedom. Once we understand the *1st law of self-preservation*, we begin to see the impact it has on how we experience and consequently interact with the entire Universe. We're all bound by the *1st law of self-preservation*: "I am incapable of making a bad decision," which causes us to make the best decisions possible at the time we make those decisions. What then, if anything, is left of choice?

Our perception of projected outcomes of the various available options guides how we make decisions. Where do we invest our energy to contribute to the best possible outcomes? Do we choose to emphasize long-term value over short-term value? Do we focus on a future outcome, or do we focus on the immediate gratification of a desire?

The better you are able to connect to the resulting feelings caused by each of your choice options the more motivated you become in your selection.

A major factor in executing choices is risk. How much detail do we need before we're willing to take a leap of faith? Being comfortable with risk means nothing more than being confident that you'll survive mistakes, accidents, misfortune and the other potentially negative influences that get in your way. Be confident about your ability to reasonably overcome risk, all you need to do is keep a clear image of your desired outcome as well as your WHY and you will lean your next decision towards your most desirable outcome.

Here is a recap of the tools you can use to create a choice filled with more knowledge and clearer feelings about the subject of your choice:

- Moving Away vs. Moving Towards
- Perspective of Returns
- Avoiding a Loss Is More Motivating than Obtaining a Gain
- Strategy: Creating More Choice Options

First Threshold – Understand

- Making Decisions That Count
- Strategy: What, Why, What Else, How

Not Just You

Remember that you aren't the only one who is governed by the built-in *laws of self-preservation*. Everyone is governed by those laws! Think of what this means! If you are always making your best possible choices, then so is everyone else. When your actions are governed by your best intents, your values and your knowledge, then so is everyone else's. While your *pot of gold* may be different than another's *pot of gold*, other people are also operating within the mechanism of choice and choose their *rathers*, every time.

When it comes to others and their choices, you must understand that their intents are not yours. Your reasons are your own and so are theirs. Judging another to be bad or good is ignoring that person's circumstances and options: it is being unwilling to understand his or her world and placing yourself in an assumed superior position. Which brings us to the *2nd law of self-preservation*: You act according to your reasons, others act according to their reasons – not yours. Everyone acts individually according to their own reasons.

Homework:

1. *Observe the people around you choosing their "pots of gold" –and allow them their experiences. Rather than saying "that's wrong," say, "in my truth, I would've done something else, I wonder what circumstances led them to choose the way they did and what alternatives they believed they had or had to choose from."*
2. *Once you begin to expand your awareness into the experience of others, you will enrich your understanding of how you make your own decisions. In order to help yourself make more informed decisions, add options to the choices you have by asking yourself the question:"what if I don't"... In the example of the aforementioned cheesecake, you initially asked yourself the question: "How would I feel if I eat the cheesecake?" If you also asked, "How would I feel if I don't eat the cheesecake?" as compared to the future consequence of "What if I do?" Look at decisions you struggle with and reword them to highlight the negative future loss, note whether this triggers you into new choice preferences.*

2nd Law of Self-Preservation

As said before, everything you do, every action you take and decision you make is the best decision you have available to you at that time. The decisions and actions you take are always from one viewpoint: <u>yours</u>. This allows a natural *2nd law* to emerge from the *1st law*.

> *2nd Law of Self-Preservation*: **Everything I do, I do for a reason; I am the reason for everything I do.**

The *1st law* is a self-centered law. It describes only how we interact within our own worlds, from our own self-centered perspectives. The *2nd law* provides insight into how we interact with the world around us and how the world around us interacts with us.

No Action without Reason

The *2nd law* contains two main statements. Firstly, everything we do we do for a reason: all effect has a cause. And secondly, all living things are motivated by their own personal reasons, their "whys." All the reasons for our actions eventually point back to us. Even seemingly selfless acts are motivated by something personal, such as the desire to feel good, to be significant, or to boost one's pride, or even to have the reward of the altruistic experience.

Why do we do things? Why do we act? What causes us to apply our energy to actions? Each action is motivated by personal reasons. This may seem quite a bold and selfish statement. Many of us were scolded by our caregivers to not be selfish, so exploring this law may cause some initial resistance. Maybe understanding this law as self-care rather than "selfishness" may alleviate some of the resistance and help us focus on the reality of this *2nd law of self-preservation*.

From the *1st law of self-preservation* we understand how the mechanism of choice operates, so it's clear that we always have the best intentions. From the *2nd law* we understand that everyone is motivated by their own reasons – not your reasons.

Once you combine these truths, you can easily understand that <u>other</u> people's acts are never motivated by <u>your</u> reasons. Simply put: Everything that happens <u>to</u> you does not happen <u>because</u> of you. Once you understand this truth within the context and viewpoint of your own life, you no longer take things personally. Often this is easier said than done, especially when you

First Threshold – Understand

don't yet fully grasp the universality of the *2nd law of self-preservation*. Once you become aware that you see the world through your own experience, you may need to adjust to the new understanding of reality in which others do the same, from their experience, not yours.

Your actions are motivated solely by your personal motivations and available choices, however limited. Your motivations are influenced by your beliefs and values, but this is a subject that deserves its own chapter.

I'd love to recommend a classic text by Viktor Frankl "Man's Search for Meaning." The original German title of this book is "...trotzdem. Ja zum Leben sagen," which more literally translates to "... despite everything, still saying yes to life." In this book Frankl clearly illustrates the *1st* and *2nd laws of self-preservation* rather astutely. At each moment during his ordeal in Nazi Germany he was forced to choose either work or death. He was aware of the mechanism of choice and understood that he was selecting his best option - his *rather* - based on the options available to him; he chose work. In his book he demonstrates his understanding of how choice is limited by the circumstances and how he was very much aware that he was selecting his best choice within the realistic parameters of his circumstances. Critics of this philosophy might say that his choices were very limited, but in the book he points out how he always selected <u>his</u> *rather* and always understood that everyone was self-motivated, including himself. Being able to understand these two primary drivers of decision and action led him to develop a psychotherapeutic method he called Logotherapy based on his findings.

Every Decision/Action Serves You
Everything we do serves us, somehow. We are unable to truly take any action without first having a motivation of some kind, a reward, however derived. It is interesting to observe people taking actions and realise that these actions are motivated by reasons that serve the people taking the actions.

The *2nd law of self-preservation* is often compared to the saying: "Everything happens for a reason," and I'd like to make a distinction between the two. The saying: "Everything happens for a reason" is explained as "The universe is designed to start a sequence of good for you, but in order to follow this path you must start somewhere unpleasant," or "something good will come from something bad." Both explanations are inaccurate. It is true that everything that happens has a cause, but it is inaccurate to say that everything that happens has a predetermined outcome. Additionally, the saying: "Everything happens (to you) for a reason" is passive and the *2nd law of self-preservation* is active, it is about why you (and others) do what you do.

Everything that happens to you, that is, every action taken "against" you, doesn't happen because of you. Really, it is that simple. While you are often being considered by others as they take actions, their primary (and eventually only) reasons for their behaviours and actions are their own. There is no need to take anything personally; everything that happens to you is externally motivated. Often the reason why you're implicated is a tangential thought rather than a primary motivation. Even if you are seen as a future investment (with a perceived outcome value) for the person who owns the motivation for the action, you are considered only as an investment to the other person's self-motivated outcome.

Don't be surprised that others' actions don't have you as their primary motivator. Your actions follow the same laws from your perspective. And therefore the *2nd law of self-preservation* is also in the first person singular tense:

Everything I do, I do for a reason; I am the reason for everything I do.

I want to include kindness to others in this *2nd law*. Every kindness to another is motivated by one of two primary drivers. We are kind to others because we are investing in the relationship, or because we want to feel good about ourselves based on moral programming. In the case of investment, being kind will provide the least resistance to moving forward. We are motivated to be kind to others by the knowledge that if we are helpful to them, they won't resist us. And our investment in the relationship can also pay back in love, kindness and care in the future.

The second driver of feeling good about ourselves stems from our moral upbringing and being punished or rewarded for doing something our parents and caregivers deemed good or bad. Most people have difficulty donating truly anonymously. Even when the donation was anonymous, they often need to tell a significant person what they did, in the hope of being judged by this person as good. Sometimes the anticipation alone is good enough to stimulate this behaviour. Even kindness is selfish.

A side note to kindness: Please understand the motivation behind acts of kindness and the results they have on the giver or helper. Keep this in mind when you need help yourself. Others are very willing to help you as long as they either see the offering of help as an investment in their future relationships with you, or as an opportunity to feel morally good. You have the ability to make another feel good by asking them for help. Please think about this in the moments you feel alone or overwhelmed on your life journey.

Giving from a Full Cup
Being selfish is a good thing. Though again, we might define this type of behaviour as self-care rather than selfishness. Before we can take care of others, we must have taken care of ourselves. Before we can give from our proverbial cups, our own cups must be filled. We fill our cups by caring for our bodies and minds and by making choices that support our health and fulfill our needs.

Depleting ourselves is not only detrimental to our wellbeing, it makes us unable to invest in relationships with others. If we deplete ourselves too much, our work, health and lives will suffer and eventually we must disconnect from others until we are at least partially replenished.

Practicing selfishness as a form of self-care does not mean that we indulge in greed or exploitation of others, or seek to cause harm. When we practice self-care before giving our energy to others, we make choices that honour our energy levels, the value of our time and work and our true needs.

Saying "no" to a request allows the requestor to find another way to solve his or her issue, instead of relying on you to fix something to which you are unable to devote adequate energy. Saying "yes," however, when we don't have enough energy, focus, or motivation to support the person, robs us of the energy we do have. If we complete the request, we find ourselves exhausted and potentially resentful. Alternatively, when we are unable to follow through, we will have done a greater disservice to the requester than if we had just said "no" in the first place.

Practicing good self-care prevents your cup from becoming too depleted. Wait to give to others until your cup is filled to the brim and overflows. From this overflow you can give freely and fully, without resentment or depletion. When your cup is full, you will not need to drink from another's cup, though you can share your abundance with others. Taking care of ourselves enables us to care for others.

Homework:
Begin by observing people in their interactions, with the knowledge that they are following their personal motivators as guided by the 2nd law of self-preservation. Allow your curious mind to wonder about their motivations. Observe how you may have a tendency to relate or attribute the other person's behaviour to you. In such a case re-evaluate your reactions based on the knowledge that the other person must be motivated by his or her own reasons, not your presence or desires.

Next, begin to evaluate your own motivators. Why do you do things you don't like to do? What truly motivates each and every action you take? Learn to observe the often partially obscured, deeper reasons behind your actions. When we are honest with ourselves, we often find that our actions are motivated by fear or the hope of personal gain.

3rd Law of Self-Preservation

The *3rd law of self-preservation* ties in with many other concepts described in this book, especially the *Hierarchy of Motivation* which is described in detail in a later chapter. The *3rd law* is particularly useful in examining where you are on your path of life and deciphering your true motivations up until this point.

3rd Law of Self-Preservation: I do what I want.

It seems quite simple, but when you observe someone's behaviour concurrently with their verbiage, you may often find that what they say they are doing does not reflect what they're actually doing. This law helps you, in many ways, to "read people's minds" and observe their *1st* and *2nd* laws in action.

Often we say one thing and do another. This law assists us in discerning our desires from our wishes. For instance, we might say: "I wish I were home" while we're at work. When we evaluate our current circumstances and the choices we have available we actually want to be at work. Using the *1st law of self-preservation* as our guide and the mechanism of choice, our path of *rathers* lead us to where we are, not where we say we wish to be.

First Threshold – Understand

It is important to observe when a person tells you they'd rather be doing one thing, while actually doing another. Often this is simply an attempt to obfuscate the truth and manipulate perceptions. In all cases, what a person actually does, not what that person says, is what matters in the end.

When I see clients, the conversation often gets a little stuck in the very first session when the client doesn't seem to be able to articulate what he or she wants from life. Once we've covered the *3rd law of self-preservation* the client is able to honestly asses "where I am now" and use it as a starting point for what they want for their future. Subconsciously that client had already been making choices with the available knowledge and options at each point, motivated by personal desires to choose the best outcomes possible for themselves, unaware that they were doing what they want all along; leading themselves choice by choice and step by step to the life they have now. This is a good basis for initiating change.

If you find yourself not knowing what you want– this law is a good starting point: You are already doing what you want. Maybe you now want something else. Maybe you want to increase the choices available to you, or shift your outlook. Start where you are in this moment. It's not very useful to observe where you should have been by now, or what more you believe you deserve to be or posses. Start with what you are and have and then look at what you want.

The difference between wish and want are the moments that follow.

Observing the *3rd law of self-preservation* in action can be eye opening. A want is followed by intent and action. A wish is followed by nothing – or maybe another wish. Only desires are strong enough to create action. Wishes remain idle wishes unless they are transformed into actions.

This is where the *3rd law of self-preservation* interfaces with every action, including how we respond to our own, internal dialogue, which we'll cover in the *Hierarchy of Motivation* chapter later in this book. It is important to understand how desire is the fuel of life. It is the driver of all action. It is the essence we use for our souls' growth. While desire is vilified in nearly every religion as the source of all evil or pain, it is essential to understand that desire is the source of all we pursue and experience. Not just pain, but everything. To avoid desire is to avoid pain, yes, but also to avoid, joy, passion, growth and life itself: the feeling of being alive.

Homework:
Listen to how others express themselves. Listen for differences between what they say and what they do. When observing yourself, also connect to the different feelings that are associated with what you say and what you do. Often what you do is connected with an actual feeling and what you say or "wish for" is associated with the anticipation of a feeling, not the feeling itself. Also observe how many of your wishes remain wishes and how few are converted to actions.

In Summary

The three *laws of self-preservation* cover the elements of Intent, Motivation and Action.

- The *1st law*: "I am incapable of making a bad decision" addresses the mechanism of choice as well as our inability to intentionally harm ourselves or others. It helps us recognise the good intent in all of us.
- The *2nd law*: "Everything I do, I do for a reason; I am the reason for everything I do" addresses the motivation for our behaviours and how to evaluate the behaviour motivators of others.
- The *3rd law*: "I do what I want" addresses the resulting action which reflects your true desire.

The triad of Intent, Motivation and Action, appears in many themes throughout this book. The Want or desire, combines with its reason to create: Motivation. Motivation is the driving force behind all our choices and actions and Desire is the essence of Motivation.

Chapter 28 – Assumptive Life

In our quest to survive, our minds have evolved a method to utilize our brains as highly efficient tools. Our minds use our brains to bring ideas together, summarize and deduct. Our brains connect similar bits of data into cohesive pictures of the world around us, sorting what we experience into something that makes sense to us. When we do not have all the data and even when we do have all the information but do not fully understand it, our brains extrapolate complete pictures from partial data. Above all, our brains make assumptions to form a perspective of reality that is familiar and comfortable to us. We connect the dots and construct assumptions in the mind space in-between the facts of data we collect, completing the picture from our imaginations. This is a highly efficient skill to have. Most information we encounter is incomplete and can neither be relied nor acted upon. Once we virtually connect the dots, however, we have a complete picture that can be navigated as *truth*. This ability to construct information from incomplete data is an evolutionary advantage, but constructing information also has negative side effects.

There is a popular belief that our minds are like little recorders, permanently capturing everything we experience and witness. This really isn't the case at all. Our minds only summarize and store information that it considers important in that moment. Our brains store the most space-efficient summary of reality they can, with the knowledge that the unimportant data that was not stored can, upon recall, be reconstructed!

The way we recall memories has been subjected to fruitful scrutiny that has yielded a lot of insight about our minds. A lifetime of research by Daniela Schiller actually shows that:

a. Each time we retell a story we "enhance" it to assist the listener in understanding the story better "within the context of the listener's world."
b. Every time we recall the same story, we are not recalling the original event, but rather we are recalling the last time we recalled the story about the event. We're playing the telephone game with our own minds.

With this new knowledge, how do we navigate our established understanding of how our minds work?

Revisit the chapter: "How We Store Memories" for a refresher.

Shaping Personal Truths

We shape the *personal truths* contained within our *foundation of reality* by using deductions, assumptions and beliefs. *Personal truths* constructed from beliefs or assumptions are different than *personal truths* derived from reality.

It is important to distinguish the difference between these thought processes that form our *personal truths*. When we use beliefs during deduction we compromise the validity of the resulting *personal truth* even if we started from reality. A belief is an unverified assumption (Reality + Belief = Another Belief).

How then do we clearly distinguish between *truths* that are deducted from reality and *truths* that are constructed using beliefs? It is important to understand this difference in order to effectively interface with reality.

Distilling Reality

How can we distinguish between beliefs and truths? *Personal truths*, within the context of brain function, are stored, perceived realities. These perceived realities are used as comparative reference material during critical thinking, behavioural self-evaluation, recreational imagery and other mind processes. *Personal truths* may or may not accurately reflect reality, but they are stored within our *foundation of reality* and are assumed to be true and reliable. We act upon *personal truths* as if they were reliable facts rooted in reality, without distinguishing their origin.

These *personal truths* are physically manifested as neural pathways that create associations between stored impressions. Most of these *personal truths* are assumptive at some level. We rely on these assumptions as complete pictures of the world we know and as such translate and filter anything we consider foreign or new to match our previously deducted or constructed and now considered reliable, *foundation of reality*.

This translation or filter mechanism is an essential tool for survival. We use it over time to build a base or *foundation of reality* allowing us to efficiently navigate our lives, without needing to re-think, re-discover, or re-learn realities we believe we already understand. As a result, we can efficiently concentrate on interacting with the few things that are new to us and rely on the things that we already know about to give us confidence to take our next steps forward into the future.

But what if our *foundation of reality* no longer reflects useful or functional information about reality? What if we realise that parts of our *foundation of reality* are no longer accurate and therefore cannot be relied upon for building futures based on reality? What if we realise that previously "connected dots" created incorrect assumptions about our realities, based on the partial data our brains collected? The answer to these questions is that we must either re-learn actual reality, or continue to live with the consequences of living with our illusions. Given the resistance to changing what we already believe to be true and the (mind/brain) work that is involved in such a shift, we resist the process of re-learning our realities. The energy that such a process would require from us would change us from highly efficient and assumptive participants into inefficient non-participants until we caught up to actual reality again. When our *foundation of reality* reflects a functional reality again, we then transition back into the more efficient, assumptive mode.

In order for us to be efficient participants in the world, our minds must make assumptions, connect the dots and hold *foundation of reality* upon which we can rely. Finding cracks in our *foundation of reality* requires us to go into emergency repair mode. This may mean spending an afternoon in epiphany, but could also mean years of "finding ourselves," with periods of severe depression.

Neural Pathways

When the synaptic connections between brain cells bundle together to work concurrently, we call this a neural pathway. Neural pathways are created and supported through focus and repetition of thought patterns. For our knowledge and memory to work efficiently, we are dependent on the brain's ability to change its neural pathways, which we know as brain plasticity. One of the amazing facts that has been observed by scientists in the last ten years is that it takes less than an hour for a brand new synaptic connection to be formed between brain cells. And there is an association between where we place our focus and the ability to change previously imprinted *truths* through the creation of new neural pathways. The more synaptic connections created for a memory or belief, the deeper the impression is ingrained within our knowledge.

Brain cells are literally addicted to these connections. When a synaptic connection is activated, the brain cell is provided with an addictive stimulus. If an existing synaptic connection is activated often, the cell will create more synaptic connections to that part of the brain to experience more of the stimulation. On the other hand, if a synaptic connection receives very little stimulation, the brain cell allows the synaptic connection to die.

Some memories require re-imprinting in order to create a long-term or permanent impression. We can become aware of this imprinting process ourselves, when the mind won't stop repeating itself. Our *personal truth* manifests itself in well established neural networks that are often difficult to break down. This is especially true when the brain is stimulated frequently by the re-imprinting and the release of the addictive synaptic chemicals.

Reality or Belief?

The *personal truths* we commit to memory are referenced without question and used in future deductions. Your energy efficient brain tells you that everything you already know is "good enough," and refuses re-examination of established *personal truths*. Only a new realisation that threatens the integrity of our *foundation of reality* successfully overcomes the brain's resistance to re-examine what we believed to be true. In order to efficiently repair our *foundation of reality* it is useful to be able to effectively separate reality-based *personal truths* from belief-based *personal truths*.

First Threshold – Understand

Reality-based *personal truth* and belief-based *personal truth* can be easily separated by recognizing permanence. Reality is permanent; it remains. When a *personal truth* exists, independent on you believing in it in order for it to remain, it is reality-based. A belief-based *personal truth* or assumption disappears the moment <u>you</u> no longer support it with your belief. Reality is independent of the observer. Reality-based *personal truth* remains therefore, whether the observer (you) are aware of it or not! Belief-based *personal truth*, on the other hand, requires the observer to add meaning, interpretations, assumptions and beliefs or it would disintegrate.

A simple strategy to distinguish between reality-based *personal truth* and constructed, belief-based *personal truth* is to ask yourself the question: "If I stop believing in this 'truth' does it remain true?" This distinction should get easier and clearer over time and with practice.

Homework:
You can practice this yourself. Just simply ask yourself this question and you'll quickly realise that the "perception" either remains or is turned into a question. There are many examples of this in our lives. For instance, when we remember an incident or a story, we often don't have all the facts. We assume parts of the story in order to make sense of it. If we analyse the story, we can ask ourselves about the parts we are filling in. "If I stop believing in this part, does it remain a truth or would I need to find out more about this part before I can factually rely on it, within my story or memory of the incident?"

Another example you could explore is when you dislike someone and judge them negatively for their behaviours. Ask yourself: "If I stop believing that this person is bad, does it remain true?" And you immediately free your brain to begin to find all sorts of reasons why this person is behaving in this way. You may imagine that they had no other choice, or that they were following their 1st or 2nd law of self-preservation or simply didn't or couldn't include the impact their behaviour might have on you, into their decisions or actions.

Participation or Control

As we become aware of reality we plan from it, use it for deductions and increase our capacity to participate in it. These abilities have been the cornerstone of human evolution. Without our abilities to deduct, predict and adapt, we would have been eliminated by evolution and natural selection.

Chapter 28 – Assumptive Life

Brains are efficient and therefore always looking for the easiest way to progress. We have long used these deductions, beliefs, rules and predictions to attempt to control our lives, others and even life itself!

Many people hold on to an *illusion of control* as a way to feel safe. I have found that these people become more unhappy and fearful over time.

The solution is surprisingly simple, yet many people find it difficult to overcome ingrained belief systems that keep them in an *illusion of control*. The answer is: Observe reality for what it is and stop interpreting it for what it's not. Do not attempt to reinterpret it, analyse it, own it, control it, or force it. Attempting to control reality is expending life energy on a futile cause. Instead, spend your energy participating in reality, wondering about it, interacting with its magic and contributing to it - without demand or entitlement. Participate in it, persuade it, entice it and collaborate with it.

Expecting an Answer

How is it that when you ask a question you often already expect a particular answer? We seem to have a strange relationship with other people. Every question has a multitude of possible answers, or might not be answered at all. And yet we ask questions that we hope will be answered in our favour, in fact we're often emotionally committed to one answer; any other answer is either a surprise to our intuition or unacceptable because of our expectations or entitlements.

What if we asked questions, allowing the respondents the freedom of:

1. Answering with their *truth*- and accepting their answers as their *truth*.
2. Answering with what they want you to believe - and accepting those answers.
3. Not answering - and accepting their decisions not to participate in your quest for knowledge.

We actually anticipate answers that fit our expectations and feel qualified to judge others' responses or understand them compared to our belief system.

When we're polite to someone, we expect them to be polite back! What if that person had a bad day? What if he or she really didn't want to speak to you, or anyone for that matter, or you interrupted a life-altering thought or awareness they are having at that moment? What if you are simply not as

First Threshold – Understand

interesting as that person's own inner world? Any or all of these might be true, yet we still expect to be treated with more civility and kindness than we received. We feel entitled to it.

Many sales people rely on this assumption. Think about the following situations for a moment and choose carefully, for your own sanity and peace.

- When the doorbell rings, do you need to drop your life/work or even sleep to address the urgency that has been created at the door?
- When the phone rings, do you need to pick it up? Do you have to answer emails immediately?

Homework:
Select three people who would be willing to participate in an experiment with you. Select people with whom you have significant relationships.

First tell them that they may choose in which of the three ways they answer your question:

1. *Tell the truth*
2. *Answer what they want you to believe*
3. *Decline to answer*

Assure them that you will accept their response to each of your questions without judgment or entitlement to a favourable response and that you will NOT follow up with a verifying or qualifying question. In other words, you will completely accept their answer.

Now ask three questions you would like to have answered honestly. Remember, their answers may not be the truth.

Then, accept their responses.

Please note, that you may judge their answers; in other words: you may not like their answers, or how they answer your questions, but you must accept their responses regardless of your judgment of them. Observe how you react to their answer but don't ask them to explain or change their answer.

Deserving Reward

You are not entitled to good health, a job, an amazing relationship...

Chapter 28 – Assumptive Life

Simply put, it may be possible to earn your good health, but before you do you are not entitled to it. And you can't pay for it, so deserving isn't a matter of "fairness" either. It's a matter of working towards and increasing the odds of obtaining your desired outcome, being present, receiving when provided and plain old good luck. But you cannot ever expect anything until the moment you actually reach the end result.

A chapter in the Bhagavad Gita begins with the idea that you have a right to action, but you are not entitled to the fruits of action. There are varied translations of this saying, but the one that I find particularly appropriate states that we cannot be entitled to our outcomes until we reach them. Feeling entitled to the outcome of our labors before we have factored in all elements required to reach the outcomes is unrealistic and a source of unhappiness. While we deserve the fruits or our labours in hindsight, we are not entitled to them in foresight. There is a great wisdom and comfort in this truth.

Until you reach a goal or reward, you are not yet entitled to it. Being *attached to outcome* means feeling entitled to the rewards of your actions before they are completed. The subsequent discontent caused by reality not meeting with your expectations becomes a cause to be unhappy. You need to work to attain your goals, but reality determines when you've worked enough towards your goals to receive the fruits of your labours. Everywhere people are saying: "I've done enough. I should have reached my goal by now." And this is simply not true. Maybe they need to work more, reconsider their HOW, overcome more obstacles, put in more effort or focus; or they simply ran out of time, resources etc.

Happiness doesn't come to you, you must work to create it and be ready to embrace it, whatever form it takes in your life. Happiness and reward will never interrupt you. You will never win a lottery if you don't buy a ticket. I encounter people who believe that all you need to do is think about what you want and it will show up in your life. For instance, when people hope to find a partner, they are really hoping that the partner one day finds them! They believe that one day, as they're watching their favourite show, the doorbell will ring and interrupt their routine and that perfect relationship will greet them at the door. No way! Even if the person standing there is a perfect candidate, it still takes emotional investment, intent, alignment and bestowing trust before anyone can begin to talk about relationship.

First Threshold – Understand

People who are looking for a relationship will NEVER find it. You don't find relationships you deserve, you find people; people with whom you can build relationships. You invest in people. With a potential partner, your investment begins a relationship that becomes more intimate over time. Not exactly something you "find," but rather something you Create, Nurture and Build.

Chapter 29 – Negative Thinking

Many people talk about *What Isn't* and what can't be done and they are surprised to find themselves getting more of what they don't want in life. I've spoken about this in a previous chapter so my focus now is on those who "can't."

For these people it's quite normal to say things such as: "I can't do this" or "it can't be done." If we examine the situation, however, we find that it <u>can</u> be done and the person evaluated the situation as "too much effort" or that "too many resources would be required" to complete the task. An extreme example might be "I can't go to the moon," meaning, of course, I could go to the moon if I dedicated all my resources and energy to making it there, but the effort it would take to get to the moon is simply not worth it to me. My brain has done a quick Return on Investment calculation and decided that the effort required is not worth the pay-off in the end; and I say <u>can't</u>.

Understanding the nuances of this mechanism would give us a better understanding of ourselves and others. Saying <u>can't</u> means "I believe the pay-off is not worth the effort" or "I don't want to take responsibility for this decision." Being honest about the reality behind "can't" allows for more authentic responses to ourselves and others. This authentic responsiveness leads to more effective personal resource management and better choices!

Learning and personal growth require energy. Our brain is very efficient in its resource-allocation and quickly responds with "Can't" to shun change and avoid what it interprets as unnecessary energy expenditure. Be aware of this when interacting with the world around you. If you want to experience the Universe, you must expend energy, passively and actively - and in my opinion the reward of participating is worth the effort.

First Threshold – Understand

Positive Outlook

To change your experience of life, you need to practice positive thinking. I do not mean just washing over the challenges of life but rather shifting your point of focus by thinking positively; instead of what you "can't" think about what you "can." Some people put a positive spin on everything by quoting a quick saying as a way to disconnect from reality. I am not an advocate of this type of thinking. I believe things happen to us, both good as well as bad, but negative thinking only helps us focus on the negative, which is counterproductive.

Our minds are only able to focus in one direction at a time and become invested in what we focus on. Focusing on what we don't want causes us to be in the realm of what we don't want and not in the realm of what we would like instead. The reason we often focus on the negative aspects of life is that our minds are capable of recognising only the things that already exist within the boundaries of our *foundation of reality* and therefore we have a tendency to focus on existing things we no longer want rather than the unknown of what we would like instead. This causes our minds to observe the world through the lens of our negative focus, instead of focusing on what we do want, even if this mechanism of negative focus is not apparent to us! Our lives gravitate towards what we are focused on. It really is that simple.

Let me give you an example:

When I say to you "Don't think about your kitchen," your mind quickly thinks about your kitchen! It actually focuses on the thing I asked you not to think about.

So, this time <u>do</u> think about your bedroom. Your focus is automatically away from your kitchen. You think about your bedroom!

This is a big deal when observing your thought and subsequent speech patterns. We often say things such as:

- I <u>don't</u> want to be poor.
- I want to be health<u>ier</u> (which is relative to less healthy)
- I <u>don't</u> want to be exhausted <u>anymore</u>, etc.

As you say these things, out loud or in your mind, you are focusing on the very thing you don't want and in some cases already have. Not only are you not thinking about the behaviour, need, or desire that you DO want, you

Chapter 29 – Negative Thinking

would be unlikely to recognise it even if you were to encounter it or a route towards it.

Now, say these things to yourself instead.

- I want to be wealthy (and visualize the lifestyle you want)
- I want to be healthy (and visualise yourself and all you would do as a healthy person)
- I want abundant energy
- Etc.

Now your mind is clearly focused on what you want and what it means to be in that new state. When any opportunity or resistance comes your way, you'll be able to recognise it easily and navigate your way towards what you do want.

This is the exact meaning of a positive outlook. It's not an exaggerated and unrealistic separation from reality. A positive outlook means focusing on what you want rather than what you no longer want. It's clear that people with positive outlooks are able to manifest their desires more easily than people with negative outlooks, as the people with negative outlooks are not active participants in creating their paths forward. People with negative outlooks waste their energy focusing on what they don't want and are incapable of recognizing opportunities that would move them towards what they do want. They are literally hoping to have their lives interrupted by something better than they have now. Unfortunately, even if these opportunities actually arose, they wouldn't be able to recognise them because their minds would be focused on what they no longer want.

Focus on what you want. Plain and simple. See all resistance to your plans as nuisances, temporary interruptions on the road to your future, which is determined by your focus. If you see it that way, you'll understand that it merely represents the necessary hurdles that must and can be overcome on your way to what you want.

Your positive outlook will affect you in other positive ways. What you envision in your mind's eye is what you reflect in your moods. If you believe in your future, your mood will reflect that belief. If you despair in your future, your mood will reflect this, too. Your mood will not only reflect your outlook, your mood will directly influence your motivation and actions. Your mood will influence how much energy and focus you are willing to

First Threshold – Understand

invest in a future towards which you have positive or negative feelings. A positive outlook will drive a more prolific future.

Furthermore, be mindful and catch yourself using sentences with negative or relative words in them. Words such as better, richer, healthier, etc. are all relative to a negative point of focus. Sentences with the words can't, won't, shouldn't, don't and other expressions of NOT in them are focused on the negative. Train yourself to quickly turn these sentences around to saying what you DO want instead! Start creating a clearer and clearer picture of the future you are working towards instead of a past you are working away from.

Homework:
First listen to others use relative or negative words in their sentences to describe positive outcomes: "I want to be richer," "I don't want to be poor," "I don't want to be overweight," "I want to stop smoking," and even sentences that imply What Isn't such as: "When you pass Bay street, you've driven too far." Even expressions of frustration such as: "I've had too much" and "I don't want to be angry anymore" could be re-evaluated with the question: "What would you want instead?"

Next, listen to how you use relative or negative words yourself, both out loud and internally and realise where you are focusing when you do that.

As you progress, start talking about what you did do, not what you didn't do. Start talking about what you want to happen. Start telling people what you want to do, not what you can't do. Start saying What Is, not what ought to be or what should be. This is a crucial exercise for creating authentic relationships with yourself, the Universe and the people with whom you interact and relate.

Chapter 30 – Effective Self-talk

One of the most direct ways that we can reinforce positive, constructive thinking and feeling is by using the power of our self-talk. Self-talk comes from the little voices "inside our heads" that constantly narrate our lives. We talk to ourselves and we talk about ourselves constantly. It is as if another self is observing and commenting on everything we do and think.

Language is a powerful force in our lives. What we say and even more what we mean and how we interpret what we say, are some of the most powerful ways to influence our thoughts, our identities and our behaviours. While we are influenced by everything we hear from outside and inside, what we say to ourselves has the most power over us. Investing in learning effective self-talk can be a highly rewarding and effective way to transform our experiences of reality.

As the brain relies on repetition to create permanence, we need to use concise, powerful phrases in our self-talk to have the greatest effect possible on our neural pathways. Affirmations are short powerful phrases that can shift our internal dialogue and help us create positive change.

Affirmations

An affirmation is a personal statement of how one chooses to perceive the world. It is to affirm something, to positively and declaratively state that something is true, for you. Affirmations use the structure of the brain and its tendency to create belief systems to create positive results; constructing belief systems that help you align with the reality you want to be living. As the brain imprints new beliefs through repetition, affirmations are repeated regularly until you behave what you believe and override old habits that no longer serve you. If you repeat them, you can reinforce those beliefs and behaviours.

First Threshold – Understand

Affirmations are particularly useful for transforming negative beliefs and thought patterns. It is the same concept as in the previously demonstrated example of thinking about your bedroom to shift your focus away from your kitchen, rather than just trying to not think about your kitchen. For example, telling yourself "I don't want to think about how I don't want to be poor" still has you thinking about poverty. A more effective way to shift your focus would be to use self-talk to affirm that you are becoming more abundant.

Examples Of Effective Affirmations

I am peacefully participating in life
I am making positive choices
I grow through resistance
I am open to receiving
I am becoming healthy
Every day at 6:30am I support my health and vitality by walking for 45 minutes

The most effective affirmations will be the ones that you create for yourself.

Creating Your Own Affirmations

Affirmations are very powerful and can literally transform the structure of your brain. Badly constructed affirmations can do more damage than good, so it is crucial to use affirmations that will change your brain in the ways that you intend. To ensure that you create and choose affirmations that will cause the most positive changes possible, you can use these rules for effective self-talk.

Creating your own affirmations is easy, as long as you adhere to the six criteria that every affirmation must follow in order for the subconscious to receive, accept and absorb the affirmation. If every affirmation you use adheres to these six criteria, you will begin to understand and connect to your own language and behaviour, your own self-talk. This will enable you to change your brain in positive ways and therefore your experience of the world.

In order for an affirmation to be as effective as possible, it needs to follow these six guidelines:

1. Framed in the Positive
2. Simple and Easy to Recall

3. Believable
4. Measurable and Direct
5. In the Present Tense
6. Rewarding

1. Framed In the Positive
The subconscious mind only hears things in the affirmative. It does not understand qualifiers or negations, it only receives the essence of our thoughts and words. What this means is that an affirmation or Suggestion must never be constructed as to deliver a negative sentence to the subconscious as though it were positive. An affirmation with a negative qualifier is received incorrectly.

Do not state what you are moving away from. State what you are moving towards. Your subconscious mind receives the sentence: "I will not smoke" without the word "not," and hears instead: 'I will (...) smoke." Changing the sentence to "I choose life filled with energy and fresh air" makes it a positive affirmation that would have the intended effect. Frame all of your affirmations in the positive, using only the words you want your subconscious to hear.

2. Simple and Easy to Recall
Long sentences with many qualifiers are great for books, but if an affirmation is too long, the power of the words can be diffused. Craft affirmations that convey the meaning that you want with as few words as possible. The exercise of concentrating your affirmations alone will help you understand your intended outcome better. The rule is: Shorter = Better and more effective. Your affirmations will be most effective if they are easy for you to memorize and say, making it more likely that you will repeat them throughout the day.

3. Believable
Read the affirmation. If <u>you</u> believe it, it will happen. If you don't, your critical brain will alter the meaning of the affirmation "on the way in," and turn it into a negative statement. This will create the exact opposite effect to what you intended. For example, saying "this week I become 30lbs lighter" is not believable and will actually be translated into a negative affirmation as it enters the subconscious. "Today, I eat six 220 calorie meals with water

First Threshold – Understand

to feel fit, lean and healthy" is much more likely to have the amazing effect you might be seeking.

To test the believability of a sentence, turn it around grammatically. For the previous sentence say: "To feel fit, lean and healthy, I eat six 220 calorie meals with 2 glasses of water per meal." If the reversed sentence still sounds right to you, the sentence is believable.

For many affirmations it is more effective to speak in terms of what is becoming, to keep them believable while still keeping them in the present tense. If you say "I am rich" when you have no money, your brain will not believe you and you will reinforce the sense of poverty. More believable is the sentence that includes a self-evident truth which facilitates the future. For instance if you say "I am opening to abundance with each passing day," you are stating something that is much more plausible for your subconscious to accept than "I am rich." Saying "I am open to abundance as I make my choices" uses the truism (I am open) to facilitate the direction component (abundance) and your thoughts will reorganize to transform the affirmation into behaviours.

4. Measurable and Direct
Do not use relative terms. Do not use words such as better, more, soon, sometime, healthier, etc. These words are relative and produce no effect. Also change any verbiage such as try, could, may, etc. into positive committed actions. The word *try* is especially dangerous as it implies failure. Replace *try* with DO.

Also avoid hidden immeasurables: "Tomorrow I will <u>find the time</u> to exercise" has a hidden *try* in it. Changing it to "Each day I wake at 6AM and exercise for 30 minutes" makes it measurable, positive and believable.

5. Present Tense
Affirmations in the future, remain in the future. "I will..." is not a positive present affirmation and the intent remains in the future. Ensure that affirmation is in the present tense. You can only change the NOW.

6. Rewarding
Affirmations are usually most effective when the reward is embedded in the wording. But if you are sure that reaching your goals every day is reward

enough in itself, you may imply it in your sentence. If, however, there is a cost and a benefit, the affirmation becomes more powerful when it is focused on the benefit. For example "Today, I eat six 220 calorie meals with water to feel fit, lean and healthy."

A few more factors that may influence your word choice:

- Facilitation: Acceptance of one suggestion always aids in the acceptance of another. If the first part of the affirmation is clear and true, the second part is more easily accepted. This is also referred to as truism.
- Grading: Suggestions are more readily accepted when they are proportionately gradual. It is easier to accept "a single step, followed by another step" than to accept "a marathon."

Using positive affirmations can be a very effective way to use the imprinting nature of the brain in your favour. Choose or create affirmations that transform your current challenges into growth opportunities, refining your perception of your reality in believable and direct ways.

Homework:

Create intimately personal affirmations of your own. What, in your life, do you want to change? What motivates you to change? What will be your reward? How will you know (measure) that you've reached your goal?

Use the six criteria of a good affirmation as your guideline. Re-write your affirmation until it adheres to all six criteria before you use it on yourself. Write it on a card you carry with you.

To create maximum effect: Sit in a quiet and peaceful location where you are unlikely to be disturbed for a few minutes. Take three slow and deep breaths while you allow your entire body to become relaxed from top to bottom. Take a fourth breath and hold it for three seconds. As you exhale, you relax your body even more.

Now, count slowly backwards from 25 to zero. On each count you take a breath and feel yourself become more deeply relaxed. When you reach the count of zero, you open your eyes in a dreamy way, without awakening from your deep relaxation and read your affirmation to yourself three times.

Then you close your eyes again, count slowly from one to three and open your eyes. Maybe stretch a little as you become fully aware again.

Second Threshold – Embody

The first threshold was all about understanding the primal drivers in our lives. We talked about the far reaching consequences of understanding the motivators that govern our decisions and actions and ultimately our personal perception of life.

But understanding isn't enough. Knowledge and understanding only become useful when we embody them. Knowledge alone is like an encyclopedia on the shelf. You look up the answer, but in a moment of decision the action you take is the action that you have practiced and felt deeply enough for it to be a truly embodied action; an action that originates from an essential part of who you are.

For example: A person wants to lose weight and understands the need to exercise more and eat better, but is constantly resisting food and rarely exercising because having knowledge is only mental. Once the same person understands and embodies the new person he or she want to become, that person's new choices require almost no effort at all. That person simply makes food and exercise choices based on that sense of embodiment. He or she may even say: "this is a habit the old 'me' would do, but the new 'me' is more interested in my new habits." The more you embody your new self, the easier it is to just be the new "you" without struggling to override the old "you."

The difference between a habitually successful person and a person who struggles is the ability to embody change; to become the person who has these experiences.

This section focuses on turning knowledge into knowing. It will help you embody the knowledge and become it.

Chapter 31 – Energy and Focus

Society seems to be in love with the idea that we can "give it more," that we need to dedicate 110%. I often find myself reminding my clients (and myself, at times) that we really have no more than 100% to give any aspect of our lives.

We need to remind ourselves that the energy required to one particular task can only be increased by decreasing the energy allocated to another task! Time and energy management are invaluable skills for creating a more efficient, realistic life for yourself.

100% No More. No Less.

To create anything you must do 100%. Don't listen to anyone who tells you that you must put in more than 100%, nor to those who accuse you of doing less than 100%.

When our minds have an unrealistic notion about the resource limits we have, we feel stress. The fact is that we simply have 100% energy and 100% focus, no more, no less. The only energy control we have is how we allocate our energy, not how much energy we have in total. We must remain aware of the limitations of our finite personal resources, while understanding that where we place our focus can create real change and move us towards our goals. Focus and follow through!

If we decide to focus more energy on one aspect of our lives, we must be realistic and understand that this takes focus away from other aspects of our lives. It really is that simple! Understanding that we must choose carefully how we spend our energy and time and that we can't do two things with the same energy or time, are fundamental skills of life that I call life management.

Second Threshold – Embody

The function of energy multiplied by time is easy to grasp:

Energy X Time = Output

You cannot change any element without affecting the other two. So let's change the way we translate our understanding of time and energy to increase our efficiency.

To start working more efficiently, you can easily regain much wasted energy by understanding that you cannot do anything in the future, nor in the past. You can affect the future: you may anticipate it or prepare for it, but you must wait for the future to become the present before you can take action or benefit from its rewards. Instead of trying to do more than 100% in any given moment, you may want to simply use your energy more efficiently in that moment. Instead of focusing your energy on trying to repair the past or doing something that needs to wait until the future, focus your energy on what you can do <u>right now</u>! Much energy is wasted on repetition, preparation and futile attempts at changing *What Is* (i.e. the past). Sometimes, all you can do is wait for the right moment (i.e. the future). Why not use your waiting time to rest, enjoy the moment and build up your strength and energy for when you will need it?

At the end of each day, pause and realistically take note of the things you were able to accomplish for yourself. Recognize that you used 100% of your time and energy that day and notice where and how you spent that time and energy. You can do 100%, no more, no less. Observing how much energy you have been able to utilize on any given day will help you understand how much energy you have available each day. Building this life management skill will help you to become realistic about your expectations and possible accomplishments with the 100% energy and focus you have available.

Working in Overdrive

When you observe your life you'll notice that some relationships fee disharmonious because they command more energy than others. The way to create harmony in your life is to re-evaluate your relationships, from your personal viewpoint. Do your relationships demand more of your precious energy than you're willing to allocate to them? Are you truly served by investing your energy into all the people in your life, or are you being coerced into allocating energy into tasks that serve others but not your best

Chapter 31 – Energy and Focus

interest? Are your relationships nurturing you, or simply depleting your energy, reserves and health and borrowing from your future?

Remember that as you deplete your reserves, you deplete your ability to give in the future! You can only assist others and contribute to the Universe when you're healthy and strong, not when you're depleted and weak.

Working from your reserves too often makes you inefficient. When we use our energy reserves, not only are we borrowing focus and energy from our futures, we have a hard time catching up and recuperating.

One of the physiological problems with being in reserve is the fact that we use adrenaline to keep us alert and in action – despite our body's readiness to enter recuperative mode. This adrenaline was meant for temporary use in emergency situations: for our survival, not just to help us push through and accomplish more. You can contribute much more efficiently to your life and the lives around you when your mind is not drugged by adrenaline and is able to open up to innovation, creativity and possibility.

Planning

Going with the flow doesn't mean you stop planning. Some people find themselves reacting to their environments and don't spend much time planning. They use their precious time and energy "fighting fires." This results in inefficient and often ineffective use of their preciously scarce energy and time.

The most effective skill to achieving your goals is effective planning. But don't plan further ahead than is necessary and do not get caught up in the planning process or its attractive cousin research either. Perfecting your plans creates prerequisites and gets in the way of taking necessary action. Examine the lives of any successful leader and you'll quickly note that they planned little, executed early and corrected along the way. Many a fine project never came to fruition due to over-planning and lack of early and sustained action.

I suggest taking specific blocks of time for planning and anticipating. The cycle that creates real and sustained progress is: plan, execute, correct – in that order. Create an overview, plan a reasonable step, execute, do not correct before or during execution. Correct last then begin the cycle again. There are times you want to plan your day and there are times you want to contemplate your entire future. Set aside times for both, but limit the time you dedicate to planning or you'll end up day-dreaming your life away. But if you spend too little time planning then you'll be "fighting fires," and have very little time left for your real priorities.

Leverage

The concept of leverage can be very helpful in managing your life. The concept is simple: if you require something to be done and someone else can do it for you at a worth-while cost you can outsource your needs and to create more with less effort. If you exchange your efficiency for something they need (don't automatically think this is money) you both create an advantage. This is called leveraging and it can help you both accomplish more than you would individually if you were to do everything alone.

Leverage is so efficient that all successful relationships, partnerships, companies, etc. are built on this very concept. Learn to delegate and trust others to assist you by leveraging the skills you each possess and you'll accomplish more with less.

Think for a moment: what small change will give you more time, more efficiency and more energy for other things in your life? Where can you apply leverage? Maybe you can pay someone to do a task, exchange favours, or even wait to tend to the dishes or paperwork until you have more to complete in a single batch.

If you're like most people who understand the world better from their own viewpoint than from others', you may find it difficult to delegate. Focusing on why you want to be more efficient and what advantages this greater efficiency will bring you, will soon sway you into letting go of minor things and keeping focused on your priorities. Use the section Making "Decisions That Count" and the "What, Why, What Else, How" strategy found in Chapter 27 to lock in on what you really want.

First Step

I've often heard the phrase: "The hardest step is showing up" or "The first step is the most difficult." There's a lot of wisdom in these sayings, yet they don't explain <u>why</u>. In my opinion, we are more afraid of the last step than the first. I believe we stop short of executing the first step in an attempt to avoid taking the last step: Finishing. When we release our efforts into the world they become subject to scrutiny and criticism. Doing anything in our fictitious minds only, means that we will never be accountable for the end result. Finishing makes us vulnerable. Finishing and releasing our efforts into the world makes us responsible for their futures, their successes or ultimate demise. Once released, these efforts cannot be changed to offset the possible negative comments, gossip and cruelty bestowed on them, which ultimately fall onto you.

We're not afraid of taking the first step. We're afraid of setting something in motion that, when finished, bares our name and affects others. Accepting the inevitability of the last step opens the door to taking the first step.

Homework:
Every night before bed make a physical list (on paper) with the major energy events (both replenishing and spending energy) of that day and the things you plan for the next day. Don't get bogged down with details, a list like this should probably have no more than four or five items. Make a separate list for groceries and mini errands, although with modern technology you might be better off to keep the grocery and errand list in your smart phone and maintain it there. The 'major items list' is much more important.

Look at the previous night's list, note which major items were completed and take this consideration to bed: "I have used 100% of my energy on today's day and therefore accomplished 100% of what I was able to accomplish." Comparing your accomplishments with your list will help you set realistic expectations for your energy based on how much you are actually able to get done.

Where Your Focus goes your Life Goes

Here is a well known fact: Our subconscious doesn't register the word *not*! The discernment of right from wrong, true from false, the sense of fairness and the qualification of negation are all functions of our conscious mind. Our subconscious mind learns in a different way. It stores impressions, regardless of positive or negative qualifiers.

As mentioned earlier, if I asked you to stop thinking about your kitchen or to "not think" about your kitchen, your mind flashes to a thought about your kitchen. Similarly, if you decide to "not focus on" your troubles, your mind goes towards the troubles.

Second Threshold – Embody

This is a natural phenomenon we have developed into a skill. Throughout our evolution we have used this ability to hold a thought or image of what we plan to avoid, in order to recognize it when we encounter it. When it comes to bettering our lives, however, this natural way of thinking can be counterproductive. When we think about no longer being poor, our focus is relative to *poor* not *rich*. When we focus on "not being single" or "quitting cigarettes" our focus is relative to being alone and fighting our cravings, rather than holding hands at a movie and fresh breath. Focusing on the positive feelings associated with the reward will help you do what it takes such as trusting someone when the time comes or foregoing that next cigarette.

Reframing

A strategy many of us have learned to use is that of reframing. In practice, this means rewording a negative event as if it were a positive experience or a lesson we needed to learn. In reframing we take a view that things happen to us for a reason; a cosmic design that keeps us aligned with a purpose we don't yet fully understand ourselves. While reframing may serve to provide fresh insight into situations, it doesn't actually make the problem itself go away.

Focusing away from a problem only serves us if it helps us to focus on solutions and opportunities. Reframing is often used to obfuscate obstacles and re-present them as desired and welcomed lessons. Reframing can transform our judgments of problems, but we are still focused on (reworded) problems. It will serve you to use your reframing skills to re-word your problem-focused self-talk into solution-focused opportunity. Your solution-focused mind will be primed to take the next step towards a solution-based future when opportunity presents itself, you will not be spending energy focussing on a problem.

Manifesting 101

A lot of information has been written about manifesting and how to attract what you want in life. Unfortunately, this information is often misinterpreted as a way of gaining advantage over others by wishing your way to riches. Manifesting in this interpretation is a quick alternative to focus and hard work; a lazy dream.

Chapter 31 – Energy and Focus

Manifesting is not a shortcut to riches, nor a way to create something out of nothing. There is no big secret to abundance that you can learn by wishing and hoping. Yet there is an essential benefit to focusing on what you want. If you have a clear image of your desires in mind, you are positively influencing your odds of attaining your goals due to the very fact that you can recognize your goals as they get closer. Here are some key points about creating traction in the direction of your choice:

- Learn what you want- not just what you think you *can have*, or should have but what you actually <u>want</u>.
- Now learn to understand your desires. Go deep – learn why you want what you want. If you do not <u>feel</u> your desire, you'll just be <u>wishing</u> your life away.
- Stop focusing on what you don't want. Instead of saying "I don't want to be sick anymore," say "I want to be healthy."
- Behave, as much as you're able, as though you already have what you want. Be reasonable, but start to include behaviours, company and situations that match a person who has what you want.
- Don't plan to take shortcuts. Do what you must to fill the gaps between the person you are now and the person you are becoming – in every way you can. Do it right now.
- Set your expectations to "reasonable progress." Don't expect shortcuts or miracles – let them surprise you.
- And measure your progress. Learn *what* gaps you must still overcome to get there – not *how* to overcome them.

Manifesting requires focus and possibly some hard work. When you understand the reasons you want something and embody the person who already has what you want, you start to become your choices. When you embody your choices, they effortlessly and naturally become essential parts of your being. You no longer struggle against your nature, or need to override your urges, you simply naturally make choices that move you towards the person you're becoming.

The Power of Focus

There is an old folk tale that evokes visions of a time when wisdom was passed from one generation to the next through stories told around a roaring fire. The fire kept everyone warm and alive through the long nights and

Second Threshold – Embody

enhanced the magic of the stories. One such old tale speaks to the struggle within every human.

In this tale, a grandfather tells his grandson that there are two untamed wolves inside every human, struggling to influence us. Different versions of the story use different animals but the most commonly used animals in this tale are wolves.

These two wolves are very different, though at first equally powerful. One wolf is full of hatred, anger, resentment, guilt, arrogance, greed, deceit and regret. This wolf wants to make everyone feel as miserable as it does.

The other wolf is full of love, gratitude, joyfulness, kindness, serenity, gentleness, patience, compassion and truth. This wolf wants to create, to inspire everyone to feel as happy and aligned with the Universe as it does.

These wolves are at the core of each of us, vying for our attention in their struggle to become the dominant force inside our deepest essence.

At this point the grandson thinks about his grandfather's words, looking into the fire and asks "which wolf wins, grandfather?"

The grandfather smiles and answers: "The one you feed."

> *You have the power to choose the wolf you want to feed.*

Hindsight

A major benefit that arises from understanding the limits of your personal 100% is a clearer, more honest and realistic hindsight. When you recognise that you truly gave 100% and were unable to allocate more resources to a task than you did without borrowing from your reserves, you will evaluate your efforts more realistically, resulting in a much more positive self-esteem. For instance, if while reflecting on your day you think "I should have put more energy into that," it will help you to realize that you would have needed to take this energy from one of the other tasks you accomplished that day, even if that was taking a nap. Think about what task you would have shorted to enable you to have this "spare" energy.

Becoming realistic with your energy resources is one of the most practical life skills you'll ever own. A quick calculation makes it clear that in order to add energy or focus to one task, you will have to take energy away from another. You get to divvy up the energy pie; you get to decide what to do with your energy based on your own reasons. But you cannot use more energy than you have each day without depleting your reserves. Learn your true energy limits and make commitments accordingly. Don't over promise and under deliver, you will end up paying for it later. Learning to evaluate your energy accurately will make you reliable, realistic, trusted, respected and healthy.

Energy Shorting

Do you sometimes feel as if you need to be omnipresent? Everything demands our attention and energy and it feels like we are being pulled in a hundred different directions. The truth is that we agree to these demands. We want to feel important and that we have an effect on the world around us, or at least maintain the *illusion of control* over our worlds. In our attempts at being present for everyone we multi-task, or at least we believe we can do everything and be everywhere.

We spend time with our children, but are actually paying little or no attention to their expressions, activities or attempts to connect with us while our minds are preoccupied with other things; we're not really present with them. We make love to our spouses while thinking about our shopping lists, work politics and other things that are completely unrelated to what is happening in the present moment. We're not present! We drive, we walk in nature, we interact with friends, all while our minds are "doing more important things," thinking about situations in the past or in the future.

The result is that we end up not doing anything well and not enjoying the reward of each task. We are shorting the relationships that need investment to remain healthy and beneficial. The relationships we short begin to demand more and more of us, to compensate for the lack of presence. Then we become so distracted by the additional demand on our energy resources that that we become even more inefficient and overwhelmed. We conclude that our relationships are broken, even to be discarded.

It becomes apparent that we haven't been present when we realize that we lack happiness in our lives. Yes, being present, in the *Here and Now* gives us the satisfaction and reward of happiness. Re-read the chapter on happiness to remind yourself of how this ties in if you have forgotten. Complete and active participation in the present moment rewards us with a sense of wellbeing that we would not be able to find any other way. And by being fully present,

Second Threshold – Embody

you satisfy the needs of your relationships while caring for yourself. Full participation allows you to fulfill the needs of the present moment with such efficiency that you'll have energy left for more full-presence participation later, plus self-care for you.

We live in a world where our attentions are constantly solicited and divided. Understand the consequences of dividing your attention and allocate your energy wisely.

Homework:
1. *Observe how much of your day's energy supply you spend on the things you do during the day. Create a log for seven days. Include the time spent on activity as well as rest or restorative activities. You will become aware of what physical activities have a mental restorative ability and what mental activities may have a physical restorative effect. At the end of each day, notice where you spent most of your energy and evaluate if there would be a better way to allocate your energies to bring you more in alignment with your desires.*
2. *How much energy do you allocate to each of your relationships? Are they rewarding? Are they driven by guilt, obligation, emotional investment, or equality? Are you in any relationships that are too one sided? Practice saying NO when you are no longer mutually benefitting from interactions.*

Look for the dysfunctional relationships in your life that don't seem "worth the effort" or "hard work to maintain." Are they really dysfunctional or are <u>you</u> shorting the relationship and robbing yourself and others of the experience of your true presence. Notice if your additional presence influences the relationship positively.

Chapter 32 – The Hierarchy of Motivation

From the years of working with my clients I've devised a tool to help us understand, in a very practical sense, what does and does not motivate us. The *Hierarchy of Motivation* helps us decipher the language we use on a daily basis to understand the reasons behind our actions. It helps us see when we're about to take real action because we connect with our personal reasons and desires, or when our actions seem to be driven by an outside force, belief system, or person.

As my clients worked with this tool it became increasingly apparent that its value reaches way beyond a simple understanding of our inner dialogue and embedded motivations. This tool helps keeps us focused on what's really important to us, what drives us and how we attempt to externalize responsibility for the actions we take to avoid accountability.

Why We Avoid Accountability

Avoiding accountability for our actions stems from childhood. We all began our lives seeing the world as a giant experiment, a resource for our abundant imaginations and a place where we could learn by simply testing our imaginations upon reality itself.

Then, one day we came to the realization that we couldn't simply experiment without being responsible for the outcomes of our experiments, whether those were the intended outcomes or not. We learned by the reactions and corrective actions of our caregivers that being accountable meant being judged as morally good or bad; not according to our intents but by the outcomes we produced, intended or unintended. We became attached to feeling that we were good people if our experiments were successful and bad people if our experiments failed. The fear of negative judgement makes us avoid taking ownership of our actions. The fear of negative judgement is so pervasive that it can prevent us from taking any action, even foregoing the potential reward of a positive outcome.

We start by telling our teachers that we won't show our drawings to them until they are "finished," as we simply don't yet know what our drawings might represent until they are completed. As adults, we end up refusing to commit to actions for fear of promising something that we will be afraid to deliver.

Language Motivates

The *Hierarchy of Motivation* is made up of three driving elements and two lesser elements. The three main elements represent the impetus behind all our intentional actions. The three core drivers of motivation are: Desire, Need and External Influence. The two lesser elements are the choice between multiple desires and the de-motivator.

Let's look at the complete *Hierarchy of Motivation*

- Rather
- **Want**
- **Need**
- **Should**
- Try

The core elements in the *Hierarchy of Motivation* are **Want, Need and Should**. These are words we use in our everyday language that indicate our motivations, or reasons, for the actions we take. These core elements are also used in self-talk. For example, we say: I want to swim, I need to eat, or I should do my homework. These core elements also appear in negative speech patterns: I don't want to practice, I don't need to run, or I shouldn't over eat.

The secondary elements in the *Hierarchy of Motivation* are Try and Rather. The word *Rather* is used when we have multiple wants or desires and we have a preference. *Try*, on the other hand, is not a motivator but a de-motivator. The word *Try* is a driving force away from action and implies failure. *Try* is used to deflect our fear of being accountable for outcomes to which we commit.

Highlight the Word TRY

Try implies failure. The use of the word *try* in a sentence implies that our minds have made peace with the possibility of failing to follow through on tasks or promises. The words "I will *try* to complete this task" are non-committal and upon further analysis show very little intent of putting forth sufficient effort to accomplish the task.

In part of an experiment, I have my students pick a task that they have planned for the next day and say the same sentence with two different verbs:

1. I will *try* [the task] tomorrow.
2. I will *do* [the task] tomorrow.

When saying these sentences out loud while monitoring our own thoughts, we realize that when we say the word *do* in the sentence, our minds start to allocate energy, time and focus to the task. We estimate the amount of effort and time required to complete the task and begin reallocating other tasks and slotting the task into the next day's schedule. Using the word *try* doesn't trigger this mind response. When we say the sentence with the word *try*, we place the task in a "to do" list along with other tasks which may or may not happen in the next little while. We may prioritize this task over the other waiting tasks, but our minds quickly tell us that *we'll get to the task when spare time appears* and no sooner. One of my students said: "My mind told the task to 'pick a number' and wait in line."

We learned to use the word *try* in our promises to others as a way of avoiding accountability; we say *try* but we already know something (not our fault) is likely get in our way. Unfortunately, we've become victims of our own trick, as we have become non-committal in our agreements– with ourselves and with others. This makes us unreliable to the people who we care about and rely on us. Worse, this non-committal language means that we no longer allocate energy and focus to things we want to accomplish ourselves! We simply place every task on the "try list" which is outside of our priority and hope that we'll have "spare time" to work on the list at an unspecified later time.

As a side problem, we don't monitor how much time and effort are required for various tasks and we become unrealistic in our estimations of energy needs. Our ability to estimate how much time and effort a task will take is a life-skill we must practice to become effective in our lives.

Second Threshold – Embody

Our first task is to eliminate the word *try* from our language. This is more difficult than you might first imagine. Catching yourself saying *try* is difficult enough, but when you do, you'll find yourself quickly justifying why in this particular case *try* is appropriate. Use the word *try* <u>only</u> when you <u>intend to confuse</u> or <u>intend to obfuscate</u> your real intention, which will always be not committing to delivering the intended request or outcome. Become very deliberate with the use of the word *try* and you will start to become realistic with yourself, your commitments and your agreements. Advising others to reword their sentences when they use the word *try* is important, too. When others use the word *try* in their sentences, understand that there is a lack of commitment and the possibility that this intention is outside of the scope of the person making the promise. Decide if the commitment matters to you or not. If it does, ask that person to reword the sentence without the word *try* in it for a more reliable promise.

Replacing Try

As the word *try* is used to indicate the understanding that a task or commitment may actually fail, we might want to replace this word with a more positive one. But we don't actually have control over each element in the future and our endeavours may still fail despite our intentions to complete the tasks or commitments.

For instance, we would love to say "I <u>will have this done</u> by tomorrow," and be a dependable source for the person with whom we're making the agreement. But how can we be sure that we will be able to deliver? So many possible obstacles could appear between now and tomorrow. We learned when we were very young that we want to avoid "being bad" as a result of failure, so we'd rather under-commit and say "I will <u>try and have this done</u> by tomorrow." This sounds safer, but actually is a way of escaping the commitment and becoming unreliable in our promises. Our allocation of resources is no longer clear and we leave room for higher priorities to interfere with the promise. Of course, we initially intend to complete the task, but we would allocate our resources more responsibly and be more likely to actually complete the task if we were to commit clearly.

Saying "I <u>will have this done</u> by tomorrow" isn't necessarily true either, as unexpected or unknown obstacles may hinder the commitment. A statement that is both true and conveys our true intent is "I <u>intend to have this done</u>

by tomorrow." This statement clearly shows commitment and direction. It shows your intention and focus, while honouring that you cannot foresee the future. This clear statement of intent means that you will allocate resources to the task and it allows you to become reliable and dependable with your word. While *try* implies failure, *intend* implies direction and determination to complete. *Intend* inspires a very different kind of relationship with yourself and your agreements.

Homework:
Eliminate the word TRY from your vocabulary. Catch yourself and others using the word TRY and spend the effort to replace the word TRY with DO or INTEND. Notice how you become more realistic with your time and efforts and how you must become realistic with your limits. You will simultaneously change your relationships with the people around you significantly as you become true to your word and clearer in your intentions.

When others use the word TRY with you, you can now decide if you want a better, more realistic commitment from them or if you don't mind that their agreement with you is lacking commitment. Depending on your priorities, you can either let it go or ask for clearer commitment from them.

Once you no longer rely on the word TRY, you may carefully and intentionally reintroduce the word TRY in your vocabulary, but only for when you deliberately intend to create confusion.

Should

The least motivating word within the *Hierarchy of Motivation* is the word *should*. This word is often used interchangeably with *ought-to*, *must* or *have to*, though for this example we will lump them all together with *should*. Sometimes *should* obfuscate an underlying desire. This is not always apparent to you and can be difficult to identify. In all other cases *should* identifies an agreement with an external, unverified belief system.

We use the word *should* to create ambiguity around accountability. Using *should* indicates that outside sources are attempting to exert forces upon us that influence our choices and make us take actions. *Should* often denotes obligation as an obfuscation of an actual preference, want or prioritized responsibility. We may even imply that these actions are involuntary or based on limited and unwanted choices. Surely, when outside sources exert unreasonable force upon us we quickly go along with the requests placed upon us. For instance, if someone asked me to hand over my wallet while pointing a handgun at me, I'd be quick to comply with that request as I clearly value my life above my wallet. But in most cases there is no external force, we just don't want to claim ownership of the true WANT hiding behind the *should*. Instead, we externalize the reasons for our actions and justify them with *should*.

It turns out that most if not all uses of the word *should* are attempts to divert or distract. Most times when we say *should* we disown the decision as an external directive. We claim that our actions or inactions are motivated externally, or by a learned belief system that we adhere to for which we acknowledge no responsibility.

With the exercise below you can quickly establish the true source of the motivation obfuscated by the *should*. For example: "I *should* go to the gym."

- Statement: "I should go to the gym"
- Question: "Says who?"
- Answer: "I say so!"
- Question: "Then why?"
- Answer: "For my health – because I want to be healthy"

This line of questioning statements that use the word *should* will reveal the ownership behind the motivator as soon as the *want* or desire is identified. We must take ownership of our desires so that we can prioritize our actions to serve us best and participate with reality rather than pretending to be victims of it.

In order to create the reality we desire, we must connect with it, take ownership of our part and be accountable for our actions. Then we'll make more realistic choices that serve us and create the progress we want for ourselves. *Should* is an excuse. We rarely have such a limited choice enforced by others, usually we're simply afraid of owning the outcomes of our actions.

Need and Want

Rarely do we truly have a *need*. While the word *should* in a sentence requires re-evaluation, the word *need* is very valid, but its meaning is often misinterpreted. A *need* never exists in isolation. Every *need* supports a *want*, a *desire*. For example I *need* a pen because I *want* to write. Even the *need* for food and water supports our *desire* to live. Often multiple needs support a singular *want*. We take a *want* and break it down into multiple *needs*, which we then seek to fulfill. It is this kind of understanding that helps us find our motivations and the reasons for our actions – any actions!

Understanding that eventually everything leads back to our *desires*– our *wants* – helps us understand the 3rd *law of self-preservation*: "You do what you want."

Want Overrides Need
In some cases we perceive a conflict between a *need* and a *want*. You'll see that this is an unfair contest. First, understand what *desire* is being supported by the *need*, then decide which you would *rather*. A *need*, on its own, is never strong enough to override a *want*. Advertisers know this very well. Pay attention to successful advertisements and you'll notice that there is very little, if any, mention of *need* without the implication of the associated *want*. Most ads show the *need* to move away from a pain and a *desire* to move towards its solution, which is the product or service sold in the ad.

Understanding that we do what we *want*, rather than what we *need* to do or say we *should* do, can be a real wake-up call. It is well worth spending time exploring what *wants* motivate each of your actions.

Rather
Strictly speaking, *rather* is not a core motivator or driving force, but it is an important element in the *Hierarchy of Motivation*. When we are presented with multiple *desires* or *wants* we always choose the *rather*.

I want to bring clarity to this idea of *rather*. A real *rather* is between actionable *wants,* not between a *wish* and a *want*. In the context of motivation, we are unable to choose an in-actionable option. *Wishes* are distinctly different from *wants*, as *wishes* are not (yet) actionable.

As said before, when we are presented with multiple *wants* we always choose the *rather*. This means that a *rather* is really a choice between multiple *wants* and even when we must choose between multiple options, the driving force behind all our actions is *desire*.

Second Threshold – Embody

Want - Fuel of Life

You do what you want. Our desire is the fuel of life itself. We experience life, our growth, our traction only through the interaction and friction between our desires and the Universe. Desire is the only reason for intent, direction and action. While desire is vilified in nearly every religion as the cause of all evil or pain, it becomes essential to understand that desire is the cause of all, including pain but also everything else. Trying to live by the belief that *desire* is to be avoided, in order to avoid pain or evil, is to pursue a stifled existence. Living cut-off from your desire puts you at the mercy of others who would use your resources to fuel their *desires*.

Growth is fueled by *desire*. We are responsible for our own growth. To avoid desire is to avoid pain, yes, but also growth and life itself; feeling desire is feeling alive.

Homework:
Be on the look-out for your own use of these "trigger words," and explore your own Hierarchy of Motivation

- *Stop yourself before you use the word "Try" and create more authentic and realistic agreements with yourself and others.*
- *Re-evaluate the word "Should," and ask yourself and others "Says who?" and "Why?" whenever "should" is given as a motivation. Elevate all expressions that contain "should" to "need" then "want."*
- *Understand the "Want" behind every "need." No "need" is on its own. When you say or hear "need" in a sentence, always fill in the blanks: "I need to___because I want____."*

Short vs Long-Term Gain

We have a tendency to select short rather than long-term gain. Our minds, while particularly good at guessing our futures, are not very good at evaluating future gain. Our minds' ability to think into the future is much stronger than our ability to <u>feel</u> into the future. We instinctively understand that our futures can change for many unforeseen reasons so we're more likely to take what we can get now than to trust in the possibility of receiving substantially more in the future.

Chapter 32 – The Hierarchy of Motivation

In an experiment conducted among university students, when asked to choose between receiving $1000 right away and various bigger amounts at a later date, the significant majority of candidates choose to receive the $1000 immediately. Varying the numbers, or length of time into the future the money would be received did not significantly change the outcome of the experiment. Most candidates' minds understood the short-term gratification as significantly more valuable than a higher amount might be in the long-term.

Long-term can be a great investment with larger potential pay-off, but because it is not yet real it may be difficult to choose long-term gain in any given moment. But focusing only on short-term gain is your mind's internal resistance to personal growth and being accountable for what we truly desire. Don't shy away from the opportunities that contribute to your growth. My advice is to look for resistance as it is an indicator of opportunity for growth. The idea you've been putting off or the question you've never dared to ask or the path you've always wanted to pursue is likely to provide the most benefit in the long run.

In conclusion to the *Hierarchy of Motivation*, how you approach your goals, the language that you use to yourself and others influences how close you get to them, if at all. Note the language you use when you describe your motivations, look for your underlying wants and pursue those. Have a closer look at the belief systems behind your motivators. Decide whether your language serves you and you truly want to continue subscribing to your belief systems or if, upon examination, you choose your new direction. This is your life; you can only assert yourself and your desires if you are honest about what motivates you. In the end, you really do what you want to do based on the choices you know are available at the time and how you value each choice.

Chapter 33 – Creating Change

We think we are unable to make anything better. There are so many reasons why we can't make something work out for us the way we want. We are faced with problems that we want to address, but we feel we lack the power or direction to do anything about them.

The following tool will help you break down a problem and see it in a way that helps you understand your ability to effect change and what steps to take to reliably cause the change you want.

Asking Better Questions

First, ask a better question. Often we ask ourselves questions that lead us directly to what we don't want. As if our brains are focused on the negative and only wanting to attract the negative. We often ask questions such as "Why does this always happen to me?" or "How can I get a better job?" and we don't realize that these types of questions keep our minds singularly focused on the problem, what we no longer want, and away from what we do want, the solution.

Because of how our minds work, we are often focused on what we already know even if what we know is something we no longer want. It is difficult, if not impossible, to focus on something unknown but this is exactly what we must learn to do. This is the core strategy in a process called *manifesting*.

Anything we focus on, think about and believe in, forms *mental-models* of our version of the world. To our subconscious minds, focus is focus. Our subconscious minds are not able to distinguish between focusing <u>on</u> something and focusing <u>away from</u> something. The primary focus is still on the "something."

Chapter 33 – Creating Change

Let me give you an example: Squint your eyes at this page and pay particular attention to all the words that contain the letter "o." You may be surprised by how quickly your mind can focus itself on the words with the letter "o" in them. Spend about 20 seconds on this part of the exercise. Now, squint your eyes again and pay particular attention to all the words that do <u>not</u> contain the letter "o." You may be surprised to observe that your mind remains pre-occupied with the words that <u>do</u> contain the letter "o." To truly begin to change focus, you must replace your mandate. For instance, focus on the words that contain the letter "a" and you'll see a shift in the words that become apparent to your attention.

It is only when we <u>change</u> our focus, not just <u>negate</u> it, that we start to see a change in our attention, environment, behaviour and results. When we want to change our lives we must create an image of what we want and focus on that rather than continuing to focus on what we no longer want.

We tend to focus on what we no longer want because of pre-occupation and choice paralysis. We're familiar with the problem. We're pre-occupied with the problem. We've become masters of our "old" lives and don't yet have the essential skills to shift our focus to our "new," unknown lives. It is difficult for a mind to live in a "better" life. We are pre-occupied with what we know and we know how to get more of what we already have, even if we no longer want it.

The other reason we have trouble focusing on something new is choice paralysis. Choice paralysis makes moving forward difficult because we make knowing the outcome a prerequisite for making the choice. We believe that one of the potential new lives must be the better choice and we stop short of choosing a single focus for fear of having chosen poorly and missing out on the other possible outcomes.

When you want to make a situation better, you must ask better, or at least different questions. Ask yourself: "What does this new life look like? What would this new life feel like?" Once you start focusing on the answer to these questions and make firm choices, you can start committing resources and focus towards reaching these goals. This is *manifesting* at its core applied to real life.

Homework:

Imagine a future for yourself. This could be a medium or long-term future, but don't mix them. When you decide to imagine a long-term future, do not add short or medium-term thoughts to the image. Stay away from what you think you CAN have or only on who you are now, but focus on who you WANT to be based on the hard work and focus you are WILLING to invest into your future. Now, fill in your image of that future to become more specific. A large house and an expensive car may require long hours at the office. A peaceful retreat in the rainforest may require you to learn another language and agricultural methods for growing your own food.

Your mind may tell you several times that you're being "unrealistic," but that is based on what you know NOW and therefore what your mind thinks it CAN do with the resources and knowledge you currently have.

Your mind may tell you that there are many possibilities. While this is true, do the exercise as if you are selecting only one future. Work with your imagination to create only one future. You can change it later. Do not become victim to "choice paralysis" as this is often just an excuse for progress. It's better to imagine a "wrong" future, than to imagine "no future at all" due to the abundance of choice and fear of making a mistake.

Remove Prerequisites

> "As soon as I have _perfected_ this step, I'll move to the next step."

Stating a goal or direction with a prerequisite is creating a barrier to action. Prerequisites of any kind are like holding the parking brake while trying to drive away. Phrases such as "If only..." or "As soon as ..." or "But before I do ..." etc. are sure ways to prevent yourself from taking the next step.

The most successful people use three main strategies to overcoming the *prerequisite barriers* they encounter: Unnecessary, Good Enough and Delegate.

Unnecessary

To remove any potential barriers, successful people eliminate all but the necessary parts to accomplish the task. Culling the unnecessary allows you to move forward and with fewer steps to accomplish your desires. Often tasks can be completed and goals accomplished without the "frills." If you spend a few minutes examining a task or goal, you may be surprised to learn

Chapter 33 – Creating Change

that there are quite a few things that can be left out or are unnecessary to accomplish an end goal.

Good Enough
Know when a task is complete to a degree that is good enough and move on to the next task. This is an essential skill for progressing in your life. Nothing will ever be completely perfect and everything is perfectible. Perfectionism is often used as an excuse to avoid taking responsibility for progress. Be generous in your declarations of "good enough" and know just to move forward.

Delegate
You can delegate or leverage almost any task. Giving general tasks to another person will free up your time to do the tasks that only you can complete, that you must do to reach the goals you have set for yourself. Unless the goal you've set yourself is to do everything yourself, in which case, congratulations, you have completed your goal!

Delegating is letting someone else do a task that benefits them and you at the same time. Think "co-parenting" or "co-owning" a project or task that benefits everybody.

Leveraging a task is when you trade your money, skills or even just gratitude to have a person who is more effective, more skilled, or faster than you complete your tasks. This strategy really puts a project on "steroids." Your excuses just melt away!

Strategy: Making Anything Better

Step 1: See Things the Way They Are
The first step to changing a situation is to perceive it as it truly is in this moment. Do not paint the situation in a way that makes it out to be better or worse than it is right now. Focus on reality in this moment without dramatizing or downplaying.

Step 2: Identify the Gap
The next step is to identify how reality is not matching your desires. There must be a difference between the way things are now and the way you want

Second Threshold – Embody

them to be, or there would be nothing to work towards and therefore no problem. But if there is something you want to change, you must state this difference: this difference is the gap between the way it is and the way you want it to be. It is not enough to just say what is wrong; complaining doesn't change things. You must clearly identify what is wrong with the current situation AND what you would like instead.

What you want is not implied in what you don't want, be specific! To help you understand the reality of your situation and find solutions that will move you towards what you want, ask yourself "So? What do I want instead?"

When working with your challenges, don't lose sight of your personal responsibilities in this step. Stating that you want someone else to take an action or change a behaviour is a form of complaining and is not actionable by you.

Step 3: Align with Your Ultimate Outcome
The third step is to name what you ideally and ultimately want to happen. Focus on the best possible outcome, your greatest desire for this situation. Don't spend energy identifying what <u>should</u> happen, nor on what you may <u>be able to</u> accomplish. Focus instead on what you <u>want</u> to happen if everything were to fall into place.

This is not the time to worry about <u>how</u> you will get to your desired outcome, nor what you think you <u>can</u> do. Focus only on what you <u>want</u> to happen. Not what you think is easily possible, but what you truly desire. Use this desired outcome as a compass heading, not as a new prerequisite for happiness; it's just a direction for now. This direction will help you know which way to go. Trust your dreams and let them fuel your actions.

Step 4: Take Action NOW
The final step is to move towards your desired outcome. These are the real step-by-step actions of *manifesting*. It may not always be easy, but it does not need to be difficult. Start right now, as soon as you identify what change you want, start moving towards it. Take a step, one step and do your best every day. Make this one step as large or as small as you need it to be. Dedicate as much energy and focus as you feel is warranted by the goal, within the context of the rest of your life. Reprioritize if necessary.

Once you've taken this one step, this immediate action, don't blindly take the next step towards your goal. Go back to step 1, understand where you are and what you want now, which may have changed. Then realign with your goals and repeat the "Making Anything Better" strategy over and over.

You can apply this strategy to almost every situation in your life you want to change.

Strategy: Forgetting How of the Future & Why of the Past

If you find yourself interested in something that you want to do, have, or become, you're focusing on the what. The what is a culmination or manifestation of the way you believe you can fill a need or want.

To create the motivation to accomplish your goal, focus on why you want to accomplish this goal: your reason. Not only will this attach the motivation to the goal and help you get there, it will also leave you open to other ways of accomplishing your why.

Often the process of figuring out how becomes very thoroughly researched. At first glance this seems like a worthy pursuit; you need to know how to proceed and succeed. You can learn from your mistakes and identify where your outcomes fell short of your intentions. Learning from the how of the past helps you make better decisions in the future. But going forward you can't solve the entire how of the future before you encounter the actual how, and the goal falls victim to wondering how you might accomplish all hows, rather than the actual how. Focusing on the how of the future slows you down and diverts precious resources from the *Here and Now*, while at the same time limiting your options for accomplishing your goals. What you need to do is make moment-by-moment decisions as you personally connect to and passionately focus on your why and progress towards your what. Forget the how of the future, the how is important in each moment, but there's no need to plan the entire method or journey ahead. As your method will likely need to evolve along the way, forgetting the how allows you to be flexible and open to opportunities that might get you there faster or more efficiently. Just take the first step, however small.

As emphasized before, looking forward in time, and concentrating on the why is extremely important for fueling our motivation and inspire actions

Second Threshold – Embody

that will create progress. When looking back however, asking "why did I do that?" is only going to stall your progress!

The *1st law of self-preservation* proves that your intentions are not in question and were valid at the time. Analysing your past reasons is useless. You can't learn from your past reasons, they were sound at the time and your future reasons may not and don't have to be the same. Allow yourself the opportunity to change and innovate.

To summarize, looking forward, concentrate on the <u>why</u> and forget the <u>how</u>, don't get caught up in preparation and details to achieve the greatest progress, looking back, forget the <u>why</u> and learn from the <u>how</u> of both successes and failures.

Chapter 34 – Connecting to Self - The Three Skills

In order to be able to be in relationship with the world around us, we must not only learn and know the world, but also ourselves. Who is the person interacting with the world? How do we relate to ourselves in a way that allows us to both understand our *personal power* and work with it and interact with the world around us <u>from</u> our *authentic core being* and in alignment with our *higher purpose*? Knowing ourselves intellectually and observing our own behaviours as if we were observing other people are valuable skills, but to authentically relate and interact with the world we must intimately know and feel our *core Selves* within us.

How do we find, communicate and work with the true self inside us? How do we engage and connect with our truest and *core Self* that contains the power and the ability to accept *What Is* and effect change into the future?

The following meditations and exercises were designed to help you support this connection. They are easy to learn because of their simplicity and they have inspired amazing effects in my clients. Practicing these meditations and exercises can effectively help you create a meaningful relationship with your deepest *core Self*, your *higher purpose* and your *personal power*.

Re-connect with *Core Self* (S-BridgeMeditation)

The first skill I would like to introduce to you is a deep exploration of self-awareness. Initially developed to create a *somnambulistic bridge* to the *sleep healing state* of our brains, the S-Bridge™ meditation is a self-training form of hypnosis that allows us to find a deep healing state. In the S-Bridge™ technique, this client-centered skill can be further utilized for various mind-body healing techniques. I have used this technique in my work to assist with fertility, fibromyalgia and inflammatory bowel disease related issues.

My clients have found this 30 minute meditation easy to follow and practice. After a period of time, usually about a month of practicing it two to three times a week, my clients found it no longer necessary to use the recording to establish deep states of meditation on their own.

This form of deep meditation is a skill that helps establish a connection with the *core Self*.

Homework:
Sit in a purposefully quiet location. Be sure to sit comfortably upright, do not lie down, or use this meditation as a sleep aid. Listen to the recording three times a week, until it is easy to find "the bottom of the pool" on your own, just by relaxing and imagining the first scene in the recording.

This recording is available for download from:
http://www.pathwithin.com/download

Connecting to Your Highest Purpose (Spirit Guide Meditation)

The Spirit Guide meditation is recommended after you have been listening to the S-Bridge meditation for a few weeks. Once the S-Bridge meditation reliably brings you into a relaxed and receptive state, the Spirit Guide meditation will be most effective.

Once you have created a reliable connection with your *core Self*, the Spirit Guide meditation allows you to make a connection with your *higher purpose*. More specifically, with a metaphor that represents your *higher purpose*. Having a relationship with your *higher purpose* or *spiritual path* becomes essential when you want to be in relationship with the Universe. The non-judgmental *higher purpose* represents our personal, highest good or mission and encourages us to live a full and purposeful life, filled with experiences and happiness.

Homework:
After listening to the recording and connecting with your Spirit Guide, re-establish connection with your Spirit Guide three times a day by simply lowering your gaze and sensing your Spirit Guide's location in the room - it is always near, it's only a matter of finding it by being sensitive to it. Once you've located your Spirit Guide again, ask it: "How am I" – and to confirm that you're connected with your Spirit

Guide and not an Ego translation of it, you will always "hear" an answer similar to "You're okay," or "fine," or "good."

This recording is available for download from:
http://www.pathwithin.com/download

Connecting with Our Personal Power

Most of my clients do this exercise twice a day until they feel their own reactions deep down inside. Begin by standing in front of a mirror.

Feeling perfectly balanced is beneficial, so first I'd like to start with a posture exercise as follows: Stand upright in front of a mirror, feet approximately shoulder width apart. Rock your body forwards and backwards until you feel even pressure on the balls and heels of the feet. Sway a little side to side to feel equal pressure on the left and right foot. Raise your head up to become slightly taller, then roll both your shoulders in unison by raising them up in the front and lowering them in the back and relaxing your spine as your shoulders relax down. Roll your head clockwise, then anti-clockwise and find the perfect balance for your head. You will feel as if your head is lighter when it is perfectly balanced. Verify your head tilt in the mirror.

We start with the *grounding and centering* meditation as follows:

Imagine rods of steel emerging from your legs and feet and burrowing down into the ground. Finding the centre of the earth. As they go down, you feel taller and straighter. Let yourself anchor the rods into the roots of the earth. Feel the strength and power that you experience.

As you feel taller and stronger, you become aware of a light above you. A big white ball of light swirling in a vortex – a wide vortex of energy and light. You can feel how the light lifts you up into the heavens and comes down to meet you in a swirling energy pool of power and light. Allow yourself to absorb this energy now, concentrating on the very entrance point, just above your head. Coming into your body and centering into the very core of your being.

Now let the two energies from the earth below and from the light above come together into a strong and balanced centre in your chest. In your heart. Let the swirling energy of the light emerge into a warm and strong feeling in a wide swirl of energy around you. Let that energy surround you – your entire being. So much energy. So much strength. You feel the strength, energy and light entering your being, moving inside you and protecting you. Creating balance and harmony from within.

Second Threshold – Embody

This recording is available for download from:
http://www.pathwithin.com/download

The next part of this exercise is a dialogue with your mirror image. The success of the exercise is dependent on how deeply you connect to your feelings. Feel your way through it. The feelings that come up may be different every time. You may feel a deeper or lighter connection. You may at times feel entranced, strange, or even frustrated. There is no particular way this will feel for you. Allow yourself to immerse in the exercise and become familiar with your feelings.

In particular, you may feel the power of the "other person" (or mirror person) wane or strengthen. This is a good sign. Match the energy level. Don't override it or succumb to it. Just match it.

Look into the mirror image and stare at the eye on your right. Talk to your mirror image as if you're talking to a real, separate person – who looks like you, has the same attributes and qualities as you, has his or her own power, abilities and feelings. As you talk to your mirror image, listen to your words as if you are hearing a person who has your best interests at heart, has gone through what you've gone through and truly understands you and what you need.

Ask the following questions of your mirror self in a firm way. Then answer the questions honestly, from the deepest *truth* you hold within you.

Ask the mirror image: *"What is your name?"* (and listen to these words at the same time)
Answer: *"My name is: _____"* (speak your name)

Then ask: *"Who owns your power?"*
And answer from deep within your gut: *"I own my power" (pause after 'I')*

Then command: *"Make a choice"*

Initially, make a choice between Yes and No, then answer: *"Yes"* or *"No"*
When you answer "Yes," step forward strongly with your dominant foot.
When you answer "No," step backwards strongly with your dominant foot.

This last step may require a little practice to complete authentically. I've observed that in the beginning there seems to be a tendency to answer with "Yes" more often than "No." I believe this is because we've been programmed to associate "Yes" with *positive* and "No" with *negative*. We want to say "Yes" to make everyone happy, but that is a form of giving away our power.

Chapter 34 – Connecting to Self - The Three Skills

This exercise is about accessing your power that has become diluted by trying to please others or follow mental programming. Decision and honesty are powerful, indecision is disempowering. Take the time to do this exercise five times in the morning and again five times at night until you no longer have a bias towards either answer and you feel your answer emerging from within you.

Avoid using your thoughts to decide "Yes" or "No." Don't try to block your mind chatter either. Instead allow your mind chatter to continue while a decision bubbles up from your gut.

With practice you will begin to feel a reaction to this exercise. At first you might feel a reaction in your chest or solar plexus area that might seem somewhat negative or defensive. It is quite normal to have a solar plexus reaction. This is a sign that you subconsciously recognise the power you have within you. As you get more used to the recognition of your own power, you can begin to direct the feeling down into your belly and below. Sooner or later you will feel your physical sensations change during the exercises and the resistance you felt initially will start to be replaced by a sense of recognition. When this happens, drive the feeling towards and below your navel.

As the sensation travels lower, towards your abdomen, you are recognizing your power but still getting used to it and you feel relatively neutral about it. When the sensation is at or below your belly button, you've connected with your *personal power* in a way that lets you use it as *power with purpose*. You can use this power to assert yourself in relationship with the Universe: to authentically collaborate with the Universe and therefore positively contribute to reality and influence the imminent Universe.

There are two main goals of this exercise. The first is to feel the source of your creative strength. Your creative power comes from deep down in your belly. Some people would call this place the creative center of our being. But there is a big difference between knowing about it and actually feeling it. This exercise can help you connect with your deepest strength and your creative power and actually feel them. Connecting to this power is what gets things moving in the direction of your desires and what gives you the perseverance to go after what you want.

The second goal of this exercise is to help you recognize the separation between the *observer in you* and the *doer in you*. The *doer* says "I'm taking

Second Threshold – Embody

action," which is called *association* when we directly interact with the world as *I*. The *observer* says "See me take this action," which is named *dissociation* when we observe ourselves interacting with the world as *me*. If we want to assert our desires upon the world around us and create any traction towards our goals, we must become *associated* to the Universe.

Homework:
Do this exercise five times per session, two sessions a day. Practice this frequently until there no longer seems to be any bias towards answering "Yes" or "No," or the feeling that you are interacting with the world as a third party. You will know you have fully integrated the exercise when you can feel your strength coming from deep within your core and you feel like you are participating directly with the reality of the moment.

Yes/No Switch
Why do we do the Yes/No Exercises?

We make the most progress in our lives when we make authentic decisions in the present moment. Once we begin moving in a direction, our progress is halted if we come upon a crossroads and can't decide which way to go. Worse, if we make all of our decisions based on habit, we will always get the same results. And when we don't understand our goals, our *core Self* is afraid to take responsibility for our lives or has a strong fear of the unknown, we can become reluctant to make decisions. This can cause us to miss opportunities that would assist us in our lives.

In doing this exercise, we begin to observe our own power, we begin to truly understand that we are the pilots of our lives and that we have the ability to choose quickly and effectively from within our *authentic core*. Becoming adept at operating the Yes/No switch from a position of deep creative power is a skill that will benefit your decision making ability.

Advanced Personal Power

The advanced version of the *personal power* exercise puts it all together. Before I describe the advanced version of the exercise I'd like to stress that it's best to become completely familiar with the basic version first and <u>not to</u> start this advanced version of *personal power* until you have become proficient in the skills you've just learned in the previous chapter.

Chapter 34 – Connecting to Self - The Three Skills

You are ready for this version of the exercise when you no longer sense a bias towards Yes or No when you answer your third question and you feel your power in your creative center in the lower belly. In working with my clients, I have found a benefit in using a two staged approach to learning the Personal Power module of this program. It seems that once the mind knows the ultimate reason we are doing this exercise, it starts opting for superficial short cuts that essentially sabotage the deep connection and relationship we are cultivating with our deepest authentic power.

In order to help you resist your curiosity, I have made this chapter downloadable from the Internet. Please go to: http://www.pathwithin.com/download to receive your free copy of this advanced chapter. When you request the chapter, there will be a two week delay before the file becomes available for download, which will give you the time required to become familiar with the basic *personal power* exercise first.

Homework:
Go to http://www.pathwithin.com/download *and receive your free copy of the advanced chapter. Do the Connecting to personal power homework from the previous chapter for two weeks, before you're able to download the Advanced Personal Power exercise.*

Chapter 35 – Action First

People often feel paralysed by choice. Their lack of foresight into the future makes them feel like they don't know what direction to go; they want to take the best road, but are afraid to commit to a choice because they don't know if their choice is the best possible one. They get stuck making no decision at all and are therefore unable to progress.

Imagine you are the driver of a car that is parked and not moving. Now imagine turning the steering wheel of the car to the left. The car doesn't actually turn directly left. It remains motionless in the same position, because the car must be moving before it will actually change direction. In fact, it must first move forward before it will go in any other direction, it doesn't simply turn on its axis.

In many ways, life is quite similar. Choice without action provides no results. The results of actions in progress provide feedback and give us a sense of whether we're moving in the right or the wrong direction. The answer to this problem is re-choice.

- First, we select a direction. Any direction at all will do.
- Then, we move.
- In short time we'll know if this direction feels right or needs adjusting and we simply re-choose!

And as the car can't change direction without moving so too our lives do not change because of choice alone. We need action for progress and progress for feedback. Only feedback will tell us if we're doing what we want to do. Action verifies our choice in reality.

Chapter 35 – Action First

Re-choice is Progress

There is an old myth that many of us were taught when we were young. This myth tells us that if we make a choice, we must stick to it. While this might create a sense of stability and judgement of "integrity," it also prevents us from making that one choice to which we must commit before we know if it is the right one for us. Choice cannot be verified in theory, only in practice. Believing in sticking it out and the "You've made your bed, now lie in it" mentality will stifle your progress and become a cage around your soul.

As was said in the section "Being Authentic" in the first chapter, being ourselves does not mean we have to be consistent. Making decisions with the prerogative of changing our choices in the future allows us to move forward. Often we put off making a decision for fear we will be enslaved by it in the future. Decisions allow us to clean up the clutter that hinders and slows down our ability to focus on what we want to create. Indecision only leads to stagnation; it doesn't create progress, traction, momentum or direction. As we free ourselves and move through our decisions, we start to feel momentum and traction. As traction develops, we become able to feel the reality of our decisions and we can then use the momentum we've created through action to make a new decision that will move us in a direction relative to our previous choice – ultimately allowing us to find our way.

Growth and progress are functions of decision and action in resistance with reality. Our ability to effect change can be felt as indecision or resistance to act in the moment and as progress or distance in hindsight. Without decision and re-decision, no action is initiated and no progress is made. Just knowing your options and taking no decision will not lead to action and progress. Making a decision, taking action and correcting your course through the power of re-choice leads to progress.

Homework:
Or food for thought - assess your flexibility- think of aspects of your life you feel are <u>non-negotiable</u> and must be the way they are. Is this <u>law</u>? Who made this law? What/who do you feel trapped by? Consider and imagine <u>breaking the rules</u> etc

Third Threshold – Relate

In the second threshold we worked on cultivating the relationship we have with ourselves, discovering who we truly are in our core and becoming our most potent Self possible. This work was to help us experience our true power and core integration and to prepare us for a more intimate relationship with our world.

This section is about being in relationship with reality, getting into the state of *flow* and interacting with the Universe in a collaborative, non-competitive assertive way; actively participating within the harmony of the Universe and ultimately experiencing bliss.

In this section I also provide tools that can help you understand and improve the interface between your *authentic core being* and the Universe, and harnessing the power of your *core Self*. Once this power is unfettered, you will be able to influence the future of our Universe through this relationship, when you are in harmony with the Universe and in a state of *flow*.

Chapter 36 – The Power and Reward of Vulnerability

As we grow up many of us learned that vulnerability is a form of weakness and that we must keep our guards up against others who might exploit us. While this fear-based advice may have been a well-meaning attempt to protect you, it may have made you too guarded. If you now have your guard up against everything, you are unable to interact with the world in a way that is emotionally rewarding to you. Raising your emotional guards won't protect you but it will imprison you.

In addition to creating resistance against the world around you, raising your guard causes you to begin to fear what might be outside this wall of resistance and as you participate less with the outside world, you begin to construct fearful, suspicious assumptions about it. You begin to imagine that your fear comes from the external Universe and you conclude it to be harmful by nature. This is a perfect recipe for anxiety.

As we navigate our lives, we come to learn that when you push someone, they tend to push back. When you fight, there is vengeance. We incorrectly assume that the Universe is also capable of vengeance and might harm us when we become vulnerable. The Universe doesn't actually work this way; when you stop fighting the reality of the Universe, it doesn't retaliate. Instead it actually embraces you and collaborates with you.

Becoming vulnerable to the Universe is the ultimate sign of strength, not weakness. Interacting authentically and vulnerably is how we relate with the Universe in a way that lacks all pretence and is ultimately freeing and rewarding.

Suggested homework: Think of parts of your life where you feel you <u>need to be strong</u> or <u>tough</u> to avoid being hurt by reality... identify people you are suspicious of. Examine why...how do you believe this serves you? Does it?

Chapter 37 – Lean into the Direction of Resistance

Resistance is a function of growth. Each time we want to grow as a person, we encounter a feeling of resistance emanating from the very thing we want to accomplish or do. It is as if our brains pre-calculated the amount of focus and energy we would need to dedicate towards achieving these goals and decided growing would take too much energy away from the familiar systems that are comfortable to our brains. So our brains attempt to convince us to avoid the work by doing something familiar that will provide more immediate gratification, and to avoid the long-term gain of growth opportunity.

Our ability to overcome this resistance relies on solving a simple equation. Ask yourself if the growth opportunity is worth the effort. And the answer may be surprisingly simple: If it is worth pursuing, it is likely to come at a cost, but the potential benefit will far outweigh the energy required. The things that offer us the most growth in our lives may serve up the most resistance and still they could prove to be the most worth-while uses of our energy.

We can use this feeling of resistance as a source of motivation and direction to help us achieve the highest rate of growth in the shortest possible time. Lean into the direction of the most resistance and take a step into that direction.

If you feel you are lacking in purpose and direction, or are unsure if you are living a life with purpose, simply start in the direction about which you feel the most resistance and life will reward you with big leaps in growth.

Homework:
Make a list of the ways you would like to improve your life. As you make this list, observe your reactions to the words you write. Be honest about your reactions, even

intense ones like fear, disgust, or horror. If you react with "I can't," "I don't want to," or "that will cost more energy/money/effort/focus than I have," you might want to take a closer look at what you <u>can</u> do to get started.

This would be a helpful time to repeat the "Making Anything Better" *strategy*, followed by the "What, Why, What Else, How" *exercise*, to get immediate direction and traction.

Highway of Life

Our self-regulating mind is always looking for the most efficient way to function, create progress, or to avoid progress if it can "get away with it." We have a tendency to forget this when we're in the midst of it all. We push forward or hold back without realizing that the resistance we are creating by pushing consumes much more energy and resources than is necessary to evolve. Being in *flow* is quite energy efficient, allowing us to achieve results without resistance.

I see this as similar to driving on a highway. When we want to go faster than the other cars, it seems as if everyone is in our way. We accelerate and brake to push ahead and when we finally make some progress, the next car is also blocking the way. The end result is that we're not much further ahead, but have spent a disproportionately large amount of energy. On the other hand, when we try to conserve energy and slow ourselves down we end up blocking the way and feeling frustrated with the others at our back who are trying to maintain their speed.

On the highway and in life, if we maintain a similar speed to everyone else and keep our awareness on the ever changing traffic as it unfolds around us, we are able to anticipate lane changes, openings and obstructions as they develop. This allows us to navigate the most efficient routes possible. We can *flow* through the nuanced changes that arise organically within the patterns around us, costing us almost no additional effort but giving us a reasonable advantage over time.

The Illusion of Control

Learning that we're not actually in control of most things is a difficult lesson for many of us and can be a source of great fear. A key aspect of successfully relating with others and the Universe is trust; letting go of your need to be in control. Unfortunately, some people have been conditioned to believe that the only way to move ahead is to ensure that the people around them are under their control. So much so, that the *illusion of control* becomes a prerequisite to their sense of safety and wellbeing. For these people, the need to grow is overwhelmed by the feeling that all of their interactions with other people are competitions. They believe that they are the only catalysts for change and creators of order in the imagined hierarchies of their lives. To maintain their illusions of control they deliberately "cut down" others around them, using insinuation and careful, often covert manipulation to maintain a picture of the world that feels comfortable to them from their assumed position of superiority.

No one was bettered by these behaviours; no one's soul experienced growth. No one, outside the perceived hierarchy of those two people, is aware of the illusory change in rank. But the hierarchy doesn't actually exist; no one became better than the other.

It is helpful to make requests of others, to invite them to participate with you in a version of reality that supports your desires but you must release the feeling that the only way to achieve that is to control others' actions. Even if they comply when you ask forcefully, approaching other people with willing collaboration brings you into a greater state of harmony and *flow* with them and the Universe than exerting your fear-based control on them ever could. This sets the stage for future collaboration and accelerated progress.

When we still believe in the *illusion of control* and desperately want to feel progress or growth, we'd rather take control, in whatever way we can, than allow growth to happen. Because allowing means participating with reality and assisting our Universe in its creation without trying to force a particular outcome, our childish egos become afraid and impatient. "What if the Universe doesn't respond?" or "what if it takes longer than I wanted?" or "what if it takes a different form than the version my mind created for my future?"

Impatient to solve our self inflicted suffering and unwilling to collaborate with the *flow* of the Universe we desperately attempt to maintain our *illusion of control* by sabotaging the outcome! We select the route that seems to put us, not the Universe, in control. Unfortunately, we are unable to force the Universe to comply with our expectations. When we blindly push ahead we actually end up forcing destruction around us, which gives us the *illusion of control*, even though it does not ultimately move us closer to our true goals. Often this is done through hurting people in our immediate surroundings or destroying situations that were once working in our favour. Imagine how much people must be allowing fear to run their lives if they believe that without holding on to control, the Universe may destroy them.

The Universe only allows contribution and growth. This is a principle of the Universe that can work to our advantage, if we learn how to align with it. The Universe heals or brings back into harmony anything that attempts to counteract it. This is why there is no regression of the Universe. There is growth and lack of growth, which we could call stagnation. There is Life and Death. But there's no regression, no changing the past or the origin of things, no moving backwards and ultimately no such thing as destruction. Even our attempts to harm any part of the Universe are simply integrated into its perpetual evolution. Every action is ultimately absorbed into the harmony of the Universe.

Ultimately, collaborating in growth is infinitely more creative and rewarding than attempting to force control. And because of the organizing principles of the Universe, we can only ever have the *illusion of control*: we can never actually impose our will on the unfolding of the Universe. Learn to trust the progression of the Universe, seeing reality as it is and your place within your world, asserting your desires, but remaining in the feeling of allowing. This will create more harmony in all your relationships and more peace in your relationship with life.

Homework:
1. *Create a list of the people and situations you need in your life to maintain a sense of wellbeing. Now observe how you are attempting to assert control over the relationships and situations you just listed. "You need that person to do... (affirming behaviour) or you will feel... (threat or pain)" Then recognize that you don't have as much control as you wish you had.*
2. *Observe yourself attempting to hold on to a situation where it is becoming apparent that you are not actually in control. How can you interact in that relationship or situation in a way that honours both your desires and the autonomy of the other people involved?*

Chapter 38 – The Power of Resistance

When we imagine ourselves taking action, we immediately encounter *resistance*, often even before we actually move; we sense *resistance* from our minds!

What is this *resistance*? Is it hostile? Is it useful? The answer to both questions is YES!

Our brains are self-regulating. It selects activities based primarily on how much return we will get for our efforts. The brain is so efficient that it requires convincing to choose actions that may have a greater long term benefit over those that offer obvious short term benefit. It decides where to allocate time and energy, constantly doing "return on investment" calculations to decide the worthiness of the next item on the agenda for its precious energy supply.

Our First Answer Is No

Our ability to intuit the future is the first cause of our resistance to change. We feel more stable when we can predictably navigate our futures and unstable when our futures are unpredictable. Change means embracing the unknown and accepting situations that require more attention, more acute awareness and more presence than our efficient brains are willing to commit to. The ability to intuit our futures is an energy-saving mechanism. As we can no longer intuit as much of our futures when we embrace the unknown and make new choices, our brains resist the additional energy use required to manage all the potential variables and possible dangers. And so, we avoid unnecessary change. Most change will be flagged as unnecessary by our efficient brains, unless our current situations are causing us significant discomfort. This efficiency is one of our primary sources of *resistance*. If we can predict an outcome we feel safe. Unpredictability feels dangerous. So our default response to change is "No."

Chapter 38 – The Power of Resistance

Same is Safe
Different is Danger

Complicated or Complex

Most often, larger problems are complex. They are multifaceted and require chunking to be understood and moved through. Chunking is the process of breaking-down a problem, working the smaller pieces and then re-assembling the smaller pieces into a total solution. Unfortunately, when our brains' "return on investment" calculations tell us that solving a new problem will put us into the unknown realm of change, the brain adds *resistance* to the complexity and we now perceive the problem to be complicated rather than complex. Complicated is when difficulty is added to a complex issue. Please be aware of the difference between complex and complicated. Most issues are not complicated – most issues are simply complex. It's our brains that add our *resistance* (to change) that then interpret the issue as complicated to test if we have the motivation and courage to continue.

Resistance is a Function of Growth

Imagine a race car suspended above the road with its engine running and wheels spinning at full speed. Everything is working but the car isn't moving. This is what happens when there is no *resistance*. There is no movement and no progress.

Now imagine the car being lowered onto the road. The fast moving wheels spin and touch the static road surface. At the point of contact, friction converts *resistance* into traction. The traction becomes movement and the movement creates progress and distance from the starting point.

Understand that all growth and change happens where there is friction and friction can only happen in *resistance*. *Resistance* is needed for growth. Find the place or issue in your life that, when touched or stirred, creates the most *resistance* and you will have found the place where you can grow the most! When you find yourself in a time of great *resistance*, understand that you are also in a time of rapid growth.

No *resistance*, no growth. It's that simple.

Resistance is the missing piece when people say "No pain, no gain." As the reverse is not true, never just look for pain. Pain does <u>not</u> equal or indicate gain. Instead look for the epicenter of *resistance* to find the greatest potential for gain. Some gain is even painless, but if there is no *resistance* there simply isn't any gain and therefore no growth.

Resistance is an undeniable ally in our quest for growth, but don't befriend it. Befriending *resistance* is giving it the power to overcome any energy and courage you may have gathered to manifest the changes and growth you seek in your life. Never befriend your *resistance*. Never underestimate or ignore it. Understand its power to cripple you and your life, recognize your need for it to help you progress and grow. *Resistance* keeps you from spinning your wheels. Use *resistance*. Use it to identify the epicenter of your growth, understand it as a force that can bring you the farthest in life.

Flow

As we think about the way we navigate our lives <u>with</u> *resistance* to create traction, we can begin to understand how *flow* also relates to *resistance*. *Resistance* creates traction and traction creates movement and a rate of growth, relative to our starting point. Once we have overcome much of the *resistance* and our rate of growth becomes relatively stable, we feel as if our momentum and power cooperate in growth. This is when we feel *flow*.

In order to feel *flow* we must first apply our focus and energy to overcome *resistance* and create momentum from traction. *Resistance* is very useful in our lives.

Outsmarting Resistance

Understanding *resistance* is the first step to working with it. *Resistance* guides us. *Resistance* seems to emanate from anything that might be worthwhile. Use it as a guide. Things that are difficult tend to contribute most to our growth.

It requires keeping our focus on creating better future outcomes and sheer determination to overcome *resistance* and sometimes we only barely succeed. Just never forget the genius thought, the possible benefit, the idea, the light and inspiration that came <u>first</u>... *Resistance* came after. Opposition, rationalization, excuses and delays... all came <u>after</u>. To accelerate your personal growth and to experience life to the fullest, do what most scares you!

Chapter 38 – The Power of Resistance

The people around you can contribute to the resistance in your growth. Not because they don't want you to thrive, but because they also want to grow in a stable environment. If you change you are less predictable than if you stay the same, which means they have to spend energy keeping up with your changes rather than spending that energy on their own growth. And your unpredictability is more dangerous than your sameness. The people around you may not want to spend the energy keeping up with your changes and some of them may even be in competition with you. It is easier to compete efficiently if the people around you are not growing and changing all the time, so competing people may even resent your efforts to grow.

Please don't let others hold back your growth, it's just their fear talking. Anticipate that you may need to spend some energy educating the people around you about your changes and they will get used to your new, growing self. With healthy communication, these people may even become sources of support in your growth.

Homework:

In the morning, resolve to lean towards your resistance and say YES to tasks or directions that seem difficult – especially directions you don't seem to WANT to go because they're difficult. Don't look for trouble or make things more difficult in an attempt to prove how you seek resistance, this is different than doing things that seem difficult because they scare you or seem "too hard" for you to accomplish.

At night before you go to sleep, recall the choices you made. Did you choose an easier road or a more difficult one? Do you believe you were rewarded by your decision? Do you believe you moved closer to a goal, experienced personal growth or more freedom? Did you become more skillful or acquire a new bit of knowledge or wisdom? Did you get the same old results, or do you feel you are moving in a direction that may serve you in the long run?

Overcome the sheer overwhelm of the size of some of your choices and your first justification for resistance, by understanding that the task may be large and complex, but unlikely complicated or impossible. Understand that the smaller steps that make up this larger and more complex task are themselves manageable and uncomplicated tasks

Did you use resistance as a guide to find your opportunities for growth?

Chapter 39 – Becoming Sovereign

If you were a country, what governance would you adopt? How would you rule your country?

- A Dictatorship (Military Rule)
- A Republic (By the People, for the People)
- A Democracy (By popular vote)
- A Monarchy (Sovereignty - with a King or Queen who has ultimate veto rights)
- A Tyranny (What you say is rule - who cares about the others)

Many people have been taught that all decisions are best made democratically. Those of us who've ever been on a committee or in a business partnership will know that democracy is all well and good for politics but nothing ever gets done! No leadership, no action!

Use this as a metaphor for your own life, it's time to become a sovereign being. Rule your life as the king or queen of yourself. See other people as sovereignties also and establish diplomatic ties, but do not let others rule you.

When another sovereign being imposes their ideas on you simply take it under advisement. You don't need to ignore the suggestion, but there's no need to take any action unless the suggestion fits your desired outcomes.

This way you can manage your own energy and decide how to divide your energy among the people and projects that serve your life.

Homework:
When someone tells you what to do, attempt to understand that person's reasons for telling you what to do: <u>that person's</u> why – from his or her viewpoint. That person may feel justified in the suggestion because it would work well in his or her life. But

that is exactly why you may not want to follow other's suggestions, they are not you! Say: Thank you for your suggestions, I will take it under advisement. Think about the suggestion and consider all factors from your viewpoint, then decide how much, if any, of the suggestion you would like to integrate into your life.

Chapter 40 – Strategy: Influencing Others

While we only have control over changing our own behaviours I would like to touch on how we are able to relate to others' behaviours. Sometimes their behaviours influence us negatively or interfere with our peace and we may feel helpless or even violated by our inability to avoid another's behaviour. We may even allow others to cross comfort boundaries, tolerate their behaviour, or experience frustration at being unable to influence their negative behaviour. The strategy described in this chapter may help you to approach other people's behaviour in a new way.

Influencing someone's behaviour is difficult yet we attempt it all the time. Beyond just protecting ourselves from others' behaviours, we may want to help people behave differently "for their own good," or simply because their current behaviours are upsetting to us or may lead to harm in our opinion. For instance, the behaviour of children, pets, your boss, a political movement, or even spouses and best friends sometimes could do with a little influence from you.

Why is it so difficult to influence other people's behaviours? Resistance. If you push, people push back. If you try to convince them, you're unlikely to be successful as they will resist your attempts at changing them. We naturally resist the influence of others at first, our default answer is "No."

The strategy we can use is very well demonstrated by baseball players or martial arts warrior. Use the approaching power of what you want to influence by redirecting the force of the opponent, not by resisting it. A baseball player grabs a ball in flight and moves his glove first in the same direction the ball is travelling, participating with the force and direction. Then he slows the ball to a stop as he winds up his body to throw the ball in the direction of his choice. The martial arts warrior allows the assailant to move towards him, connects with his assailant in the direction of force and

Chapter 40 – Strategy: Influencing Others

uses the assailant's momentum as energy while redirecting his opponent into a controlled position, arresting the attack and often disabling the assailant in the process, without inducing further harm or wasting his own energy.

When working in relationship with others use this three step method for influencing behaviours):

1. Participate / Engage

First participate. Behave in a way that is very similar to the thing you would like to change. Being similar builds rapport but also gives you an opportunity to learn the behaviour you're about to change from the inside out. You will instinctively understand the strategy, direction, speed and possibilities of the following two steps. Merely resisting a behaviour will cause you to be met by equal and opposite resistance. Participation brings you into a position of influence. Participate in any way you can.

2. Attenuate

Attenuation means gradually slowing down, sometimes to a full standstill. Not everything can simply be stopped. You must account for the kinetic energy and anticipated momentum. Once you are participating you can often slow it down and use the stored energy for the next step.

3. Redirect

While the behaviour is slowing down, you must realize that the stored energy wants to go somewhere. You can't usually replace a behaviour with nothing. Reusing the behaviour's energy to fuel a desired new behaviour is an excellent strategy to create sustainable change. While energy is being used to fuel the new behaviour, there's little energy left to sustain the old, unwanted behaviour.

A wonderful example of this is a client who couldn't stop her children from jumping on the bed. Once she had understood that every time she told them to stop, the children resisted and had no alternative behaviour to direct their energy, she jumped on the bed with them, had some fun and laughed with her children, then said: "Come, let's play tag in the back yard." She tagged her youngest and ran away to the back yard. Of course both children followed her and they spent their energy in the back yard.

Third Threshold – Relate

Homework:
Identify behaviours in others that annoy you or that you find inappropriate. Use the strategy of "Engage, Attenuate, Redirect" to change the direction of their energy and focus.

Chapter 41 – Human Needs Psychology

I believe one of the most useful tools that has recently emerged in the mental health field is the classification system used by Cloe Madanes and Tony Robbins, made popular in their Strategic Intervention program. I do not intend to teach their work in this book, but I do want to show you an adaptation that has helped my clients experience more effective relationships.

In order to effectively work with my adaptation of this tool, it will help you to understand the relevant parts of this tool. To learn the entirety of Strategic Intervention and Human Needs Psychology, I recommend that you explore the Robbins Madanes Training Institute or some of the books written by Cloe Madanes, in particular Relationship Breakthrough (Published by Rodale ISBN:978-1-60529-581-7)

The Six Human Needs

Within the Human Needs Model there are six basic needs that all humans are thought to have: stability, variety, significance, connection, personal growth and contribution beyond ourselves. Each need is significant to our sense of wellbeing and we therefore seek to fulfill them all throughout our lives.

The need for stability is fulfilled when we feel reliability, stability, safety, clarity, etc. We feel stable when we have a reliable income, a safe home, friends we can count on, etc.

The need for variety is fulfilled by adventure, exploration and trying new things. It is also fulfilled through testing the stability of the structures and relationships in our lives. The need for variety is also known as the need for instability.

Third Threshold – Relate

The need for significance is fulfilled by the understanding that we matter, that we make a difference in our worlds, that our voices are heard and that we influence others. The need for significance is the feeling we have about how we feel as a result of the impact we have on others.

The need for connection is fulfilled by nurturing the relationships we have with others and receiving love from other people. The need for connection is how we feel towards others and how they influence our feelings.

The need for personal growth is fulfilled by learning and evolving. This need can be tended after the first four needs are met to a reasonably satisfactory level.

The need for contribution beyond ourselves is fulfilled by giving our energy and focus to other people. We feel ready to find ways to express this need when we feel abundant.

We primarily find ways to fill these needs through relationships with other people, as well as through our jobs, the food we eat, the activities we pursue, etc.

From this model I would like to highlight the following scoring exercise, which provides insights into how each of our relationships meets our Human Needs. Once we have a clearer understanding of the ways we are affected by our relationships, we become empowered to evaluate and change the ways we interact within these relationships.

Evaluate your relationships by scoring each relationship based on the Human Needs Model. For each need, give that relationship a score from 1 to 10. A low score means that the relationship is only minimally meeting this need or not meeting it at all and a high score means that this relationship is more effectively meeting this need.

Relationship with:				
	A	B	C	D
Stability				
Variety				
Significance				
Connection				
Growth				
Contribution				

Chapter 41 – Human Needs Psychology

First, fill in the name of the relationship you are evaluating. This could be the name of a person such as Sally, Mom, or James; or a group of people such as your parents, colleagues, or the Jones'. It could also be a conceptual group such as "friends," "neighbours," or "audiences." You can also use your relationships with food or work. Be careful to keep your relationships clear and distinct while using this tool. "Mom" is different from "my parents," and "work" is not the same as "my colleagues." It is often interesting to create a Human Needs analysis for both parents as a unit and for mom and dad individually. This may shed some new light on these relationships.

To fill in the columns please answer the following questions, based on your gut feelings.

In column A: on a scale of one to ten, how much <u>does</u> the relationship with (relationship name) contribute to your need for (Human Need)? Example answer: "My relationship with Mom contributes to my need for stability by a factor of seven out of ten." Do this for each of the six Human Needs in column A.

In column B: on a scale of one to ten, how much <u>should</u> a relationship with (relationship name) contribute to my need for (Human Need)? It is important to answer this question based on how you believe you would like this relationship to be scored.

In column C: subtract the number in column A from the number in column B and write it in C.

Column D is only to be used if the other person/people in the relationship will also be using the exercise to evaluate the relationship. If so, then in column D write the number you believe (relationship name) would write in column A if that person were asked the question "on a scale of one to ten, how much <u>does</u> the relationship with (you) contribute to (his or her) need for (Human Need)?"

The value of this exercise is increased when both you and the other person/people in the relationship complete it. Once both exercises are completed independently it can be an eye opener to compare how you both believe you meet the Human Needs of the other and how that person's degree of need fulfillment in your relationship may differ from yours.

Third Threshold – Relate

Column C

Select the Human Needs that show a difference of more than two in column C and write down the answer to the following question for those needs: "In what ways can *I* change my behaviour and how I contribute to the relationship so that the answer in column A shifts to more closely meet the answer in column B?" Or you may find that on further evaluation you overlooked some aspect of the relationship that would change your answers. Either way, this is a wonderful opportunity to learn in detail how your involvement in the relationship influences the relationship and affects its ability to meet your needs.

Homework:
Use the Human needs Psychology exercise to evaluate your most important relationships. You will gain valuable insight into your role in each relationship and how you can help shift them into the relationships you want, over time.

Use Column D when you can ask the other party in the relationship to do the same for you.

An interesting way to learn about certain habits and how you might change your behaviours is to do this exercise with Money, Food, Your Work, a habit such as shopping or even an addiction such as cigarettes.

Further Study: "Date with Destiny Event" – Anthony Robbins http://www.tonyrobbins.com, *Relationship Breakthrough* – Cloe Madanes (Published by Rodale ISBN:978-1-60529-581-7), *Strategic Intervention Certification* – Robbins Madanes Institute http://www.rmtcenter.com

Chapter 42 – Forgiveness: An Act of Power

We sometimes feel shorted in our relationships. That is, we feel that we put more resources and focus into a relationship than we receive in return. It is as if our minds keep score of how much we invest into our relationships, but the relationships do not provided sufficient return on the investment. In essence, we feel our relationships owe us.

Throughout our lives we invest in relationships with the belief that one day they will provide us a good return on investment. This may seem a perfectly reasonable belief, considering that most relationships reciprocate what we put into them. Trading our skills with others creates a generally favourable balance. For instance, <u>we</u> as parents are good at providing the safety of food and shelter, a baby is good at giving us love and joyful feedback and each party benefits from the relationship. This type of mutually beneficial relationship is more than the sum of its parts. We create relationships with people in much the same way, but we also have relationships with our jobs, food, money, etc. Our jobs, for instance, promise us monetary rewards for investing our work. But what if we feel we were cheated? What if we feel that we invested energy and focus into a relationship that shorted us by returning less than we anticipated?

In our eyes, when we feel shorted on our investments, we believe the other parties still owe us something and our relationships do not feel equal. When the "loans" remain outstanding over time, we may even feel entitled to increase the interest they owe. Even if they completely repaid the loans in full - if we were able to quantify such things - we still believe those people owe us endless apologies for hurting our feelings or leaving us in uncertainty for such a long time.

Relationships with people we deem close, such as with our romantic partners or close family members, often suffer from unresolved "agreements" that

Third Threshold – Relate

resemble such an unpaid loan. While we may go about our lives waiting to be repaid, the other parties to the "agreements" often have no idea what, exactly, they still owe us. They may even believe there are outstanding loans that you still haven't repaid to them. The word "agreement" is used rather loosely, as there is usually no actual agreement among people. In most cases one of the parties decides what would be fair by that person's own standards and waits to be reimbursed, often without communicating any of this to the other party. These one-sided agreements are at the core of the division in many of the couples who come to me to work on their relationships. Creating consensus about the outstanding loan and the required level of repayment is a sound way to begin to restore peace, but I find that forgiving the "loan" altogether is much more healing to the relationship.

Forgiving is for the giver. For-giving is a decision to disconnect from the agreement, forgive the loan and start from a new foundation of strength. A clean slate for the relationship can be achieved almost immediately. And when the other party is unwilling or unable to participate in a future relationship, forgiving frees the giver – that's you – from the "agreement" and allows you to move on with your life. The other party doesn't even need to be informed of your new found freedom. Allowing yourself to disengage from old agreements gives you the power to create new ones that are based on a truly mutual understanding.

We have a notion that in order to be able to forgive the other party, that person needs to be present to thank us for our benevolence, but the truth is that forgiveness is a personal act of releasing the old agreement. By severing ourselves from the old agreement, we take our power back in an assertive act of self-care. This is a gift to self that empowers us, without needing the awareness, approval, or acknowledgement of the other party.

Homework:
Make a list of the most important relationships in your life. This list will include all relationships you currently hold responsible for some of your current attitudes, beliefs, behaviours and habits. Include ex boyfriends/girlfriends who were mean to you, far removed uncles who made comments about you or your behaviour, dead parents, influential teachers, books, food, work. Begin to take back your power by forgiving them. Let go of your need for them to repay their debts or to equalise wrongdoing. There's no need to forget the past, just don't let your need to be repaid and therefore the connection you have with those people be excuses that keep you from

Chapter 42 – Forgiveness: An Act of Power

moving forward in your life. Reclaim your personal power by deciding to forgive and letting go of the agreements and the people, WITHOUT restitution of any kind.

Once you have mastered the art of forgiveness and understand the freedom of forgiveness fully and deeply, you will forgive your mirror image and inner narrator as well.

Chapter 43 – Bestowing Trust

We sometimes feel betrayed by people or situations and don't quite know how to mend the situations. We know and understand that we are unable to have authentic relationships when we treat the relationships with suspicion. We want to return to trust, but we fear being hurt again. How do we regain the trust we need to reengage fully in the relationship?

Unfortunately, we learn from popular media and our social circles that when we are "betrayed" we must cut-off all relations with the person or situation that betrayed us. This strategy may leave us disconnected from relationships that could actually serve us. When we burn ourselves on the stove we are more careful in the future, but we don't stop using the stove. We start using the stove with the respect we should have used in the first place. It is us who begin to use the stove again and trust ourselves with the stove. The feeling of trust is built by us, trust is bestowed not earned.

Trust is a feeling that comes from us. So in situations where another person has betrayed our trust, we may have overlooked our roles in the trust relationships. We may have created expectations about how the other people should behave and made our trust conditional on this expected behaviour. This is why we feel anger paired with a betrayal; our anger is our recognition of our unmet expectations.

If you make the continuation of the relationship dependent on the other person "earning" your trust, you give away your power. You wait until the other person has "paid back" the loan (with interest) and you can't have a relationship based on equality until that person meets the criteria you have set. Regardless how measurable or attainable the measure, making trust conditional, places you in a perceived elevated position of judge. This either stops the relationship due to inequality or makes trust an unattainable prerequisite to the relationship. Understanding how trust flows from us gives

Chapter 43 – Bestowing Trust

us the key to finding a solution. Decide to bestow your trust and forgive the illusion of debt created by your expectations.

Seek to understand how the trust was broken and learn from it. Seek to understand why you want the relationship to continue and use this as your motivation. Then decide to forgive and bestow your trust again, to create a new and equal agreement. Then you can move forward in the relationship with renewed faith, new knowledge and clearer understanding of the mutual agreements you're creating together.

Homework:
Decide who in your life you wish were trustworthy (even if it seems like they are not at the moment). Decide WHY you want to entrust them with the ability to hurt you. What will you gain by entrusting them with the ability to hurt or harm you? Then, if it is important that they can be trusted, decide to BESTOW your trust upon them and inform them of this fact. Share this information without threatening them – "if you betray my trust again," etc. Simply TELL them that you trust them and give them the power to betray that trust. Do not test them by giving them the opportunity to betray your trust, just give them the power that comes with being trusted and treat them as trustworthy. Being vulnerable to the people you decide to trust can be very rewarding.

Chapter 44 – Circle of Potential

We live in an abundant world of infinite potential and unlimited opportunity. Our potential is only limited by how much focus and effort we're able to assert upon the world. The opportunities seem endless – bound only by our ability to cut the knots that limit us and move in the directions we want to pursue.

Unfortunately, the reality of our lives is often marred by our caution, which inhibits our ability to move forward. Instead of making strong headway on our paths to success, we feel held back by the overwhelming evidence that progress requires great effort and the absence of proof that our efforts are likely to produce results.

As we cautiously begin a new project or head in a new direction, our minds calculate a return on investment and look for reasons to move forward. But then at a certain point we realise that we are not as successful as we had hoped and extrapolate that additional effort may not yield the success we had anticipated when we began the endeavour. And we don't invest further, often leaving the project to fail in the absence of our continued input.

In studying people who started new companies there were two kinds of people: those who had been laid off and those who were looking to move up from their jobs or looking to become independent. The strategies that were used by people who were "down sized" to find themselves with redundant skills and those that were started by people who had a reasonable income but were looking to move up or become an independent entrepreneur were significantly different. The people who had been laid off went "all-in;" they put all their efforts into making their plans work, no matter what. In other words, they were present, persistent and tenacious, while remaining flexible and resourceful. The other group devoted significantly less time to their new goal and was not eager to facilitate change.

Chapter 44 – Circle of Potential

They knew there was a lot on the line and felt as if they simply had no other choice than to keep going. This motivated them to put much more effort and focus into their projects than, maybe warranted based on calculating only the initial return on investment.

What fueled their persistence and tenacity? What prevented them from throwing in the towel when it seemed like their efforts might not yield results? Faith. Not idle hope, but faith. They were able to augment the lack of guarantee-of-success with faith; faith in the future, faith in the viability of their ideas and faith in their abilities.

There is a cycle that can either fuel or destroy the success of a project. This cycle starts with virtually unlimited potential. Our potential is unfathomably large. People are capable of enormous feats and accomplishments when the stakes are high enough. We begin a project by turning a small amount of this potential into effort and focus.

Some, not all, of our effort and focus is converted into success. As we continue to learn what works and what doesn't, we become more efficient, effective and successful; this takes time, however and even more sustained effort and focus.

As we begin to measure our return on investment from the success of our efforts, we also increase the faith we have in the possible success of our efforts based on tangible evidence. And our ability to continue to put so much of our potential into effort and focus is determined by how much we believe in the project. This also means that as our successes decline, our faith declines. As this happens, we continually decrease the amount of our potential that we apply to the project and our resulting success continues to decline.

Once we understand the model of success, we learn that the key to increasing your success is to focus on the reason why you want to achieve the success, not on how much effort will yield the success you want. When you pursue those goals which are truly important to you deep down you stand to put more effort into the unpredictable process and are therefore more likely to have better results. If we look at any successful person, we learn that he or she almost completely ignored the return on investment calculation and simply believed that the outcome was worth <u>any</u> effort to achieve the goal that they valued above anything at the time.

Third Threshold – Relate

As mentioned in the previous chapter, we must observe that no amount of effort will actually guarantee success at any level. We are never entitled to outcome; we are only entitled to desire outcome and work towards fulfilling our desires. But if you find yourself unmotivated to put in the effort and focus required to bring about the success you intended, regardless of initial success, then you need to go back to the reason: the why. Because to even have the possibility of experiencing success, you need to fuel your project, your future and your potential - and the only true motivator is your desire.

This is where positive thinking can benefit you. Believe that your dream is possible; cultivate your faith, even if it's challenging. Let that faith carry you through the hard work. Know that you will be there along the way as an active, flexible participant who can solve the unforeseeable issues and that you are uniquely skilled to assist your projects to fruition. Believing in the outcome is not done by ignoring the bad parts, but by observing each situation in your life as a project that can be solved, regardless of its current state. Keep a clear image of your world the way you desire it in your mind and above all focus on why you desire it. Dream big, seeing the situation unfold towards your desired outcome to establish a positive direction for the belief. This increased belief transforms more potential into effort and focus, which drives more success, creating a positive cycle that can carry you to your goals.

Homework:
Reread "Strategy: Making Anything Better" and "Strategy: Forgetting How of the Future & Why of the Past" in Chapter 33 to integrate your knowledge with this chapter. The strategies will enable you to propel almost any project forward at an accelerated speed. Find a project you want to manifest or an issue in your life you want to address and take yourself through these steps to propel yourself forward.

Chapter 45 – Being Yourself

There is a common element of struggle among the people I counsel through this program. They want to build a future that reflects who they truly are and what they want, but they don't know how to move forward and choose a direction for themselves. They're not able to get a good grip on what they truly want, nor are they able to describe their true selves.

As all our actions begin from our desires, we must connect deeply with our *core Self* before we can understand what we want. Then from our deepest sense of self we will tap into our deepest heartfelt desires. Connecting with our heartfelt desires is not necessarily a conscious practice. As we hold intimate connections with our *core Self*, our behaviours become manifestations of our deepest good and heartfelt desires. We no longer need to design arbitrary futures filled with "goodies" that were marketed to us. Instead we focus on what truly matters to us and our most authentic behaviours will automatically reflect our true selves. There is no need to override our natural responses. I would encourage you to observe your own natural responses, as they most deeply reflect your *core Self*.

Instead of telling yourself who you **should** be, you can observe yourself making choices, learn why you made those choices and what parts of those choices truly reflect your *authentic core being*. Staying connected with your *core Self* and keeping a connection open to your *authentic core being* allows you to reflect on your behaviours and learn from your reactions. This will make it so that you will be able to say: "That was how I reacted before my behaviours were guided from my *authentic core being*. Now I feel my *authentic core being* and my *higher purpose*, I choose to behave in a new way. My way!" You may be surprised to find that your behaviours are naturally different than before, without the need to override urges or habits. You will simply make new choices based on your new, more connected, more present, more authentic state of being, without any force or undue effort.

Third Threshold – Relate

Do not make your old behaviour wrong. Growing is a process in evolution. Your less evolved self was never wrong, just less evolved. Be accepting of the various versions of yourself as you evolved throughout your life. This may initially be a conscious effort, as you may be overriding how you were raised to think about yourself by your parents and caregivers. Now understand that our new behaviours are rooted from our new knowledge and abilities, based on our newly formed relationships with our *authentic core being* and our *higher purpose.*

Observing your own choices and behaviours with this new awareness of yourself can be the most effective way to learn about what you want for your future. Amplify the positive feelings you desire by continuing to nurture the connection with your *authentic core being* and *higher purpose*. This amplification will unleash your passion and fuel your desire, direction and drive to move ahead.

The three elements that facilitate your true desires that drive your life are: Your ability to connect with your *authentic core being*, your ability to feel your *higher purpose* and your ability to extrapolate an understanding of your desires from these elements into actions that serve your reality.

The Universe is both assistant and resistant in your life. The Universe can assist you in manifesting the future you want, provided that you make timely choices that lean into the direction of your desires. But the Universe resists any attempts to force your control upon it and will not respond in a way that matches unrealistic expectations. Connect with who you truly are inside, your *authentic core being* and *higher purpose* and observe your subsequent choices and behaviours. Begin by observing your current choices and behaviours – as you choose and behave according to who you are in this moment.

Exercise: Recalling the Present

"Find a comfortable and quiet location where you are unlikely to be interrupted for a little while. Allow yourself to drift and dream your way into a better time. A future time. A time where everything in your life aligns with your true essence.

Imagine yourself in the not too distant future, maybe a few weeks, or months from this moment, having already overcome all the obstacles and difficulties that seemed to have stood in your way. Now, tap into the triumphant feelings and freedom of having accomplished this liberation for yourself.

How do you feel? Become aware of how you feel in this moment. Explore the feeling of how your accomplishments and dedication paid off and brought you many steps closer to your ultimate dreams and desires; many of which have yet to be manifested into your life but that feel much closer in this imagined near future moment. Many of these goals have already brought you joy and a sense of accomplishment. This moment is filled with a sense of completeness, a sense of reward and a motivation to reach for more after having done the work that was required to persuade the Universe to lean towards your desired goals.

Feel how you would feel. Imagine how you would walk. Imagine talking to friends and colleagues. Imagine the faces of people with whom you would interact. Imagine the happy and supportive faces of family members and friends who have watched you grow and live your life, successful in all you have moved towards and proud in all you have accomplished. Maybe curious to see what you will accomplish next...

Now, for a moment, think about the effort it took to get to this place. Understand, without getting specific, how you overcame all the obstacles and crossed all the bridges to get to where you are now. Notice that while some obstacles were more difficult or more complex than others, you still overcame them! Through sheer belief, determination, persistence and agility, you arrived at a place of accomplishment and pride. Fuelled by the rewards of what you have accomplished so far, feel the need to move forward and find new ways to experience your life to the fullest."

This recording is available for download from:
http://www.pathwithin.com/download

I have personally coached people who live truly amazing and inspiring lives. Once they reach the level of self awareness that they can do this exercise on a regular basis, they accelerate their growth and align with their true potential.

I suggest that at this stage of the Path Within Program you create the time do this exercise regularly, maybe a few times a month to benefit from its full potential.

Chapter 46 – Identities and Belief Systems

So who are we? This question has been on the minds of many a philosopher and scholar. While I don't want to dismiss this important question, for the purpose of this book I would like to approach this subject in a more practical manner. I'd like to work from the perspective of identities and behaviours rather than the question of existence itself. When we understand how we view ourselves and behave according to this self image, we can learn how we navigate our world and sort what matters to us.

We carry a sense of who we are in the forms of identities. We identify ourselves as human, male, female, teacher, biker, carpenter, actor, etc. We even identify ourselves as **not** being something, such as, not a loser or the all too persistent: not good enough. We also add identifiers such as: "person with a drivers license," "poor," "sick," "coffee addict," "joker," etc.

These identities define how we behave and even what we believe. In some cases we have been given identities by others and choose to live up to those expectations. In most cases, however, we self-identify and hold this identity as a measure against which our belief systems and behaviours are weighed on an ongoing basis.

Our behaviours reference our identities and we label our behaviours based on their adherence to the identities they represent. The attachment to a particular identity and associated behaviours creates a boundary that determines whether we would or would not engage in certain behaviours; whether a behaviour is representative of its identity or not. The judgment of representation regarding the behaviour is what we commonly know as our *belief system* or values. We perceive our *belief system* as an internal compass by which we compare "who we are" to "what we would do," and control our behaviours accordingly.

Chapter 46 – Identities and Belief Systems

We also use identities when we need to make a decision. We ask ourselves the question: "Would a good girl do this?" or "Would a working class man do this?" Rather than looking at all the possible ways in which we can proceed we limit ourselves and restrict our decision by filtering it through the identities we currently subscribe to.

What is holding you back from making important decisions and actions that would allow you to move forward? Consider your finances, your relationships and your business.

Do you find your belief systems influenced by society? Do you find yourself purchasing clothes, gadgets, computers, etc. that fall within your identities? What about the neighborhood you live in or the car you drive? Do you find yourself going beyond your budget to afford things that match your identities?

By the time we are adults we hold onto many such identities. That is, once we learn to recognise a set of behaviours, we lock in the summary of these behaviours as an identity and refer to these identities as part of our *foundation of reality*. Once we have assimilated behaviours we no longer question them as being part of an identity, belief system, or value system. We often refer to those behaviours as being part of "who we are." They become our story and we often find many of our stories difficult to abandon for fear of failing to be "who we are" and having to re-examine everything about ourselves.

While it can be efficient to navigate life using pre-established *truths*, this prevents us from being open to new experiences and personal growth. We prejudge all of our experiences and how we are likely to react, often, without questioning belief systems that were created at a very young age. In many ways we still behave according to belief systems that were useful and safe for a toddler or a pre-teen! Many people become enslaved to old identities that prevent them from incorporating new wisdom, adult behaviours, and experiences. Our belief systems effectively cut us off from learning new skills and moving forward in our lives.

Three strategies

If we stop growing we no longer feel alive. When our belief systems make us unwilling to engage in experiences outside of our current acceptable behaviours, we miss out on many opportunities to engage in life, learning

Third Threshold – Relate

and growing. Finding ways to work with our belief systems gives us the tools to move beyond our outmoded self-imposed restrictions, without needing to actively override our old behaviours by creating coping strategies. Instead, we embody the new belief system to naturally incorporate the behaviour that allows us to grow and experience.

Expansion

When you feel restricted by your belief system, or the values associated with "who you are" prevent you from taking action that you know would help you grow because it is outside your previously practiced behaviour pattern, one of the strategies you have at your disposal is *temporary expansion*. You may assign a temporary or evaluative status to your proposed behaviour. You simply allow the behaviour, regardless of your values, belief systems or identity, for a limited time. Regard the behaviour as a possible candidate for incorporation into the belief system after experimentation. "You don't know until you try it," and you may learn first-hand that you either want to permanently add the resulting experience to your identity, or reject it as "an experiment gone awry."

Re-evaluation

There are circumstances where you are able to see that the values you hold are either based on external influence or old stories that may no longer serve you. For instance, the societal conditioning that "good girls" behave in certain ways. Re-evaluating the belief system may help us to incorporate new behaviours in our idea of what a "good girl" does.

This kind of evaluation may also be relevant in the case of generalizations, when we encounter a singular set-back and generalize that attempting the same thing in the future would always yield the same result. For example, when we are rejected in love, we may create the story that we are un-lovable and incorporate this into our identity, which prevents us from taking another chance.

While working with my clients, I pay particular attention to the people who self-label. They say things such as: "I know myself, I would never do that" or "I'm not that kind of person" or "I always...." or "I consider myself to be a (insert label here) person"

Chapter 46 – Identities and Belief Systems

Re-evaluating our identities and belief systems means asking ourselves the question "Is this true in this context? Or "Is this still true?"

Often, for lack of insight into the future, we might be tempted to err on the side of status-quo. But if you're honest about your inability to accurately predict how you might learn from a new experience, you can open up to embracing new experiences just to see if you might expand your self-awareness and enjoyment of life as a result of allowing yourself to re-evaluate what you believe about yourself.

Shifting

A surprisingly efficient way of overcoming the limits imposed by our belief systems is to shift identities, if only temporarily. Changing your identity to an identity that incorporates the behaviours that caused you hesitation, is a quick and efficient way to get a feel for the consequences of the new experience. Often all it takes is to shift our identities a little to allow ourselves to succeed.

One of the biggest obstacles to change is our inability to abandon our old identities, in other words to make our "new selves" different from our "old selves." We have the hardest time redefining ourselves, especially when this new identity is different from "how we've always been." So expansion and re-evaluation can be difficult endeavours to undertake, especially in the brief moment of a decision. Shifting identities, however, gives us the opportunity to experience momentary breakthroughs and appreciate the rewards of our potential "new selves" before permanently deciding to remain the "new self."

The conflicts we create and mind-energy we must expend to employ the previous two strategies of *temporary expansion* and *re-evaluation* may prevent us from using them, but shifting identities is fast (and often fun) to do. Simply take on the identity of a person who would engage in the behaviour you are contemplating, or take on the identity of a person who would be successful, who would dare to say "hello," or who dares to love himself or herself and feel how it feels to be that person.

We already shift identities naturally, all day long. From one moment to another, we are fathers, husbands, scholars, teachers, homeowners, businessmen, etc. Why not slip into identities such as adventurer, lover, philanthropist, healer, magician, leader, assistant, MVP, VIP, etc.

Third Threshold – Relate

There's a lot of truth in the saying "Fake it 'till you make it," or the alternative "Fake it to make it," which is more in alignment with the idea of shifting and lacks the persistence the first saying implies. Everything we initiate, we must imagine first and then take action based on our imagination. In order to go to sleep, we must first enact being asleep. In order to be better, we must first agree that we can do better, then imagine actually being better and feeling the rewards. Taking the next step of doing better serves to reward us with the feelings and feedback we need to motivate further progress. If, however, shifting our identities doesn't give us the rewards we anticipated, we do not need to be persistent. We can consider the experience as an opportunity to learn what we do or don't want to pursue further.

Inversely, changing behaviour will change how we see ourselves. We are able to improve our lives much faster than we could possibly have imagined before, just by shifting our identities to incorporate the behaviours we need to accomplish the results we desire.

Homework:
1. *For 15 minutes, walk on the street as if you're depressed. Shoulders down, not talking much, looking down. Notice your mood and the reaction of people around you.*

    For the following 15 minutes, walk on the street as if you've just won the lottery. You're upright, looking out, smiling and chatting with everyone. Looking them straight in the eye and even walking lighter. Notice your mood and the reaction of people around you.

    We wear different identities based on what we <u>believe</u> we should be; you're a different person at work or at home... change your identity and your mood, your behaviour, your world, your life will react accordingly.

2. *Think about characters from books, film, stories, or even real life that you admire. Create a list for each character to identify what character traits you would like to incorporate more into your own life and behaviour. Write these traits down without limiting yourself to what you can do, but what you desire. An example would be: "I'd like to give away money" – disregard that you don't have money to give away. You don't need to limit yourself by creating a prerequisite excuse.*

Look at the common elements in each list and think about ways for you to become a person who also engages in these behaviours. Imagine already being the person with these characteristics.

Spend some time in the character of this person and allow your subconscious mind to figure out the difference between the identities and resulting states.

Shift your identity to become the person who behaves in this way, regardless of whether you have the resources or skill or luck or heritage to do the things you want, just behave as a person who <u>would</u> behave in this way.

Conclusion

Thank you for taking this journey with me. If you have made it this far, take a moment to think about the ways you have transformed since you began this process. Do you feel more connected to your own inner wisdom? Do you understand yourself more, your challenges, desires and highest potential? Are you more curious about your life, your interactions and your relationship with the Universe?

This book is a culmination of over 20 years of study, combined with working with my clients to help them understand themselves and the Universe with more clarity. But ultimately your journey is yours. You will take from this work what you choose.

In this book, we have explored the depths of human motivation and desire, the ways our brains process impressions and the natural laws of the Universe. We have looked at conditioning, shame, anxiety, depression, fear, motivation, desire, manifestation and many other aspects of creating and enjoying our lives. Remember, all of these aspects of your being are a part of your nature. Don't fight yourself or reject parts of yourself as undesirable. Understand and accept them and allow yourself to be a whole and essential part of *What Is*. Hopefully, you have delved into the many exercises that were designed to help you with some of your own limiting habits and beliefs and are experiencing a clearer understanding of *What Is*.

The true wealth of this work lies in its integration. Theory and knowledge can only take you so far. To really integrate these teachings into your life, you will need to engage in the exercises and commit to an ongoing practice of observation and transformation within the context of reality. You will need to change how you perceive and interact with your loved ones and colleagues, your Universe and especially yourself.

Conclusion

My intent is that this book will serve as a reference that you can return to again and again, each time discovering deeper levels of self-awareness. I have faith that through interactions with your loved ones you will share the results of this work and they will be impacted by the benefit you receive from your own personal growth, harmony and authenticity.

Where you go from here is up to you. By now you have probably learned to trust life more, to take ownership of your desires and act upon them, to ride that delicate balance of knowing that you cannot control life, but you can influence the unfolding of the Universe through active participation and deliberate, focused action. I am curious to know how you will use your embodied wisdom in your life.

In gratitude, Anthony Santen

Index

Numbers

1st law 150–153, 161, 163, 167, 169
2nd law 162–165, 167, 169, 174
3rd law 167–169

A

abundance 167, 179, 186, 197, 212
acceptance 69, 100, 140–141, 187
addictions 4, 78, 110
affirmation 183–187
agreements 6, 52, 78, 147, 203–205, 208, 247–249, 251
amygdale 82, 84–85
anger 4, 77, 80–85, 100, 113–114, 182, 198, 250
anxiety 1, 4, 20, 23, 77, 80, 87–91, 94–95, 110, 113, 229, 265
assumptions 40–42, 44, 71, 73, 78–80, 87, 92–94, 138, 148, 170–172, 174, 176, 229
attached to outcome 177
authentic 1, 3–4, 6–7, 9–10, 16–18, 120–121, 179, 182, 208, 217, 222–223, 227, 250, 255–256
authentic core 10, 16, 121, 217, 222, 227, 255–256
authentic core being 10, 16, 121, 217, 227, 255–256
awareness vi, 1, 11, 14, 16, 18, 29, 31, 35, 41–42, 44, 55, 67, 71, 88–89, 91–95, 100, 111, 120–121, 127–128, 138, 143–144, 146, 148, 162, 175, 217, 231, 234, 248, 256–258, 261, 266

B

balance 18, 21–24, 54, 156, 219, 247, 266
bargaining 100
belief system 3, 6–7, 17–18, 28, 42, 75, 83, 117, 120, 144, 147–148, 150, 175, 183, 201, 206, 258–261
betrayal 250
blame 63–66, 103–104, 120, 123, 127
bliss 49, 68, 137–138, 142–145, 227
brain cells 173

C

chemical imbalance 75, 96, 98
choice paralysis 211–212
collaboration 23–24, 38, 46, 49–50, 69, 75, 79, 121, 232
construction 42–45, 92, 112
contentment 5, 130, 137–138, 141–143
core being 16, 149, 255
core self 120, 217–218, 222, 227, 255
courage vi, 28, 56, 60–62, 235–236
creation 49, 52, 62, 142–143
creative power 221–222

D

danger 28, 43–44, 54–56, 58, 61, 82, 87, 89, 108, 125
delegating 213

denial 100
dependency 88
depressed 77, 97, 110, 115–116, 262
depression 1, 4, 20, 23, 71, 77, 80, 88, 96, 98–101, 103–107, 112–114, 116–118, 172, 265
desire 3, 5–6, 9–10, 47, 51, 56–58, 78, 110, 120, 130–131, 134, 141–143, 146, 150, 157–159, 161, 163, 167–169, 180–181, 197, 200–202, 206–209, 212–214, 221–222, 233, 254–257, 262, 265–266
doctor 87–88, 127
download 218–220, 223, 257
dream vi, 10, 58, 109, 196, 254, 256

E

ecstasy 137
embody change 189
emotional issues 80
emotionally unavailable 103–104
emotional reactions 78
emotional response 78–79
entitled 6, 24, 48–49, 127, 132–134, 139–140, 176–177, 247, 254
entitlements 121, 132, 134, 147, 175
evolution 54, 77
evolve 25, 36, 38, 77, 231
expectations 87, 91, 132, 134, 137, 141, 147, 175, 177, 192, 197, 250–251, 256, 258
external forces 202
externalizing 12, 125, 127, 201, 206

F

facilitator 11, 16
failure 70, 83, 125, 142, 186, 202–205
faith 3, 99, 160, 251, 253–254, 266
fear 3–4, 6, 14, 20, 28–29, 40, 42–43, 47, 54–56, 58–62, 65, 74, 77, 86–87, 89–91, 95, 126, 138, 142–144, 154, 167, 202, 222, 229, 231–233, 237, 250, 259, 265

fearful 29, 41, 54, 58, 77, 175, 229
flow 49, 121, 150, 227, 231–232, 236
forgiving 18, 247–249, 251
foundation of reality 10, 30, 97–100, 103–106, 110–111, 117, 172, 259
freedom 89, 147

G

generalizations 74, 260
God 1, 49
grateful v, 13, 90, 92, 150
grief 23, 100
grieving 96, 98–100, 112, 114
grounding 219
growth 5, 7, 9, 47, 52, 66, 69–70, 74, 89, 112, 131, 134, 138, 168, 187, 208–209, 230, 232–233, 235–237, 243–244, 257, 259, 266
guilt 63–64, 120, 198, 200

H

happiness 3–5, 7, 9–10, 13, 43, 49–51, 57, 68–70, 104, 125, 127, 129–137, 139, 141–144, 177, 199, 214, 218
harmony 3, 8, 18–24, 49, 52, 55, 62, 69–70, 84, 92, 97, 99, 120–121, 134, 137, 144, 192, 219, 227, 232–233, 266
healing 11, 14, 20, 24, 71, 75–78, 87, 96–98, 100, 104–105, 107, 111–114, 116, 118, 128, 248
healing response 24, 75–78, 96–97, 100, 104, 107, 113–114, 118
here and now 9, 29, 51, 89–92, 95, 136, 199, 215
Hierarchy of Motivation 168, 201–202, 207–208
higher purpose 121, 217–218, 255–256
hippocampus 39–41, 107–108, 111
horizon of awareness 58, 88–89, 91, 94
hypnosis 11, 41, 217

I

identities 7, 83, 103, 147, 183, 258–259, 261–262
illusion of control 18, 65, 100, 175, 199, 231–233
illusions 14, 31, 36, 51, 68, 117, 138, 140–141, 172, 232
immune system 75
imperfection 92
impotence 81–82, 85
inability 77, 81–83, 85–86, 103–104, 109, 138, 169, 240, 261
inferior 86
intend to 20, 204–205, 243
intuition 26, 42, 61, 97, 106, 175

J

judgment 6, 23, 68–69, 88, 100, 117, 139–140, 142–145, 148, 150, 176, 258

L

law of attraction 3
laws of self-preservation 146
leverage 130, 158, 194, 213
limiting belief 28
loneliness 48, 96

M

magic v, 35, 68, 139–140, 142, 144, 175, 198
manifesting 3, 10, 24, 27, 56, 58, 61, 86–87, 140, 142, 173, 181, 196–197, 210–211, 214–215, 236, 254, 256, 265
manipulate 26, 48–49, 108, 144, 168
meaningful relationships 15
meaning of life 4, 20
medication 87–88, 113
medicine v, 76, 87, 97
meditation 4, 14, 41, 106, 112, 114, 217–219
mental health 23, 67, 77–78, 90, 113, 243

mental illness 20, 23, 76–77
meta-cognition 25–29, 38
metaphors 1, 11, 14, 52
mind-control 11
mood 88, 181, 262
motivation 15, 61, 81, 154, 158–160, 164–166, 181, 202, 207–208, 215, 230, 235, 251, 257, 265
moving away 154, 185
moving towards 44, 154, 185, 214
Murphy's Law 3, 133

N

need 1, 7, 9, 12, 14, 16–17, 24, 28, 35, 38, 43–44, 47–48, 55, 57, 62–63, 65, 71, 74, 80–81, 84, 88, 91, 98, 103–104, 107, 109, 111–112, 117, 119, 129, 131–133, 135, 138–139, 143–144, 155, 158–159, 161, 164–166, 174, 176–177, 180, 183, 189, 191–192, 194, 197, 199, 202, 206–208, 214–215, 220, 224, 229–231, 233, 236–238, 243–245, 248, 250, 254–255, 257, 259, 262, 265
negative speech patterns 202
negative thinking 180
negotiation power 48
neural pathways 173
neuroplasticity 75
nightmare 58

O

omnipotence 31, 47
original miracle 49
overwhelmed 48, 109, 166, 232

P

participation 12, 15, 35, 49, 120, 129, 138, 142–145, 199, 266
path of life 56, 60, 102

The Path Within v, 1, 3, 7–10, 12–18, 24, 27–28, 33, 35, 50, 66, 119–120, 128, 257
permanence 53
persistence 253, 257, 262
personal power 10, 217, 221–223, 249
pharmaceutical 78, 87, 96
positive outlook 181
positive thinking 180, 254
potential 142, 252
pot of gold 153, 162
predator 48, 85–86
prescription 88, 113
pretend 56
the problem 13, 22, 46, 48, 65–66, 81–82, 84, 107, 117, 139, 196, 210–211, 235
psychiatrists 87
psychological homeostasis 75, 96–100, 110–111, 114
psychology 58
psychotherapy 17
pursuit of happiness 132

R

rather 24, 149, 162, 202, 207, 259
re-choice 150, 224–225
reframing 196
regret 64, 66, 120, 198
regret circuit 66
relationships 1, 6–8, 14, 16, 20, 48, 57, 59, 69, 85–86, 89, 98, 103–104, 121, 139, 142, 165–166, 175–178, 182, 192, 194, 199–200, 205, 217–218, 221, 223, 227, 233, 241, 243–248, 250–251, 256, 259, 265
religion 3, 13–14, 18, 119, 140, 147, 168, 208
resistance 11, 17, 19, 22, 27, 30, 52, 70, 144, 163, 165, 172, 181, 184, 209, 221, 225, 229–231, 234–237, 241
resolution 86

return on investment 179
root causes 4, 20, 24, 87–88, 97, 113

S

sadness 78–80, 96, 98–99
S-Bridge 217–218
scratch pad 40, 108
self 5, 7, 14, 16, 66, 83, 88, 128, 146, 163, 167, 183–184, 217
self-awareness 88
self-care 67, 166, 200, 248
self-confidence 16
self-deprecating 147
self-esteem 16
selfishness 163, 166
self-preservation 146–153, 161–165, 167–169, 174
self-talk 36, 83, 183–184, 196, 202
self-worth 16
severance 98–99, 102, 110, 112
shame 3, 63–66, 88, 151, 265
should 63, 74, 77, 113, 133, 141, 147, 151–152, 168, 174, 177, 182, 195, 198, 202, 205–208, 245, 250, 255, 262
sleep cycle 106
sleep healing state 217
the solution 22, 36, 47, 65, 83–84, 87, 94, 210
somnambulistic bridge 217
source of your creative strength 221
spirit guide 218
spiritual 9, 13–14, 218
stage of life 39, 43, 45, 107, 109, 111
stress 64, 89
subconscious minds 108, 110, 210
success 9, 13, 26–27, 60, 70, 83, 138, 160–161, 220, 252–254
suffering 8, 52, 64, 75, 123, 130
superiority 68–69, 139, 141, 144, 148, 150
super power 25–28, 36, 38, 42, 61, 97

survival 4, 20, 22, 40, 54, 56, 61, 71, 77, 79, 97, 106, 108, 146, 161, 170, 172, 193

T

temporary expansion 260–261
threat 44, 55, 82, 86–87, 89, 91, 110, 233
triggers 8, 16–17, 79, 82–83, 88, 97, 129, 135
trust 89, 99, 157, 159, 177, 194, 208, 214, 231, 233, 250–251, 266
truth 11, 15, 17, 24–25, 28, 30–31, 46–49, 60–61, 63–64, 68, 71, 74, 93, 103–105, 119, 127, 131–132, 138, 147–149, 151, 162–163, 168, 170–171, 173–177, 186, 198–199, 220, 248, 262
try 47, 64, 86, 120, 131, 133, 186, 202–205, 208, 221, 231, 240, 260

U

ultimatum 86
unhappiness 4, 7, 24, 69, 121, 129–134, 137, 140–141, 177
unintended outcomes 147
universe v, 3, 6, 9–10, 13–14, 18, 22–24, 46–47, 49–51, 61–62, 68–70, 81, 84, 92, 97, 101, 120–121, 134, 138, 140–141, 144, 161, 182, 193, 198, 208, 218, 221–222, 227, 229, 231–233, 256–257, 265–266

V

victim 48, 85–86, 123, 212

W

want v, 4, 6–7, 9–10, 12, 15, 17, 23–24, 30, 55–58, 63, 70–71, 82, 84–86, 94, 113, 115, 117, 119, 125, 127–128, 130, 132–133, 135, 140, 157–160, 165, 167–169, 175–177, 179–184, 193–194, 196–199, 202–211, 213–215, 218, 220–222, 224–225, 230–232, 237, 239–240, 243, 246, 250–256, 258, 260, 262–263
what if 26, 44, 66, 103, 106, 108, 162, 172, 232, 247
what-if 94, 98, 111
what is 6, 49–53, 68, 74, 91–92, 94, 98, 100, 115, 137–138, 140–144, 182, 192, 217, 265
what isn't 6, 51, 91–92, 179, 182
wishes 167–169, 207